Photoshop for Nature Photographers

A Workshop in a Book

Photoshop® for Nature Photographers
Photographers
A Workshop in a Book

Ellen Anon

Tim Grey

SYBEX®   San Francisco • London

Publisher: DAN BRODNITZ
Acquisitions Editor: BONNIE BILLS
Developmental Editor: PETE GAUGHAN
Production Editor: LESLIE E.H. LIGHT
Technical Editor: PETER K. BURIAN
Copyeditor: SARAH LEMAIRE
Compositor: FRANZ BAUMHACKL
Graphic Illustrator: TONY JONICK, RAPPID RABBIT
CD Coordinator: DAN MUMMERT
CD Technician: KEVIN LY
Proofreaders: NANCY RIDDIOUGH, AMY MCCARTHY, JIM BROOK
Indexer: NANCY GUENTHER
Cover Designer: INGALLS + ASSOCIATES
Cover Photographer: ELLEN ANON

Library of Congress Card Number: 2005924830

ISBN: 0-7821-4427-6

SYBEX and the SYBEX logo are either registered trademarks or trademarks of SYBEX Inc. in the United States and/or other countries.

Some screen reproductions produced with SnapZ Pro X. © 1994–2004 Ambrosia Software, Inc. All rights reserved.

The CD interface was created using Macromedia Director, COPYRIGHT 1994, 1997-1999 Macromedia Inc. For more information on Macromedia and Macromedia Director, visit http://www.macromedia.com.

Internet screen shots using Microsoft Internet Explorer reprinted by permission from Microsoft Corporation.

SYBEX is an independent entity and not affiliated with Adobe Systems Incorporated, the publisher of Adobe ® Photoshop ® software. This is an independent Sybex publication, not endorsed or sponsored by Adobe Systems Incorporated. Adobe ® and Photoshop ® are trade marks of Adobe Systems Incorporated.

TRADEMARKS: SYBEX has attempted throughout this book to distinguish proprietary trademarks from descriptive terms by following the capitalization style used by the manufacturer.

The author and publisher have made their best efforts to prepare this book, and the content is based upon final release software whenever possible. Portions of the manuscript may be based upon pre-release versions supplied by software manufacturer(s). The author and the publisher make no representation or warranties of any kind with regard to the completeness or accuracy of the contents herein and accept no liability of any kind including but not limited to performance, merchantability, fitness for any particular purpose, or any losses or damages of any kind caused or alleged to be caused directly or indirectly from this book.

Manufactured in the United States of America

10 9 8 7 6 5 4 3 2 1

Wiley Publishing, Inc.
End-User License Agreement

To my husband Jack and sons Josh and Seth—
thank you for being so supportive; and to my parents for
planting a love of nature and photography within me.

—Ellen Anon

To Nature.
May we take care of her so we'll always have not just
a place to live, but beautiful places to photograph.

—Tim Grey

Acknowledgements

Ellen Anon

First, I must thank my family for their patience with me when I am away taking photos or teaching workshops or when I'm holed up in my study working; I appreciate your support and the extra burdens I sometimes place on each of you. An extra thank-you to Josh for explaining some of the more esoteric computer concepts.

Second, I realize how fortunate I am to have so many friends in the field who have gone out of their way to further my career. Arthur Morris is my close friend, mentor, and colleague who prompts me on to new levels of excellence and productivity. He has opened doors for me that have had major impacts on my life. Peter Burian is a good friend and colleague who continually shares opportunities with me. He has encouraged my writing efforts for years and prodded me to get published in a variety of venues. A friend of Peter's, Jon Canfield, became my friend as well. Not only has he graciously put up with my ruthless tech editing of his books, he guided me through some of the rough spots in this book as well, and even shares writing opportunities with me. Joe and Mary Ann McDonald took a risk and hired me to teach at their digital institute (www.Hoothollow.com) before even meeting me. Teaching with them is an honor and the bonus is that they have become cherished friends. Rick Holt, who teaches Photoshop workshops with me at Hoothollow, is my buddy. Together we learn more of the secrets of Photoshop as we weather the storms of life. Freeman Patterson has become a friend and mentor as well, and is a source of constant inspiration.

Tim Grey, my co-author, warrants his own paragraph. Way back when, I took a course from Tim at the Lepp Institute and asked him a minimum of 500 questions per day. Because he answered each one patiently and thoroughly, I filled in the gaps in my Photoshop knowledge so that I could go on to teach others. When I approached him about doing this book, he graciously agreed, despite the fact he had more than enough other projects to keep him busy. Thank you, Tim.

Of course I am thankful to the folks at Sybex for seeing the value in this project. They are an amazingly supportive and professional group of people. Some authors have horror stories to tell about their editors. I feel extremely lucky that my team has been absolutely wonderful. Beginning with acquisitions editor Bonnie Bills, whose encouragement and suggestions helped shape the idea for the book; to developmental editor Pete Gaughan, who skillfully molded each chapter; to technical editor Peter Burian, who made certain our explanations were accurate and clear; to copyeditor Sarah Lemaire who gently made certain we were writing in English; compositor Franz Baumhackl and proofreaders Nancy Riddiough, Amy McCarthy, and Jim Brook—each person has done an excellent job. Production editor Leslie Light gets a special thanks for always knowing when to pick up the phone and coach me with a few kind words as well as being accommodating with deadlines.

Our fellow photographers were incredibly generous with their time, writing, and images. Josh Anon, Peter Burian, Greg Downing, André Gallant, Charles Glatzer, Darrell Gulin, Rick Holt, Lewis Kemper, Joe McDonald, Arthur Morris, Michael

Reichmann, and John Shaw all graciously contributed and made the book that much better. They are all busy professionals, yet they made time to help us. Thank you!

Thank you also to the Adobe prerelease team and forum members who were always responsive to questions and concerns and who made learning CS2 a pleasure.

Lastly I want to thank my friends, including Art Becker, Dee Cunningham, Charlotte Lowrie, Michael Lustbader, Michael Nadler, Alan Parry, Patty Raydo, and Rocky Sharwell, as well as all the participants in workshops who've asked when I would write a book. And for anyone I've forgotten to mention, I apologize. It's not that you're not important to me; it's that I'm at that certain age …

Tim Grey

Those of you who have read my previous books (or more appropriately, actually, read the Acknowledgments in my previous books) know that I always thank my lovely wife Lisa for tolerating my crazy work schedule. This book found me at the crossroads of three book projects as well as a demanding travel schedule, so it called for a much higher level of support (and tolerance) than anyone would consider reasonable. I appreciate her patience, and look forward to a family vacation with not even a moment's thought to books, work, or Photoshop (well, OK, maybe to Photoshop). For all who have expressed their appreciation for my books, I assure you my wife deserves most of the thanks! I'm a lucky man to have her.

I also want to thank the many photographers who have inspired me with their own work, and even in some cases provided images or text for us to include in this book. These include John Shaw, Art Wolfe, Dewitt Jones, Art Morris, Jeff Greene, Ira Meyer, Alice Cahill, and the many amateur photographers whose images I've had the pleasure of seeing at various presentations and workshops. I'm fortunate to be able to see so many incredible images from so many excellent photographers.

I'd also like to add a special thanks to Pete Gaughan and Leslie Light at Sybex. These are the editors who had to endure my delays as I tried to stay on schedule with this book despite so many other obligations. While they may never admit it, I know I tested their patience. And yet they were always exceedingly polite in nudging me to finish a chapter even after the deadline had past. I'm lucky to have such great editors.

About the Authors

Ellen Anon

Ellen got her start with photography at age five; it remained a hobby as she took a very long fork in the road, eventually earning a Ph.D. in clinical psychology. Finally in 1997 a broken foot forced her to take a break from work as a psychologist, and she used the time to study John Shaw's photography tapes. (Thank you, John, for starting me on the road to photography as a career.) She debated briefly between building a traditional darkroom in her home and creating a digital darkroom. Since she's not fond of being closed up in small dark spaces with strong smells of funky chemicals, she opted for the latter. Ever since, photography has been a two-part process for her. Making the image in the field is step one, and optimizing it using Photoshop is step two. Being creative with it is the icing on the cake!

Photography and Photoshop are shared passions for Ellen. She has been fortunate to co-lead photography workshops with Arthur Morris, Photoshop workshops for Joe and Mary Ann McDonald, and her own Photoshop-in-the-Field workshops. She also presents seminars in various locations and is an instructor for the high school scholarship programs at the North American Nature Photography Association (NANPA) summits. Her articles and images have been published in a variety of venues, including *Natures Best*, *eDigital Photo*, *Popular Photography*, Sierra Books *Mother Earth*, Photoworkshop.com, and various calendars, billboards, etc. In addition she was runner-up for International Wild Bird Photographer of the Year in the digitally altered category. Ellen has also been the technical editor for several recent books on Photoshop and digital photography.

Photography has taken Ellen to locations from Hawaii to South Africa and has paved the way for her to meet all sorts of wonderful people. Her husband and two sons sometimes travel with her, all of whom are quite skilled with cameras. Fortunately they adapt to her crazy schedule and willingly plan vacations around her photographic destinations.

Tim Grey

A lifetime of working with computers and a love of photography combine as the perfect passion for Tim Grey. He got started with computers at the age of ten and took his first photography class in high school. In college, he started tinkering with Photoshop, helping others learn how to use the software. Since then his passion for all things related to photography and digital imaging has grown exponentially.

Tim loves learning as much as he possibly can about digital imaging, and he loves sharing that information even more. He does so through his writing and speaking appearances. His articles have been published in *Outdoor Photographer*, *PC Photo*, and *Digital Photo Pro* magazines, among others. He is the author of *Color Confidence: The Digital Photographer's Guide to Color Management* and of the e-book *Photoshop Sharpening*; he's a co-author of *Real World Digital Photography, 2nd Edition* and of *Photo Finish: The Digital Photographer's Guide to Printing, Showing, and Selling Images*. He also presents seminars and workshops at a variety of industry trade shows and other venues.

Tim publishes a regular "Digital Darkroom Questions" e-mail list, where he answers questions related to digital imaging for photographers. To add your e-mail address to the list, visit www.timgrey.com.

When he isn't working to meet deadlines on his latest book, Tim enjoys venturing out with his digital SLR to find new subjects. When traveling on business around the country and the world, he capitalizes on any "down time" to go out walking with camera in hand capturing whatever catches his eye, which typically includes urban subjects.

He also enjoys photographing nature's beauty during outings with his family near their home in Redmond, Washington. And one of these days, when caught up on book projects, he plans to pick up his guitar again to really learn how to play, and get current on his pilot's license so he can once again take to the skies in the pilot's seat.

Foreword

Adobe Photoshop has changed the world of photography immeasurably. It is an amazing, powerful tool, now at the hands of nearly every photographer. I don't claim to be an expert in the program, but that doesn't change my admiration for its depth, its scope, or what talented artists can create with it.

For nature photographers, the biggest reason for excitement is being in control of your process. Shooting with digital equipment means that the artist controls every step, from being in the field to "processing" using your digital darkroom and even to printing. With the artist in control of these steps, the final product—your art—will more closely reflect your vision.

Digital's convenience allows new opportunities beyond Photoshop. I'm able to shoot in India and nearly instantaneously send photos back to the office for posting on my website. Recently when I was giving a talk in Asheville, North Carolina, my laptop was stolen, along with the slide show I was to give. If these had been slide carousels, my only choice would have been to cancel my talk; there would have been no way to get replacement slides picked, processed, and sent to me quickly enough from my office in Seattle—and that's assuming the slides weren't originals and lost forever. In this day and age, though, it was a minor setback. My office managed to upload new files for me to a web server, and I borrowed a laptop to make the presentation, all within eighteen hours.

But digital's most important benefit for me is that it enables me to view a photo in the field just after I've shot it, instead of having to wait weeks until I'm back home and have the film processed. It has opened my work up to new possibilities, and it allows me to be more spontaneous and take risks that are impossible with film, thanks to instantaneous feedback.

Currently, digital photography isn't necessarily more convenient than traditional film photography. Instead of hauling bricks of film across the world, I'm hauling USB external hard drives for redundant backups, and I'm hauling solar-powered chargers for batteries to power my laptop.

But the smart photographer knows that comparing today's digital equipment against today's film equipment is a losing game. The true revolution of digital is in its infancy. You may not be quite ready to switch your entire photographic workflow over to digital right now, but there will come a time when it will be much more convenient and much less expensive, and in the end you, the artist, will have much stronger control over the final product by shooting digitally.

This is exactly why *Photoshop for Nature Photographers* is so timely. Every evolution in the technology of photography—and I think it's worth remembering that photography in any era has always been concerned with the newest technology—comes with a learning curve. I'm very impressed with the scope of the work in this book, the depth of the knowledge, and the clear instruction. Tim and Ellen do a fantastic job of guiding the reader through the technical maze of digital photography. This is a book for all levels of photographers—from those who have shot for years on film and are transitioning, to those who are at the beginning of their craft and starting out using digital cameras. It's a book about digital workflow and related issues, but first and foremost it's a book about photography.

In the end, that's the most important thing: the photograph. The rest is a means to an end; my true love—and I suspect yours as well—is not the technology or the tools but the image. What really matters is looking at the photos we take and being reminded with awe of the beauty and fragility of our natural world.

—ART WOLFE

World-renowned nature photographer, artist, and author; recipient of numerous photography honors, and publisher of award-winning books

Contents

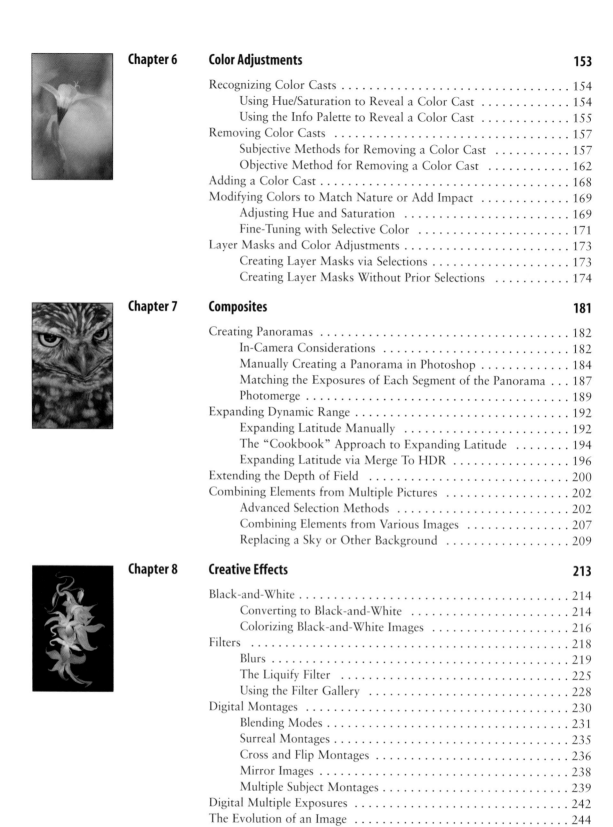

 "Making the best possible picture in the field,

and creating the  best possible output from

that capture"

Introduction

Photoshop and nature photography are a logical marriage. Although there are some people who regard Photoshop as an evil that degrades the purity of nature photography, in reality nature photography has long been a two-step process. The first step involves making the best possible picture in the field. The second is creating the best possible output from that capture. Ansel Adams is widely acclaimed as one of the greatest black-and-white nature photographers of all times. Yet if you had a chance to view some of his prints before he optimized them in his traditional darkroom, you might not have looked twice at them. Although he was an excellent photographer, he was truly a master of the darkroom. Today, Photoshop enables many more people to become masters of the darkroom—the digital darkroom.

Becoming a master of the digital darkroom can be a daunting task. Trying to learn the program by trial and error is a most time consuming—and frustrating—approach. Finding the time and money to spend a week at a workshop devoted to Photoshop for photographers involves a major time commitment, to say nothing of the significant expense involved.

There are lots of Photoshop how-to books on the bookstore shelves, but many address the needs of graphic artists more than photographers. Graphic artists need to use vector tools such as the Pen tool or Shape Tool, which aren't of much use to most photographers. And while there are some books that do target photographers, none specifically address the unique needs of nature photographers. Many of these books focus on areas unimportant to nature photographers. For example they may spend many pages dealing with retouching portraits or repairing scans of old photos.

Most nature photographers need to know how to take their images from scans or off CF cards into the computer and use Photoshop to edit and optimize them. They need a straightforward workflow that pertains to nature photography, that's easy and efficient to follow. That's the goal of *Photoshop for Nature Photographers*.

Further, this book addresses some of the unique concerns nature photographers experience, such as white balance and color corrections. Of course all photographers deal with white balance, but many are concerned with making their images truly neutral. As nature photographers, we often get up before dawn to capture the beautiful early morning light. That light that we go to great lengths to capture is far from neutral. In fact it's the warmth of it that makes so many of our images. If they were portrayed as neutral, many would lose their impact.

Photoshop offers a multitude of ways to accomplish almost every task. Which method is the best to use in a specific situation often depends on the type of image you are modifying. Throughout the book we bear in mind that your subjects are nature and gear the techniques to those that are likely to give you the best results the most easily.

We want this book to be easy to use, and have organized it to follow the basic workflow. Each chapter lays a foundation for the following chapters. You'll also notice that we incorporate an element called Try It! in this book:

Try It! These sections offer a chance to take a break from reading and practice the techniques that have just been covered using your own images or those that we provide on the companion CD. Reading about a technique is one thing, but for most people, it doesn't sink in until you actually do it. By providing you with images to practice on, we hope to make this book more like a workshop.

You'll notice that most of the book is written in the first person plural, meaning that both Tim and Ellen recommend the technique or approach that is being described. Occasionally we break into first person singular when one of us is describing a personal experience or preference. Although generally we provide you with clear guidance for how to proceed, there are a few times where Tim prefers one approach and Ellen favors another. We have opted to present both approaches to you because both are viable options; it's not that one is right and the other wrong. It's simply a matter of each of us having certain preferences based on the types of images we regularly work with. You too may find one or the other approach more useful with your images. By providing both, we offer you the best of our joint experience.

Who Should Use This Book

Every nature photographer who wants people to look at their pictures and say, "Wow!" should use this book.

Photoshop for Nature Photographers: A Workshop in a Book is designed for nature photographers who want a straightforward workflow customized to make their images have the most impact. If you are new to Photoshop, you'll find we start off with the basics and gently build your abilities. We give you plenty of opportunities to practice what you're learning using images we provide as well as your own. We write in an informal, casual, but clear way, providing lots of examples and color illustrations to help you develop your skills.

If you already have some familiarity with Photoshop, but find that you don't always get the best results or that your workflow is inconsistent, we'll help you hone your skills. We'll provide techniques that will allow you to efficiently optimize your images. And if you'd like to get some ideas of how to be creative with your images, this is the book for you! We cover a variety of ways of compositing (combining) images as well as creating various digital montages, filter effects, and even digital multiple exposures.

If you take other types of photographs as well as nature photographs, our workflow and techniques will still work well for you. You'll gain the tools and abilities you need to make your pictures come alive.

What's Inside

The organization of this book follows the general workflow that we recommend. Here is a glance at what's in each chapter.

Chapter 1: Thinking Digitally in the Field discusses the photographic techniques you need to use in camera to get the best results. It covers choosing RAW versus JPEG, exposure, (including histograms), white balance, shooting for composites as well as ethical considerations.

Chapter 2: Making Photoshop Work for You lays the foundation to make Photoshop work in a predictable way for you, including color management issues as well as setting the Preferences. It also shows you how to use Bridge to manage and process your pictures.

Chapter 3: Basic Tools is an introduction to the selection and brush tools that you'll be using in later chapters to optimize your images.

Chapter 4: First Steps begins the actual digital workflow, starting with using Adobe Camera Raw to create the best possible converted image. It goes on to cover the initial steps in Photoshop including cropping, rotating, and image cleanup. The concept of layers is introduced.

Chapter 5: Exposure Adjustments introduces you to using layer masks and guides you through making various tonal adjustments including Levels, Curves, and Shadow/Highlights.

Chapter 6: Color Adjustments continues the use of adjustment layers to help you fine tune the color in your image using Hue/Saturation, Selective Color, and Color Balance.

Chapter 7: Composites covers a variety of ways to combine images to create effects not possible in a single image including replacing skies, panoramas, extended depth of field, extended exposure latitude (including creating using Merge to HDR to create 32-bit images), and combining parts of various pictures into a single image.

Chapter 8: Creative Effects presents ways to become more expressive with your images including converting to Black and White or partially colorized images, using various filters, creating digital montages and even digital multiple exposures.

Chapter 9: Output covers the workflow after you have created your Master File in order to size, reduce noise, and sharpen your images for print or web.

Chapter 10: Additional Techniques presents some ways to become more efficient including actions and batch processing. It also covers practical applications for your images including making greeting and business cards and preparing slide shows.

What's on the CD

The companion CD contains sample images for you to practice the techniques in the book. Use them to follow along with the instructions and try out each new technique as they are presented. Taking the time to use these images will reinforce what you're reading.

How to Contact the Authors

Both of us welcome feedback from you about this book or about books you'd like to see from us in the future. You can reach Ellen by writing to ellenanon@aol.com or Tim by writing to tim@timgrey.com. For more information about Ellen's workshops and photography, visit her website at www.sunbearphoto.com. To learn more about Tim's writing and appearances, visit www.timgrey.com.

Sybex strives to keep you supplied with the latest tools and information you need for your work. Please check their website at www.sybex.com for additional content and updates that supplement this book. Enter the book's ISBN—4427—in the Search box (or type **photoshop and nature**), and click Go to get to the book's update page.

Thinking Digitally in the Field

Getting the most out of Photoshop really begins with taking the best pictures you can in the field. Many digital neophytes think they no longer have to worry about being careful while photographing because they can "fix it later in Photoshop." The reality is that there is much truth to the adage "Garbage in, garbage out." The more careful your photographic techniques, the better your final image, and the less time you will spend on the computer. Use Photoshop to optimize your images and as an outlet for creativity, but not as a panacea for sloppy photographic techniques.

This chapter considers some of the things you can do in the field to capture the best digital files possible to work on later in Photoshop.

Chapter Contents

Photographic Techniques

It really doesn't matter if you are using film or digital to capture your images—the basics remain the same. We've been appalled to hear one well-respected professional nature photographer, who wouldn't think of photographing without a tripod with his film camera, announce he didn't bother with a tripod with his digital camera. Shortly thereafter he realized his foolishness and now employs the same careful photographic techniques when using his digital cameras that he used to use with film.

Digital photography and Photoshop are not excuses to be sloppy in the field. You still have to do everything possible to take the best pictures you can in the field. That way, the time you spend at your computer will be devoted to optimizing images and being creative, rather than trying to compensate for mistakes you made while taking the pictures.

For example, use a tripod whenever it's reasonable to help ensure the sharpest pictures possible. In fact, using a tripod is essential when you want to combine images to expand exposure latitude or create a panorama by stitching together several individual photographs. If you don't use a tripod when taking several pictures at various exposure settings in order to capture the highlight and shadow detail, then when you try to combine them into a single image (discussed in Chapter 7, "Composites"), the images won't combine properly, and possibly they won't merge together at all. And if you try to shoot a panorama without a tripod, you're likely to encounter all sorts of complications when you try to stitch them together, a topic that is also covered in Chapter 7.

With digital capture you still need to use most of your photographic tools to help create the best images possible, including mirror lockup and cable releases when appropriate. Although we claim to sharpen images in Photoshop using the Unsharp Mask or Smart Sharpen filters (techniques described in Chapter 9, "Output"), this sharpening is not a substitute for accurate focusing and capturing a sharp image. Also, you'll still want to use split neutral density filters, even though it's essentially possible to create a custom neutral density filter by combining exposures or by using adjustment layers and layer masks, all of which are covered later in this book. If the scene lends itself to using a split neutral density filter, as in Figure 1.1, it will save you time and effort later, so use it!

Throughout this book, we've asked some of the top nature photographers in the world to share some of their insights and favorite tips for using Photoshop effectively. Here, in the first of these "pro" sidebars, Charles Glatzer, M. Photog., briefly shares some thoughts about shooting digitally. Glatzer, a professional photographer and teacher for more than 20 years, hosts "Shoot the Light" instructional photographic workshops throughout the U.S.A. and abroad. His images are recognized internationally for their lighting, composition, and attention to detail.

Figure 1.1 Use good photographic techniques, including tripods, cable releases, and even split neutral density filters when appropriate, to capture the best images possible and then optimize them in Photoshop for impact. (Photo by Ellen Anon.)

Getting It Right in the Camera

by Charles Glatzer

© Charles Glatzer

Consistency is key to my livelihood. When capturing images in the field I eliminate as many variables as possible.

To consistently transpose the images we see in our mind to the capture medium, it is necessary to pre-visualize the result. Pre-visualization is possible when one has gained technical proficiency. Knowing the photographic fundamentals and being able to see and understand light, its quality and quantity, physical properties, etc., and how they relate to your subject and capture medium will allow you to take control of your imagery.

And, while Photoshop affords me the ability to apply levels, curves, contrast, and saturation adjustments while tweaking exposure and color balance to an image, I prefer to get it right in the camera. In doing so, my workflow is now faster and more productive, allowing me to transpose the image I captured on my CF card to the printed page more efficiently.

Translation: I can spend more time in the field.

© Charles Glatzer, www.shootthelight.com

Similarly, you need to choose your camera settings such as Aperture Priority, Shutter Priority, or Manual to create the type image you have in mind. Planning to use Photoshop is not an excuse to suddenly rely on the fully automatic program shooting modes. Many nature photographers shoot in aperture priority or manual because controlling the depth of field is their primary concern. If you envision a picture with a shallow depth of field, photograph it that way, using a wide aperture to begin with rather than relying on one of the blur filters within Photoshop. Use a filter later to accentuate the effect if desired. Occasionally, nature photographers may choose to use shutter priority for a specific need such as to create a blur of birds in flight (like the ones shown in Figure 1.2). Although you can create motion blurs in Photoshop, planning your image ahead of time (for example, using a slow shutter speed combined with panning) enables you to capture images with motion effects that would require a lot more time to make digitally. In some cases, you can capture motion effects (like the one in Figure 1.2) that would be nearly impossible to recreate in Photoshop, because objects closer to you blur more than objects that are farther away.

Figure 1.2 It is doubtful you could re-create this blur effect in Photoshop because the closer the birds are to you, the more they appear to be blurred. (Photo by Ellen Anon.)

Compose carefully. Of course you can crop the image later, but that means you will be cropping away pixels, leaving fewer pixels and therefore less detail to work with. With fewer pixels your final image will have less detail and may not be able to be printed as large as you hoped. Take the time to create a pleasing composition so you can use all the pixels your camera is capable of capturing.

Careful metering is as important as ever, even though you now have histograms to give you immediate feedback as to whether the exposure is correct. Meter as you always have, but make it a habit to check the histogram, at least for the first image in a series, to see if you need to tweak your exposure.

Choosing RAW versus JPEG

It's funny how this has become such an emotionally charged topic for some, almost akin to the classic which-is-better debates, such as Nikon versus Canon or Apple versus Microsoft. The truth is there are advantages and disadvantages to both formats. In fact, since Ellen's camera (at the time of writing, a Canon 1Ds MKII) allows her to shoot simultaneously in RAW and JPEG, she does both. If she had to choose, she'd choose RAW most of the time.

Before considering the benefits of each format, let's define what each one is. RAW is actually a pseudo-format used to refer to a lot of camera manufacturer proprietary formats: Canon .CR2 and .CRW, Nikon .NEF, Olympus .ORF, Minolta .MRW, Fuji .RAF, and more. It's a category of files rather than a specific file format like JPEG and TIFF. Raw files are similar to film negatives. They're files containing all the information about the amount of light that was captured by each sensor. Parameters such as color space, white balance, sharpening, saturation, contrast, etc. are recorded as metadata or tags but they're not applied to the image in-camera. You can still modify all these parameters at the time of conversion.

JPEG is a file format that uses lossy compression each time you resave your file in order to decrease the file size. This means that as the pixels are compressed, data is thrown away, even the initial time when the camera first writes the image. Each time thereafter that you resave your image it is recompressed and more data is lost. Although you may not notice any problem with the initial image, if you resave an image often, you are likely to see some degradation in image quality. Figure 1.3 presents sections of the same image at 100 percent magnification. The first image was a raw file saved as a TIFF file; the second image was resaved numerous times as a JPEG to illustrate the potential image degradation that can occur.

Figure 1.3
A section of an image originally captured as a raw file, and the same section after being resaved multiple times as a JPEG. (Photo by Ellen Anon.)

TIFF is a generic file format people often use to save their raw files after conversion or to save images that were initially shot as JPEGs. TIFF files can be compressed, but they use lossless compression, so you can resave your files with no loss of image quality. TIFF files are larger than JPEG files.

Another difference among these formats has to do with something called *bit depth*. Many nature photographers start to feel over their heads when computerese slips into the discussion, but bit depth isn't very complicated. In simple terms, a bit is the smallest unit of information that can be recorded digitally—either a 1 or a 0—and refers to black or white. In an 8-bit image each color channel (red, green, and blue) contains 2^8 or 256 possible tonal values. Since each channel has 256 possible tonal values, there are 16.7 million ($256\times256\times256$) possible color values for each pixel, as shown in Table 1.1.

▷ **Table 1.1** Colors and Bit Depths

Bit Depth	Typical Format	Possible Colors per Component	Possible Colors per Pixel
8 bits	JPEG	256	16.7 million
12 bits	RAW	4,096	68.7 million
16 bits	PSD, TIFF	65,536	281 trillion

Now 16 million may seem like more than enough, but in reality, at times the transitions between tones in an 8-bit image are not smooth, which is called *posterization*. 12-bit images, which is what most cameras can capture in RAW, have 4,096 tonal values for each color channel, which means a choice of 68.7 million ($4096\times4096\times4096$) possible colors. Tonal gradations are much smoother with so many possible values for each pixel.

JPEG images are limited to eight bits, so some JPEG images may demonstrate posterization. Clearly, more detail can be accurately conveyed the higher the bit depth. 8-bit color is common, but with raw files becoming more standard, 16-bit images are also becoming common. Even 32-bit files are starting to emerge and can be created using Photoshop's Merge To HDR (high dynamic range), which is covered in Chapter 7.

It can seem confusing initially that in Photoshop you have options to use 8-bit or 16-bit images (32-bit if you've created an HDR image). If you have a JPEG image, it is clearly an 8-bit image. When you convert a raw file, which is usually a 12-bit file, you can convert it as either an 8-bit file or a 16-bit file. Converting into 8-bit results in a smaller file in which you have discarded 3,840 possible tonal values per color channel. That's a lot to throw away!

Photoshop 7 offered minimal support for 16-bit images, but Photoshop CS and CS2 offer considerable support, making it logical to convert into 16-bit space. Converting a 12-bit image into a 16-bit space retains all of your data. That way when you make tonal or color adjustments, there are plenty of tonal values to use.

What's so great about RAW?

A lot of things! As just described, you have many more possible tonal values, which offer the possibility of more accurate detail in your photos and smoother tonal transitions. But there are other advantages as well. For example, you can "expose to the right" (as will be described shortly) and then correct the exposure in the raw converter to optimize the signal-to-noise ratio and have the most accurate tonal information with the least problems from noise.

More importantly, all the information captured by the sensor is available, and during the conversion process, you get to determine how it appears. For example, with the exposure, you can make it lighter or darker, even several stops lighter, although more noise may become visible in the image when it is lightened. For best results, try to limit lightening to one stop or less. In most cases you can tweak the exposure such that there is rarely a need to bracket exposures by a third of a stop in the field anymore, except when you are in danger of clipping your highlights. Clipping highlights means that you have overexposed your image and captured no detail in the highlights.

There is a tremendous amount of flexibility and control available to you as to how to present the information you captured on the sensor, as you can see in Figure 1.4. The raw capture (left) was converted with settings that revealed significantly more color than was captured in the JPEG version (right) of the same image. No pixels have been damaged, and yet the image is significantly more dramatic. Although you can instruct the converter to distribute the information the sensor captured in ways that will maximize the contrast, decrease it, or change the white balance, etc., what you can't do is to re-create information that isn't there. So if you have highlights with no information or shadows with no information, you may be able to lighten or darken them, but you won't be able to recreate detail within them unless you captured it in the first place.

Figure 1.4 The raw capture (left) was converted with settings that revealed significantly more color than was captured in the JPEG version (right) of the same image. No pixels have been damaged, and yet the image is significantly more dramatic. (Photo by Ellen Anon.)

In addition to making final decisions about parameters such as exposure, contrast, white balance, color saturation, and more, you can even select the color space here. Usually you will want Adobe RGB (1998), which is a wide color space that correlates well to the colors most ink jet printers can print. When capturing as JPEG files, most cameras use the sRGB color space, which has fewer colors available. sRGB is particularly suited for web use and projection use. We'll talk more about color spaces in Chapter 4, "First Steps."

Note: If your camera allows you to select a color space, Adobe RGB (1998) is a good choice for nature photographers.

RAW also offers you the ability to easily fix some problems that occur in some images, such as noise reduction for images taken using higher ISOs, chromatic aberration that occurs with some lenses resulting in fringing, and vignetting. We'll explain how to identify these potential problems and how to easily minimize or eliminate these issues using Adobe Camera Raw in Chapter 4.

The downside of all this flexibility and capability is that in order to use raw images you have to convert them. This takes time. Many people are happy using the converter in Photoshop called Adobe Camera Raw, noting the ease of workflow with Adobe's Bridge program. (We will look more closely at using Bridge—which replaced the File Browser used in versions of Photoshop prior to CS2—in Chapter 2, "Making Photoshop Work for You," and at Adobe Camera Raw in Chapter 4.) Some users prefer a separate program, whether developed by third-party software makers (for example, Capture One, Bibble, or BreezeBrowser) or supplied by camera manufacturers.

The other major downside of shooting in RAW is you will need a lot more storage space, both in your camera and on your computer, when you capture in RAW than if you use JPEG.

Capturing in even high-resolution JPEG means you need less storage space; a 1 GB compact flash card will make you feel like you can shoot forever. Also convenient is the fact that JPEG images are ready for you to edit or resize and show others in slide shows, e-mails. or whatever you desire. But there are two *huge* downsides: One is that whatever your camera settings are, including color space, contrast, sharpening, white balance, exposure, and saturation, they are applied to your image at the moment of capture. Any changes must be done within Photoshop itself to this 8-bit image and will result in some destruction of pixels and therefore image degradation. In reality, this may often be so slight that it's not noticeable, but it's there. However, there are times when the differences may be huge. For example, if you accidentally use the wrong white balance, a JPEG image may seem nearly useless at first and at best may require extensive corrections in Photoshop. But the extent of the exposure corrections you'll be able to make will be less because you'll have only an 8-bit image to work with, and extensive Photoshop corrections may result in posterization or noise. Furthermore, as discussed earlier, a JPEG file is compressed lossy, which means that even when you first open it on your computer, it has already thrown away some information the sensor captured when you took the picture. Sometimes this is not noticeable, but at other times it can result in banding and other strange artifacts.

Which is right for you, JPEG or RAW? If you make large prints and want the best images you can get, RAW is the way to go. If time and convenience are your priorities, then JPEG may be for you. If you plan on selling your images or entering contests, check with your intended clients or the contest rules, because some will require you to provide the original RAW file as well as the converted image.

Try It! Shoot a series of images in RAW and in JPEG. Expose them to the best of your ability in JPEG and then use the same settings for the RAW version. Then shoot one set with an incorrect white balance setting. Capture a variety of scenes, including some with shadow areas, some with significant highlight areas, and some more average-toned scenes. See if you can detect a difference in the optimized versions. You may have to wait until you finish a few more chapters so you can optimize both versions of the pictures to their maximum potential for your final decision.

Understanding Histograms

Without a doubt one of the most important advantages of shooting digitally is the ability to check the histogram to ensure you are exposing your images correctly. In the old days—that is, just a few years ago, before digital was so common in the field—wherever there was a group of photographers shooting similar subject matter, you'd inevitably hear someone ask, "What are you shooting at?" People felt comfortable with their compositions but always worried about setting the exposure correctly, knowing that as little as 1/3 stop difference could mean the difference between an awesome image and a throwaway.

With digital cameras you can review your shots on the small LCD screen on the back of the camera. While this may be helpful to double-check your composition and to a certain extent to check for sharpness, the real value lies in displaying the histogram. Get in the habit of checking the histogram in the LCD on the camera back (like the one shown in Figure 1.5). If your camera has a flashing highlight overexposure alert feature, be sure to enable it. That way you'll know immediately if you need to modify your exposures.

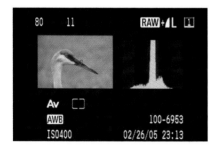

Figure 1.5
The major value of the LCD screen on your camera back is the chance to review the histogram and double-check your exposure.

What is a histogram? A histogram is simply a bar graph showing the distribution of the tonalities (lightness/darkness) of the pixels you captured in the image. They range from pure black on the far left to pure white on the far right, with the different tonalities in between. This means that dark tones are toward the left, middle tones are in the middle, and light tones are toward the right. The higher the spike corresponding to any particular value, the more pixels there are of that particular tonality within the image.

Some people mistakenly think that an ideal histogram would be a bell-shaped distribution of pixels. *In fact, there's not a single ideal histogram for all images*. Rather, the ideal histogram for an image is one that captures all the data within that particular image. Let's look at a series of pictures and their histograms.

Figure 1.6 shows a good histogram for an average scene with a full range of tonalities. Note that the pixels extend across the entire histogram, but there are no spikes at either end. Spikes at the ends would mean you have pixels that are overexposed and/or underexposed and therefore areas with no detail. Since all the pixels fall within the bounds of the histogram, this picture will have detail throughout.

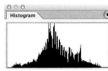

Figure 1.6 This is an ideal histogram for a scene with a full range of tonalities. (Photo by Ellen Anon.)

Figure 1.7 shows an underexposed picture. All the pixels are in the left portion of the histogram, indicating no light tones. Since you know that the pelican is in fact white, a proper exposure would have the pixel distribution moved to the right. If you are shooting a subject with a large light area and see a histogram that looks like Figure 1.7, you need to add light to your exposure.

Figure 1.7 This picture is underexposed. Note that all the data in the histogram is skewed towards the left and there are no light tonalities. (Photo by Ellen Anon.)

Compare the image and histogram in Figure 1.7 with those of Figure 1.8. The latter is a well-exposed picture with an ideal histogram of an overall dark scene with a few bright areas. If the exposure had been any brighter, the whites would have been *burned out* or *blown out* and lost their feather detail. *Blown out highlights* means that no detail has been captured in the brightest areas of the picture.

Figure 1.8 Overall dark scenes with small bright areas will have histograms that look like this. This is *not* underexposed, even though the data is skewed towards the left, as in Figure 1.7. (Photo by Ellen Anon.)

Figure 1.9 shows an overexposed image. Note the spike on the right side of the histogram indicating blown out highlights. Unfortunately, no amount of Photoshop magic can restore data that was not captured. Checking your camera's histogram regularly can avoid the frustration of taking an entire series of pictures like this.

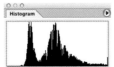

Figure 1.9
The whites in this image are blown out, as indicated by the spike on the right side of the histogram. (Photo by Ellen Anon.)

Now compare the histogram and picture in Figure 1.9 with those in Figure 1.10. This picture of white birds on a nearly white sky day is not overexposed, although most of the pixel data is skewed towards the right. This is the type of histogram you want in this type of situation—light background and light subject with minimal dark areas.

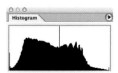

Figure 1.10 A light subject with a light background will have a histogram that is skewed towards the right. (Photo by Ellen Anon.)

Figure 1.11 shows a histogram of a high-contrast scene. There is a spike on the left side of the histogram, although the data extends through the tonalities all the way towards the right of the histogram. There is no way to capture this shot at this time of day without losing either some highlight or shadow detail. Normally it's better to preserve the highlights and sacrifice some shadow detail, as was done in this image. An alternative appropriate for some situations, which we will discuss later, is to shoot multiple exposures and combine them in one image.

Figure 1.11 This scene has too much contrast to capture in a single shot. The spike on the far left of the histogram shows that there is some loss of information in the shadows, but the highlights have been preserved. (Note that the small spike on the right is just before the end of the histogram.) (Photo by Ellen Anon.)

Finally, let's look at the histogram of a silhouette in Figure 1.12. As you might expect, there is a spike on the far left side of the histogram, but in this case it doesn't mean the image is underexposed. On the contrary, we want silhouettes to be pure black!

Figure 1.12 Silhouettes will have histograms that have a spike on the left side indicating areas of pure black. (Photo by Ellen Anon.)

The bottom line is that there is no single ideal histogram for every situation. You have to think about the tonalities in your image and where they should fall on the histogram to know what is ideal for any particular situation. It's vital to make sure that you don't have spikes at the extreme ends of the graph, since that would mean shadow or highlight areas without detail. Of course, if you are shooting a silhouette, you want a spike at the left side of the histogram indicating blacks for the silhouettes, while any specular highlights may be fine as pure white. But for most images, in order to capture detail in both the shadows and the highlights, you want the tonalities to fall within the boundaries of the histogram.

Note: Many photographers new to digital and Photoshop think they don't have to worry about exposure anymore because they can "fix it later" in Photoshop. The harsh reality is if you blow out the highlights or totally block up the shadows, the only "fix" will be to clone in pixels from other areas. Photoshop allows you lots of ways to tweak the exposure, which we'll explain in Chapter 5, "Exposure Adjustments," but if the data isn't there because of overexposure or underexposure, Photoshop isn't going to create it for you.

Exposure

If you check the histogram and see that you have a spike at the far right, you need to modify your exposure to have less light. If you are shooting in aperture priority, you might choose to put in some minus exposure compensation, or if you are using manual mode, either use a smaller aperture or increase your shutter speed. Since you're shooting digitally, there is a third option—to switch to a slower ISO. Although you still need to set the correct exposure compensation, you can use the same depth of field/aperture setting as you originally wanted (perhaps in an effort to keep the background out of focus) or the same shutter speed (perhaps in an attempt to blur your subject). Similarly, if the histogram is indicating a spike at the black end, unless you're shooting a silhouette, you want to add light via plus exposure compensation, slower shutter speeds, wider apertures, and possibly also a faster ISO to allow you to use the desired apertures and shutter speeds. Faster ISOs—those with the larger numbers—mean that less light is required to hit the sensor to achieve the proper exposure. The problem with this is that the faster the ISO, the more noise the picture is likely to have. Use the slowest (smallest number) ISO that you can.

 Note: Usually, the lower the ISO, the less noise you will encounter. Noise is in many ways the digital equivalent of film grain, except that it tends to be more evident in darker shadow areas. It appears as variations in color and tonality in areas that should be smooth.

Technically, the ideal histogram for a raw image should not only contain all the pixels with no spikes at the ends, but also it should be exposed as far to the right as possible with no blown out highlights. This is to obtain the best signal-to-noise ratio possible. (It is important to keep in mind that this applies to raw images but not to those captured as JPEGs because the main benefits occur in the process of the conversion. If you are shooting in JPEG, make the most accurate exposure you can and make sure you're not clipping data on either end.)

Michael Reichmann does an excellent job of explaining this, so we asked him to share that explanation with you. The following section, "Expose Right," was written and contributed by him. For more information on Reichmann and his work, please visit his website, www.luminous-landscape.com.

"Expose Right" by Michael Reichmann

In the beginning there was the light meter. Photographers used them and saw that they were good. Then there was through-the-lens metering, and the people rejoiced. Automatic exposure followed, and photographers thought that the millennium had arrived. Eventually the millennium actually did arrive, and with it digital cameras with histogram displays; and the world changed again.

What hasn't changed over the years is the need for accurate exposure, which all of this technology is ultimately in aid of. But what constitutes proper exposure is quite different between film and digital. In this section you'll see why, and how to take best advantage of it.

Don't Blow It

Digital is very much like color slide film in that you want to avoid overexposure. While it's often possible to recover some information from the shadows of an underexposed digital image, especially if a low ISO is being used, once overexposed beyond 255 there is no information to be retrieved. The individual photo sites or pixels have simply recorded 100 percent of the information that they can absorb, and this is a featureless white.

© Michael Reichmann

Note: We authors interrupt Michael here to say the following: The exposure scale of a histogram goes from black at 0 to white at 255 in 8-bit capture; the same principle applies for 12-bit capture, where the maximum value is 4,095.

This would lead most people to think that the best thing to do would therefore be to bias their exposure toward the left of the histogram—toward underexposure. This would avoid the risk of blown out highlights, and since it's often possible to retrieve detail from underexposed shadow areas, what have you got to lose?

A lot actually, as you'll see.

Signals and Noise

Film has *grain*. These are particles of silver or organic dyes that, when exposed to light, turn dark to varying degrees. Fast films have more grain because they have more of these light-sensitive particles with which to absorb light.

Digital uses very tiny photo sites—sensor elements made of silicon that are sensitive to light. Essentially, if no light hits a sensor element, no voltage is generated, and a value of 0 or black is recorded. If the sensor element is flooded with light (overexposed), it records a maximum value of 255 (in an 8-bit image) and a corresponding voltage level is produced. Light levels in between are recorded as some value between 0 and 255.

While silicon doesn't suffer directly from what we describe as grain, it does have a comparable issue. This is described as *noise*. Noise in this context is any form of non-image-forming energy (light is just one form of energy). Various things can cause noise to be recorded by the sensor. These include heat, cosmic rays, and several other exotic sources. There is an inherent noise level in all silicon chips. As a percentage of the total signal being recorded, it is usually quite small and unnoticeable. But it's always there, and depending on the exposure being recorded, it can become visible and annoying. This is somewhat akin to the noise that one sees on a TV screen when there's no channel broadcasting or antenna attached.

 Note: We authors interrupt to add that, usually, the energy that causes noise is low enough in its intensity that it falls to the left (dark) side of the histogram.

This is where what we call the sensor's *signal-to-noise (s/n)* ratio comes in. If there's a lot of signal (data to the right side of the histogram), then the s/n ratio is high, the signal predominates, and the noise isn't visible. But if the signal is low (to the left of the histogram), then the s/n ratio is low, and one sees the noise because it represents a relatively high percentage of the total signal present.

So the solution is clear. Take a photograph, check the instant review histogram, and make sure that the exposure is as far to the right of the histogram as possible without touching the right edge.

But wait. There's a problem. If you do this, and you're shooting JPEGs, you'll see some fairly nasty looking exposures—ones that appear very bright, inappropriately so. Of course, you can try and fix the shot in an image-editing program such as Photoshop. But because JPEGs are pre-baked images (reduced to 8-bit mode and with predetermined exposure and color balance characteristics embedded in the file while in the camera), such adjustments can't really be performed while still retaining decent image quality. So with JPEGs at least, the idea of biasing your exposures to the right of the histogram appears to be good in theory, but not terribly practical.

Raw Mode

The answer is to shoot in raw mode. In raw mode the file contains the data that the sensor recorded. In addition, there are *tags* that describe the camera's settings, such as white balance, sharpening, contrast saturation, and the like. But these tags are just that. The raw file itself is not changed in any way. It is also in 12-bit or 14-bit mode, in a 16-bit space (more on this in a moment). Finally, a raw file isn't compressed the way a JPEG file is. If it is compressed, which a few manufacturers do, it's done so losslessly.

Dynamic Range and Bit Mode

The concept of *bit mode* is important to properly understanding digital image quality.

Let's assume for the purposes of illustration that a digital SLR has a dynamic range of five stops. (It's usually closer to six stops, but let's not quibble.) When working in raw mode, most cameras record a 12-bit image. (Yes, we say it's in 16 bits, but the reality is that the camera's only recording 12 bits of information in a 16-bit space. Better than 8, but not as good as a real 16-bit would be.)

A 12-bit image is capable of recording $2^{12} = 4,096$ discrete tonal values in each component. One would think that therefore each f/stop of the five-stop range would be able to record some 4,096 divided by 5 = 850 of these steps. But, alas, this is not the case. The way that it really works is that the first (brightest) stop's worth of data contains 2,048 of these steps—fully half of those available.

Why? Because CCD and CMOS chips are linear devices. And, of course, each f/stop records half of the light of the previous one, and therefore half the remaining data space available. Table 1.2 tells the tale.

▷ **Table 1.2** Where Light Levels are Stored on Chips

F/Stop	Number of Levels
Within the first f/stop, which contains the brightest tones	2,048 levels available
Within the second f/stop, which contains bright tones	1,024 levels available
Within the third f/stop, which contains the midtones	512 levels available
Within the fourth f/stop, which contains dark tones	256 levels available
Within the fifth f/stop, which contains the darkest tones	128 levels available

This realization carries with it a number of important lessons, the most important of them being that if you do not use the right fifth of the histogram for recording some of your image, you are in fact wasting fully half of the available encoding levels of your camera.

But, we all know (or at least should by now) that the worst sin in digital imaging is to blow out the highlights—just as it was when shooting slide film. Once they're blown (past the right edge of the histogram), it's bye-bye data.

The Lesson

The simple lesson to be learned from this is to bias your exposures so that the histogram is snuggled up to the right of the histogram (as illustrated in Figure 1.13), but not to the point that the highlights are blown. This can usually be seen by the flashing alert on most camera review screens. Just back off so that the flashing stops.

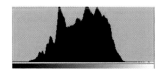 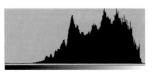

Figure 1.13
A normal exposure shows a centered histogram (left). This histogram is shifted to the right for maximum signal/noise ratio (right).

Now when you look at the raw file in your favorite raw processing software, like Adobe's Camera Raw, the image will likely appear to be too light. That's OK. Just use the available sliders to change the brightness level and contrast so that the data is spread out appropriately and the image looks "right." This accomplishes a number of things: First, it maximizes the signal-to-noise ratio. Second, it minimizes the posterization and noise that potentially occurs in the darker regions of the image.

Please be aware though that for proper results you need to make these corrections while working in 16-bit (12-bit) mode in a raw converter. Unlike what some people think, in raw mode, the camera is not doing any nonlinear processing. All nonlinear processing is done in the raw converter. This is why if you're going to try this trick, you must shoot in RAW and then manually readjust the image in the raw converter before exporting the file into Photoshop. By doing this you'll be maximizing the data bandwidth of your entire system.

Also be aware that by doing this, you are in fact effectively lowering the ISO used to capture the image, requiring slower shutter speeds and/or larger apertures. If you are hand-holding the camera or shooting moving objects, the tradeoff may not be worth the reduced noise level.

But, if ultimate image quality is your goal, and you have the ability to control all of the variables, *exposing to the right* is a technique that will serve you well.

© 2004 Michael H. Reichmann, www.luminous-landscape.com

White Balance in Nature Photography

With film cameras you used specific types of film according to the lighting conditions, and you used filters to further control the color casts. With digital, you have a somewhat equivalent, but more flexible, choice and that is white balance. As you know, the color (or temperature) of light varies throughout each day. It's a "warmer" color in the morning, and the world takes on a reddish/yellow glow. Your eyes adapt to that and compensate because you know that white is still white. (Think about when you put colored glasses on and a few minutes later the colors look "normal" again.) Later, when the bright sun is overhead, the color appears "cooler" or bluer. Your eyes continuously adapt so that you see neutral colors as neutral, and most people are rarely aware of color casts.

Your cameras are more literal—they record the colors exactly as they see them. With digital cameras you can use the white balance setting to render the neutral tones (any shade from white to black) neutral rather than having them have a color cast. For example, you need a different white balance in the cool bluish light of an overcast day than in the warm reddish light of a sunset. All digital cameras offer an automatic white balance setting in which the camera makes a best guess as to the correct lighting temperature. Surprisingly, most do quite a good job, as shown in Figure 1.14.

However, some photographers feel the best way to be certain of getting the correct white balance is to set it yourself. Most nature photographers are content to use one of the presets that are supplied with the camera such as flash, sunny, cloudy, shade, fluorescent, etc. With many cameras, using these settings ensures that the image you capture will appear as neutrally colored as possible, while other cameras tend to have a warm bias. You do have to be vigilant to changing lighting conditions and change your white balance accordingly. As you can see in Figure 1.15, if you use the wrong white balance setting, your picture may have a strong color cast. If the image is shot in RAW, this is easily corrected during the conversion process; but if it's shot in JPEG, a mistake like this could ruin the image.

Figure 1.14
Auto white balance was used to capture this photo in the warm light of early morning. (Photo by Ellen Anon.)

Figure 1.15
The white balance here was accidentally set to Tungsten. A mistake like this can be deadly if the image is shot in JPEG.

But if you've ever gotten up before dawn to go out and photograph in the beautiful, warm, early morning light, you know that we nature photographers aren't always seeking to make neutrally colored images! Often, we want a color cast in our images, particularly a warm cast, as shown in Figure 1.16. This is one of the reasons I prefer to shoot in raw mode (Ellen Anon writing at this point); I don't have to make a final decision about the white balance until I'm converting the image, whereas with JPEG mode, the white balance is "baked" into the image. My decision may be based more on the mood I want to portray than on what the actual lighting conditions were at the time.

Figure 1.16
This picture, taken at dawn, actually has a warmer color cast than I saw at the time, but I like the result. Altering the white balance lets you effectively convey a mood. (Photo by Ellen Anon.)

If you are shooting in JPEG, you may want to try using the auto white balance feature, along with setting the white balance specifically. You may not only want to set the white balance for an accurate rendition of the scene, you may want to experiment a little. For example, if you use the cloudy or shade settings in fairly sunny conditions, it's similar to adding an 81A or 81B filter to your camera lens; these settings will add a warm cast to your picture. Product photographers must be concerned with absolute color accuracy in their photography. Nature photographers have the luxury of being able to be creative with the white balance and create, augment, or remove color casts as it suits their vision. You can use the white balance settings rather than filters to do this both with JPEG and RAW.

When you capture your images as raw files, because the white balance you selected in the camera is not actually applied until you convert the image, you have the luxury of time to adjust the white balance as you wish. Most raw converters provide a continuous temperature slider to set the white balance that best fits the mood of the image. You can tweak it in small increments to precisely obtain the effect you are after. Because of this, many photographers elect to leave their cameras on auto white balance and then use the sliders in the converters to impart or remove color casts. Others still select what they believe is the best white balance setting while in the field so they can recall what the lighting was and how the image actually appeared. They prefer to have their images be as close to accurate, realistic color as possible. Who's right? Both are! It's a matter of your personal goals and preferences with your photography.

Note: If you are using auto white balance, using a warming or cooling filter may have no effect, because most cameras will compensate for the filter and try to make everything neutral!

Photographing Elements to Composite Later

How many times have you looked up and commented on the great clouds or beautiful sunset but not taken the picture because foreground elements were missing? Or the opposite—you found a great subject, perhaps a bird posing wonderfully or a gorgeous scene, but the sky or background was completely blah? Or you could tell there was just too much contrast to be able to capture the picture? When you are in the field with your camera, it's important to remember that Photoshop enables you to combine images in a seemingly infinite variety of ways. You have to adjust your thinking to include seeing the potential for an image.

Skies, Clouds, and Moons

There are a number of situations that lend themselves to photographing parts of a picture that you will later combine in Photoshop. You can create libraries of these image elements to use at some later time. Perhaps the most obvious elements to store are skies and clouds. Whenever you see a dramatic sky, photograph it! Place the images in a special folder labeled skies. You'll need more than one replacement sky, because one of the keys to creating believable composites is to match the direction and quality of the lighting. Sunsets are great to photograph, as are clouds—the blue sky with puffy white cloud types as well as the impending storm clouds. This way, when you find a great subject (perhaps that leopard in the tree while in Africa) or a beautiful scenic, you'll be able to remove the distracting white sky and make it appear that luck was with you in the field.

Figure 1.17 shows a picture that could have occurred but didn't. Capturing all these landing cranes in one shot was wonderful, but unfortunately the sky behind them was boring. A few minutes earlier, the sky in the very same spot had been dramatic, but there were no birds. This image is a combination of the birds with the sky that had been there a few minutes earlier.

Figure 1.17
Sometimes nature doesn't cooperate and gives you a great subject but a boring sky or vice versa. In Photoshop you can combine them to have the best of both worlds. (Photo by Ellen Anon.)

Don't limit yourself to just skies and clouds, though. There are all sorts of things that can be added to pictures to add impact or create a sense of your own style. Ellen likes to keep a folder of moons to use as accent elements in pictures. She shoots full moons, crescent moons, moons against black skies, and moons in daylight skies. You'd be amazed at the variety of color casts in the moons. Then when she thinks a picture needs a little extra pop, she puts one in. (We'll explain how to do that in Chapter 7.) Sometimes she makes them a realistic size, and sometimes she enlarges them. Another person we know adds docks and has a collection of docks to add to scenic water pictures! You're the artist and the choice is yours. Use your imagination and keep your eyes open for other elements to collect to add to your images.

When photographing something that you're likely to want to later extract from the picture and use elsewhere, try to design your photograph so as to make it easier to remove the desired object. For example, it will often be easier to remove an item from a blurred background rather than a cluttered one, so consider using a wide aperture. You may need to take a step or two left or right, or perhaps get down a little lower to help separate the offending object from the subject. A little care in the field can make your work in Photoshop much easier!

Expanding Camera Capabilities

Sometimes you see a scene and know that you can't capture it in a single shot because of the technical limitations of your equipment. Photoshop provides ways to combine shots to create images not possible with a single exposure.

Your eyes can see a much greater range of tonalities than can your camera, where the dynamic range is limited to between five and six stops of lights for digital captures and slide film. This means that although your eyes might be able to see detail in both the highlights and the shadows, today's cameras may not be able to do so within a single exposure. The solution is to take a series of exposures, making sure you capture detail in all parts of the pictures. This could mean two or more exposures varying at least one stop each.

Some Helpful Definitions

Dynamic range   The range between the brightest and darkest points of an image.

High dynamic range (HDR) images   An HDR image contains a far wider dynamic range than can be displayed on a screen or printed on a printer. They are often created from multiple exposures of one image and are stored in special file formats. They are of interest to photographers because you can convert them back to 8-bit or 16-bit images and compress the dynamic range, allowing you to get images with detail in both shadow and highlight areas of an image, more like what your eye saw when looking at the scene rather than what your camera captured.

If you're dealing with a static subject and shooting from a stable platform, you can take a series of exposures to later combine using Merge To HDR to create a 32-bit file. This file is called a high dynamic range (HDR) file and will be discussed more in Chapter 7. Unfortunately, most nature photography does not lend itself to this because if any element in the scene changes—even a shadow or a leaf—Merge To HDR may not work correctly. However, there are still ways to combine exposures within Photoshop to extend the latitude. So even if your subject matter is not completely static, take at least two or three exposures: one for the shadows and one for the highlights. You will need to keep your camera in precisely the same spot and not change the focus or aperture between the exposures, and vary only the shutter speed. Chapter 7 will explain how to put these pictures together to create a picture with as much or more detail than your eyes are accustomed to seeing.

Photographing Parts of the Scene Individually

Another limitation of your cameras sometimes arises when you need more depth of field and shutter speed than what the amount of light will allow. This happened to me (Ellen Anon) in Bosque Del Apache, New Mexico, when I saw the beautiful mountains and sunset in the distance with the cranes flying fairly close to me. Although I could see it, there was no way to capture the entire scene with adequate depth of field to have the cranes in focus as well as the mountains and have enough shutter speed to freeze the motion of the birds. My solution was to photograph the birds in one frame and the background separately. Then I combined the two in Photoshop, as shown in Figure 1.18. In reality, the moon was behind me while taking those shots, but in the end, I decided to add it to the picture because I wasn't trying to create a documentary image but rather, one that captured how it feels to be there. Photoshop made that possible.

Figure 1.18 There was no way to capture the birds and the mountains in a single shot due to the low light levels. Instead, individual shots were combined in Photoshop. (Photo by Ellen Anon.)

Ethical Considerations

Is the image "manipulated?" It sounds like such a straightforward question. But to answer honestly may be more difficult than it appears, especially when responding to people not well versed in digital.

If you shoot in RAW, you essentially have a negative that needs to be processed during conversion. The settings you apply determine the appearance of the image, but these really aren't manipulating it any more than the chemicals did in a darkroom. Similar adjustments done in Photoshop are considered by some to be manipulations. Many accept that it is necessary to clone out dust and to perform some sharpening since there is some slight softening of digital images by their very nature. A few people are bothered by basic exposure and color modifications, but most accept this as part of the processing as long as the overall intent of the capture remains the same.

Although cloning out dust is usually acceptable, there is debate about how much of an object one can clone out before the image is considered manipulated. Sometimes it's more environmentally responsible to clone out an object rather than remove it in reality. Sometimes it's impossible to remove it in reality. Unfortunately, for some this crosses the line into a manipulated image. Maybe it's an area that needs to be thought through more carefully.

There are many gray areas. For example, it's common practice when photographing hummingbirds at feeders to put up a man-made background so that the birds are photographed against a pleasing non-distracting background rather than clutter. This is acceptable. But if you took the image photographed with the cluttered background and, in Photoshop, replaced the background with a simpler one, many would insist the image is manipulated.

For me (again, Ellen Anon), if I composite elements, it's manipulated, and I am careful to indicate this whenever reasonable. When asked, I respond honestly and label images accurately. The bottom line for me is that photography is an art form, and it's my goal to create images that express what I feel. For those of you who are more inclined towards scientific documentary types of nature photographs, the lines may be different. You have to decide what's right for you!

Removing Objects in the Field or Later in Photoshop

There's an old adage that reminds us to "Take only pictures and leave only footprints, and barely those if possible." But as nature photographers we know that sometimes there are distracting elements that are interfering with our picture. It may be an ill placed stick, a wayward branch, or maybe a rock that's too light and bright. It seems harmless enough to move it and create a cleaner photo. Many times it may be fine. But have you considered that perhaps that rock or branch was serving a purpose to one of the many critters in our world? Perhaps the branch provided some protection against winds or shielded visibility from a predator; maybe the rock provided a safe resting spot while looking for food. We know and see the world though our human perspective and what seems inconsequential to us may actually have a significant impact on a variety of wildlife.

Does that mean you should never move anything in the environment? That would be an extreme and unrealistic position, but the reality is you may want to consider whether it would be smarter to remove the offending item later in Photoshop. Although it may create more work for you, you will be creating less stress on the nature around you. You are going to have to use common sense in making this choice. (We'll cover how to remove objects in Photoshop in Chapter 4.)

Making Photoshop Work for You

Believe us, we know what it's like to get started with a new book on Photoshop, and no doubt you're ready to dive right in and start working on your images. We're almost there! But first we want to make sure you have Photoshop configured in a way that is most efficient for you, and that you understand some of the basics of working with your images. In this chapter we'll show you how to configure Photoshop, work with your images, and sort through those images to find those you want to optimize to perfection.

2

Chapter Contents
Color Management
Setting Preferences
Views and Zoom
Sorting and Editing with Bridge

Color Management

For any photographer, achieving accurate color is a key concern. While you may take artistic license in how you optimize an image, you want to ensure that the print is an accurate reflection of your interpretation of the image. That means producing a print that matches the monitor display to the extent possible. This is the job of color management, and it can help you achieve greater consistency in your workflow.

Note: For more information on a complete color-managed workflow, see Tim's book *Color Confidence* (Sybex, 2004)

Monitor Calibration

The first step in a color-managed workflow is to calibrate and profile your monitor. We can't stress how important this is. If you don't have a calibrated display, the images you are evaluating and optimizing are likely to be at least slightly—and possibly significantly—inaccurate. If you don't calibrate your monitor, you also have no valid reason to complain about prints that don't match your monitor. Calibrating your monitor is a critical first step to producing the results you are looking for with your images.

As far as we're concerned, calibrating your monitor is only done properly if you are using a package that uses a colorimeter (a type of sensor) to measure the color values of your monitor so that appropriate compensation can be applied (see Figure 2.1). There are several packages available that include a colorimeter, and we're perfectly comfortable with any of them.

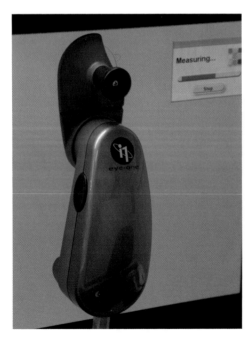

Figure 2.1

For monitor calibration, use a software package that includes a colorimeter sensor to measure the color behavior of your monitor and apply compensation to ensure an accurate display.

Three of the most popular monitor-calibrating packages are as follows:

Spyder2   This package from Color Vision (www.colorvision.com) is perhaps the most user-friendly available, making it a good choice for those of you who are just getting started with a digital workflow and feeling a little intimidated, without compromising on the quality of the results.

EyeOne Display 2   This is an advanced package from GretagMacbeth (www.gretagmacbeth .com) that produces exceptional results, including automatic compensation for ambient lighting in your working area. EyeOne Display is slightly complicated in operation, but it produces highly accurate results.

MonacoOPTIX ^{XR} This package from X-Rite (www.xrite.com) is also an advanced solution, and one of the most thorough in terms of the calibration process. It guides you through a large number of adjustments of your monitor settings to help ensure the widest dynamic range and best results possible.

Regardless of the solution you choose, the key is to calibrate and profile your monitor display, and to do so on a regular basis. This is necessary because the monitor's display will shift over time. For CRT monitors, we recommend calibrating at least about every 30 days; for LCD monitors, about every 60–90 days should be adequate.

Working Conditions

A calibrated monitor display ensures accurate color (to the extent possible), but doesn't ensure consistent color. That may sound a bit contradictory, but it emphasizes the importance of working under consistent conditions. As a nature photographer, you are well aware of the considerations of good lighting. You look for optimal conditions, with the sun at an optimal angle to produce a golden glow, for example. Just as varying lighting conditions can affect the ultimate quality of your photos, the conditions under which you work can affect the appearance of your monitor display.

It is very important that you work under lighting conditions that are as consistent as possible, and ideally somewhat dim. The monitor you are using as the basis of all your evaluations about an image emits light, and that light can be influenced by the light in the room. If the room is too bright, you won't be able to see subtle details on the monitor. If the light isn't relatively neutral, it can have an effect on the color appearance of the monitor display.

The ideal situation is to work in an environment that is consistently dark. That doesn't mean you need to work in absolute darkness. It just means that you want to minimize the lighting to the extent you are comfortable with, and do everything you can to ensure the lighting is neutral and remains consistent from one session to the next. If you work on an image with early morning light filling the room and making the image on your monitor look warmer than it really is, you may overcompensate by adjusting the image to look too cool.

If you can minimize the amount of artificial light in the room, perhaps by using a dimmer to keep the light at an appropriate level, that is an excellent start. If you have windows in the room where you're working on your images, it is a good idea to close the blinds (or install blinds) so you can minimize the influence of outside light.

The bottom line is that you want to be working in an environment where the monitor is accurate by virtue of the fact that it has been calibrated, and is consistent, because your working conditions are likewise consistent. This helps ensure that you are seeing accurate color on your monitor, which is the reference both for adjustments you're making to your images and for evaluating the accuracy of your prints.

Color Settings

Photoshop allows you to establish color management settings that determine its behavior related to the color in your images. Establishing appropriate settings is important to ensuring that your workflow results in accurate color and maximum image quality. These settings can be adjusted by choosing Edit > Color Settings, which brings up the Color Settings dialog box shown in Figure 2.2.

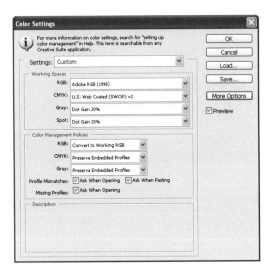

Figure 2.2
The Color Settings dialog box allows you to establish settings related to color management within Photoshop.

The Color Settings dialog box includes a More Options button that, when clicked, enlarges the dialog box to include additional controls. (It also enlarges the list of profiles on the Working Spaces drop-down menus to include all profiles available rather than only those designated as working space profiles.) Once you've clicked this button, it changes to Fewer Options, which returns you to the "basic" dialog box. We recommend leaving the advanced settings at their default values anyway, so for most users there is no need to access the More Options version of the dialog box.

Note: In versions of Photoshop prior to CS2, the More Options settings are accessed by selecting the Advanced Mode check box.

A *working space* profile defines the range of colors (the color *gamut*) that will be available for your images. The Working Spaces section includes options for specifying which profile should be used as the working space for each of the color modes available (RGB, CMYK, Gray, and Spot). For most photographers, the only working space you need to be concerned with is RGB, which is the mode we recommend working with for all images until there is a reason to convert them to a different color space (for example, if a printer insists that you perform the RGB-to-CMYK conversion). In most situations (including printing to most desktop printers), you will work on your images in RGB and keep them in RGB for the entire workflow.

Note: You want to work in RGB, because either you're printing to what is effectively an RGB device (such as a photo inkjet printer, even though it uses CMYK inks) or your print service prefers to receive RGB images and perform CMYK conversions for you.

For the RGB working space, we generally recommend using the one named "Adobe RGB (1998)". This is a good general working space with a relatively wide gamut, providing an appropriate space for a wide range of output options. That doesn't mean it's the best answer for everyone, but when it doubt, Adobe RGB (1998) is a good choice, and it is what we recommend unless you have a good reason to use something else. For example, some photographers may want to utilize the space named sRGB as their working space, if their printer uses a workflow based on sRGB or if their images will be primarily displayed on the Web or via digital slideshows.

Note: If you are using Adobe RGB (1998) as your working space in Photoshop, it makes sense to capture in the same color space if it is offered by your digital SLR.

Within the Color Settings dialog, the Color Management Policies section provides settings that allow you to determine what Photoshop should do when you open an image that has a different embedded profile than the one you are using for your working space. As with the Working Spaces section, here you only need to be concerned with RGB. We recommend using the Convert To Working RGB setting here, with the assumption that if you've decided on a working space profile that's appropriate for your workflow, it makes sense to use that as the working space for all your images. Should you decide to use an image on a website, you can always convert to sRGB as part of the process of preparing the image.

We generally prefer to have images converted to the working color space when they're opened. But in order to maintain maximum control over what is being done to our images, we also prefer to be given the option of what action should be taken for each image. Therefore, we usually select all three check boxes next to Profile Mismatches and Missing Profiles at the bottom of the Color Management Policies section. The effect is that the options selected from the drop-down menus will be the default (for instance, RGB images will be converted to the current working RGB space), but each time an image is opened that has a different profile embedded than your working space or no profile embedded at all, you'll be prompted so you can apply a different action on a case-by-case basis.

Note: If you select the check boxes in the Color Management Policies section but find you are always confirming the default action, clear the check boxes to prevent the extra step of dealing with the Missing Profile or Profile Mismatch dialog boxes.

Once you've established the preferred options in Color Management Settings, click OK to apply the settings. There is no need to restart Photoshop for the changes to take effect.

Setting Preferences

In addition to the Color Settings, there are a large number of preference settings you can establish within Photoshop. As the name implies, many of these are a matter of personal preference. However, we do have recommendations on some of the settings. The Preferences dialog box can be accessed by selecting Edit > Preferences > General from the menu (Photoshop > Preferences > General on Macintosh).

 N o t e : Because there are so many settings within the Preferences dialog box, we won't cover all of them. Instead, we'll focus on those settings we feel are most important.

General Settings

The General page includes a variety of settings that affect your overall experience in Photoshop, as you can see in Figure 2.3.

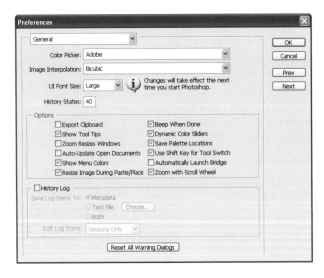

Figure 2.3
The General section of the Preferences dialog box includes settings that affect your overall experience in Photoshop.

Here are the settings you should be concerned with:

Color Picker: Adobe   Leave the Color Picker set to the default of Adobe rather than using the color picker from the operating system.

Image Interpolation: Bicubic   This is the best general option for interpolation, with other settings being useful in specific situations. We'll address the details of interpolation in Chapter 9, "Output."

UI Font Size: Large   This is a welcome new setting in Photoshop CS2, providing relief for the tiny text size that results from running our monitors at extremely high resolutions.

You'll find it very helpful from a readability standpoint to set this to Large. Note that this setting does not take effect until you restart Photoshop.

History States: 40 to 60　This determines how many steps you'll be able to undo on the History palette. In other words, if you've made a mistake, how many individual steps can you undo in order to get back to the point where you actually made the mistake? The default setting of 20 is relatively low, especially for certain tasks such as image cleanup with the Clone Stamp tool. However, setting the value too high consumes a relatively large amount of memory when you are doing a lot of work on your images. Therefore, we recommend that you strike a compromise, using a value of around 40 to 60. This is usually adequate for being able to go back and correct a mistake even if it takes some time to realize what you've done, while not consuming a huge amount of memory.

Options Check Boxes

The General page in the Preferences dialog box is dominated by a large number of check boxes that allow you to set a range of preferences. Here are some of the settings we find helpful in this section:

Export Clipboard: Off　This setting determines whether anything copied to the clipboard in Photoshop will be exported so other applications can use it. We recommend turning this feature off to reduce the amount of memory being used.

Show Tool Tips: On　This setting displays the tooltip text when you hover your mouse over a tool or control. These are very helpful for reminding you about what a particular tool is, so we suggest keeping this option turned on.

Zoom Resizes Windows: Personal preference　This determines whether a document window will automatically be resized as you zoom in or out. When this setting is turned on, as you zoom out on an image, the document window becomes smaller when the image no longer fills the screen; when you zoom in, the document window enlarges until the image exceeds the space available on the screen. This setting is a matter of personal preference, with some photographers (including Ellen) finding it helpful and others (including Tim) finding the automatic resizing annoying.

Beep When Done: On　Some tasks require a fair amount of time to process, and it isn't very productive to just sit there waiting for the Photoshop to finish. By turning on this setting, Photoshop beeps when a task is completed. That way, you can turn your attention to other matters while waiting for a major task to complete, knowing you'll be alerted when you're ready to continue.

Dynamic Color Sliders: On　When selecting a color in the Color palette, it can be helpful for the sliders to change color as you adjust the color value so you can get a better sense of what color you'll achieve by moving a slider in a particular direction. We don't use the Color palette very often, but we keep this setting enabled for those situations where we put the palette to use.

Save Palette Locations: Personal preference　This setting determines whether the palette arrangement you see when you start Photoshop will be the same arrangement you set when you last closed Photoshop. In general, if you moved palettes within Photoshop, you probably did it for a reason, so this setting is probably a good thing. On the other hand, if you have saved a particular palette arrangement (as discussed later in this chapter), you may want to have Photoshop always return to the setting you've established, even if you've since shifted things around. In that case, you'd want to disable this setting.

Use Shift Key For Tool Switch: On   Each tool in Photoshop has a shortcut key associated with it, allowing you to activate the tool very quickly. Some tools actually have more than one tool associated with the same shortcut. By default, to switch among tools with the same shortcut key, you need to add the Shift key. We recommend leaving this option set, because otherwise you can get some unexpected changes in tools when you press the shortcut key.

Automatically Launch Bridge: Personal preference   If you select this option, the Bridge image browser automatically launches whenever you start Photoshop. This can save time when you decide you want to launch Bridge, but it also slows down the Photoshop launch. If you use Bridge all the time, enable this setting. Otherwise, we recommend leaving it off.

Zoom With Scroll Wheel: On   If you have a mouse with a scroll wheel, this setting can be very helpful. It allows you to zoom in and out on your image by scrolling the wheel. We recommend turning this setting on.

History Log

The History Log section provides settings that can help you figure out how you performed a particular action on an image. When you enable this setting, you can have every step you perform on an image recorded in metadata, so you can review the information later. *We generally prefer to leave this turned off* because there isn't an easy way to remove the information later. However, it can save the day if you apply a series of steps on your images and then want to know how to apply the same changes on another image. It is particularly helpful, for example, when applying a series of filters to an image or when experimenting with any creative technique.

When you check the History Log check box, additional settings become available. If you're going to use this option, we recommend setting the Save Lot Items To option to Metadata, so the information will always be saved with the image file. We also recommend you set the Edit Log Items option to Detailed, so the information you collect is actually useful.

 Note: If you save the log information to a text file, the information for *all* images is saved in a single file, which isn't very efficient.

If you use the History Log option, you can review the saved information (which only accumulates after you enable the setting) by selecting File > File Info from the menu and clicking the History option in the left column (see Figure 2.4).

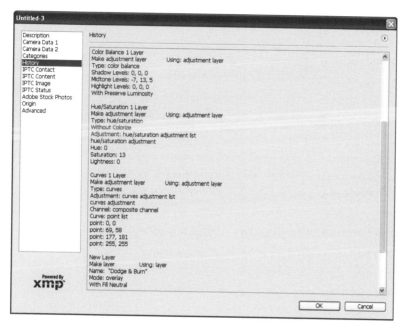

Figure 2.4
If you use the History
Log feature, you can
review everything that
has been done to your
image in the File Info
dialog box.

File Handling Settings

When you're finished with the General settings in the Preferences dialog box, click
Next to continue to the File Handling section, illustrated in Figure 2.5. This section
contains options related primarily to how files are saved.

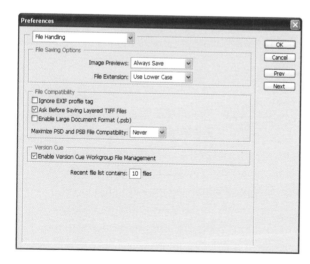

Figure 2.5
The File Handling section
of the Preferences dialog
box contains settings
that affect how files are
saved.

In the File Saving Options section of this dialog there are two settings, Image
Previews and File Extension:

Image Previews: Always Save   The Image Previews setting determines whether a small preview thumbnail will be stored as part of the image file. We leave this setting on Always
Save except for when we are saving files for display on the Web and concerned about
file size. If you save a large number of images for the Web, you may want to use the
Ask When Saving option or even Never Save.

File Extension: Personal preference   The File Extension dropdown allows you to choose between uppercase and lowercase file extensions. This is really not a significant concern, as either will work fine with current software. Frankly, it doesn't make any difference which setting you use, especially since you're not likely to see the file extensions very often.

In the File Compatibility section, there are several options:

Ignore EXIF Profile Tag: Off unless necessary   We recommend you leave this option off *unless* you're encountering problems with the color space embedded in your captures. This option in the File Compatibility section shouldn't be an issue for most photographers. If activated, it causes Photoshop to ignore the embedded color space in your digital captures. It's only an issue for images that have problems caused by their embedded profile, which is rare.

Ask Before Saving Layered TIFF Files: Personal preference   This controls the display of the TIFF Options dialog box. This setting is based on your particular workflow. Because Tim usually saves his TIFF files flattened (saving the master file with layers as a PSD), he leaves this option turned on so he has the choice to save without layers. Ellen, on the other hand, tends to save her TIFF files with layers (or flatten them manually), so she turns this option off to avoid the extra click on the OK button in the dialog box.

Enable Large Document Format (.psb): Off unless necessary   This option determines whether you'll be able to save files in the PSB format, a special Photoshop format for extra-large files that is necessary for images with pixel dimensions greater than 30,000 pixels on a single side. While it's nice to be able to create such large images for certain applications, these large images can't be printed, so we don't find them particularly useful. If you're not going to use the PSB file type, turn this setting off just to reduce the length of the list of file types when saving images.

 Note: The PSB file format can only be opened with Photoshop CS or later.

Maximize PSD and PSB File Compatibility: Personal preference   This option essentially controls whether a full-resolution composite image will be saved as part of the image file in Photoshop's native formats. The primary reason to enable this feature are to ensure that you're able to open the image as you intended it to appear with later versions of Photoshop—even if the algorithms determining how adjustments are applied get changed—or to enable applications that aren't able to build a thumbnail or preview from the layered file to utilize the full-resolution composite instead. It also provides a solution for situations where you have created a PSD file in a recent version of Photoshop and are sending that file to someone using an older version that doesn't support all the latest features. The disadvantage to using this setting is that file sizes are increased considerably (potentially doubled) when this option is used.

There is one check box under Version Cue:

Enable Version Cue Workgroup File Management: Off unless necessary   Version Cue is a separate Creative Suite application (not included with the stand-alone version of Photoshop) that allows multiple people to work from one set of files without conflict, or one person to work on a file with multiple versions.

The final option in the File Handling settings concerns the recent file list:

Recent File List Contains: 10   This option allows you to specify how many files should be listed on the Open Recent list found on the File menu. We find the default of 10 to be more than adequate.

Displays & Cursors Settings

Click Next when you're finished with the File Handling settings to access the Displays & Cursors options, as illustrated in Figure 2.6.

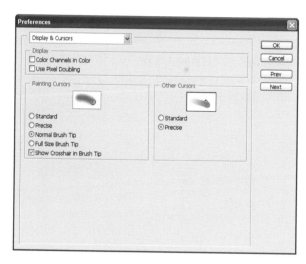

Figure 2.6

The Displays & Cursors section of Preferences is used primarily to adjust the display of mouse cursors within Photoshop.

In the Display section are two check boxes, both of which we recommend leaving turned off:

Color Channels In Color: Off   Turning this on causes the channels viewed through the Channels palette to be displayed in their actual color (red for the red channel, for example), rather than as a grayscale image. While this sounds like a good idea in terms of being able to interpret the color values for each channel, it actually becomes a challenge, because each of the component colors has a different perceived tonality, making comparison (and even viewing at times) difficult.

Use Pixel Doubling: Off   This check box speeds up image display by working with reduced image resolution. The performance benefit here isn't significant for any computer that is really capable of handling Photoshop, and there is a quality disadvantage in the display when the setting is used.

Cursors

In the Painting Cursors section you can adjust the cursors used for your mouse pointer when working with brush tools within Photoshop. *We recommend Normal Brush Tip and Precise.*

Standard   The Standard option causes the mouse pointer to display a small icon of the tool you're using. While this helps remind you of which tool is in use, it doesn't help much in evaluating the size of the brush being used or the specific area to be affected.

Precise   The Precise option uses a "target" display that makes it easy to see exactly where you'll paint on the image with a given tool, but it doesn't give you any size information.

Normal Brush Tip   The Normal Brush Tip option uses a mouse pointer that matches the shape and size of the brush you're using, with softness accounted for by showing the perimeter of the brush as the point where the opacity of the brush edge is 50 percent. (See the left-hand image in Figure 2.7.) That means the soft edge of the brush actually extends beyond the shape shown for the brush, but the shape represents the primary area being affected.

Full Size Brush Tip   The Full Size Brush Tip setting uses a full display of the actual brush size, with a fuzzy edge to the mouse pointer representing a soft brush. (See the right-hand image in Figure 2.7.) However, this brush size represents the full extent of the brush, which can be a bit misleading for soft-edged brushes since they generally have no effect all the way out to the edge of the full brush size.

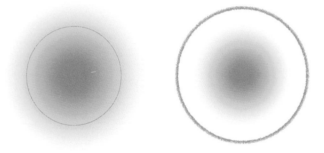

Figure 2.7 The Normal Brush Tip setting (left) causes the brush edge to be defined at the point where the opacity of the brush is at 50 percent for soft-edged brushes. The Full Size Brush Tip setting (right) causes the full extent of the brush to be shown (including a representation of a soft edge) even though there may not be any effect out to that distance when painting

There is one additional option under Painting Cursors:

Show Crosshair In Brush Tip   The Show Crosshair In Brush Tip check box allows you to specify whether you want to see a crosshair in the center of the brush, so it's easier to see exactly where the center of the brush is. There are a variety of situations where this can be helpful, and we don't find it to be a distraction, so *we recommend leaving it turned on.*

Note: The Caps Lock key toggles the display of brush cursors between the precise and brush options, so if you're not getting the display you expect based on Preferences, check the status of your Caps Lock key.

For Other Cursors, the Precise option should be used so you can see exactly where in the image you're clicking when using one of the non-brush tools. In most cases this option displays a crosshair or "target" for the non-brush tools.

Plug-Ins & Scratch Disks Settings

In the Plug-Ins & Scratch Disks section of the Preferences dialog box, it's important to establish appropriate settings in the Scratch Disks section to ensure optimal performance for Photoshop (see Figure 2.8). Whenever Photoshop doesn't have adequate memory to perform a task, it depends upon hard drive space to simulate additional memory; the hard drive space used is referred to as a *scratch disk*. (Think of it as providing a scratch sheet of paper for Photoshop to use for figuring out complicated problems.)

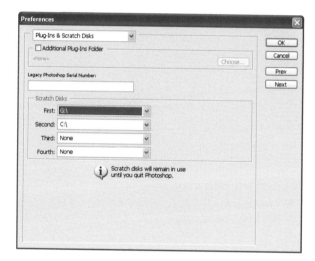

Figure 2.8
The Plug-Ins & Scratch Disks section of Preferences is important for ensuring maximum performance in Photoshop.

When Photoshop must resort to scratch disk space, you want to make sure it's working optimally. To maximize performance in this situation, point Photoshop toward a secondary internal hard drive that isn't being used by the operating system for system purposes. As a general rule, that means if you have more than one physical hard drive installed in your system, you should set the First scratch disk to the secondary hard drive, and the Second scratch disk to the primary hard drive. If you have more than two drives installed, you can also establish settings for Third and Fourth, keeping in mind that you want to set these in order of optimal performance, with the fastest drive first and the drive used by the operating system listed last. Most external drives offer much slower performance than internal drives, so they should either not be used for this purpose or should be last in the order.

Memory & Image Cache Settings

The Memory & Image Cache section contains two settings that can affect overall system performance (Figure 2.9):

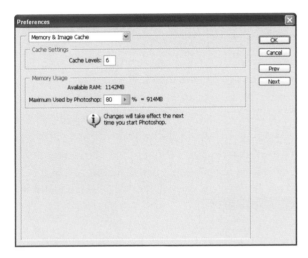

Figure 2.9
The Memory Usage setting in the Memory & Image Cache section of Preferences is important for overall system performance.

Cache Levels: Default (6)   The Cache Levels setting determines how many zoom settings are stored in memory for your image so the image and histogram can be drawn more quickly when zooming in and out on your image or performing adjustments. The performance difference here is minimal, so we generally leave the setting at the default value.

Memory Usage: 80% or less   The Memory Usage setting is much more important for overall system performance. As you have no doubt figured out, Photoshop wants to have access to as much memory as possible. The Memory Usage setting determines how much memory Photoshop reserves for its use. While you would generally expect to benefit from setting this to the maximum value, that can actually lead to problems. Very high settings can lead to stability issues, and on many computers, setting the value to 100% can even prevent Photoshop from loading. We recommend setting the value to no more than 80% to provide as much memory to Photoshop as possible without running the risk of system stability problems.

Note: The Type settings aren't generally of significant concern to nature photographers, and we consider the default settings to be appropriate for most users.

Views and Zoom

With Photoshop set up just the way you like it, you're ready to start actually looking at your images. Photoshop provides a variety of ways to do just that. They include ways to display the image with Photoshop and ways to navigate around within your images with various tools.

Windows and Workspaces

The first thing we recommend doing when you open an image is to size the document window appropriately. In general, this means maximizing the document window so you can see as much of the image as possible (as illustrated in Figure 2.10). If you're only working with one monitor and therefore have Photoshop's palettes on your primary display, you can press the Tab key to toggle these palettes on and off. Other users prefer to resize the document window to fit within the available space defined by the palettes, instead of maximizing the document window for each image.

Figure 2.10
It's generally best to maximize your document window so you can see as much of the image as possible while working in Photoshop.

You can also adjust the arrangement of the various palettes within Photoshop to suit your own preferences. Throughout this book you'll become familiar with many of the palettes you can use, and you'll start to develop a preference for which palettes you want to have visible and how you want them arranged (see an example in Figure 2.11). You may even find that you prefer to have different configurations established for different tasks or for different types of images. Fortunately, it's very easy to switch between various palette arrangements.

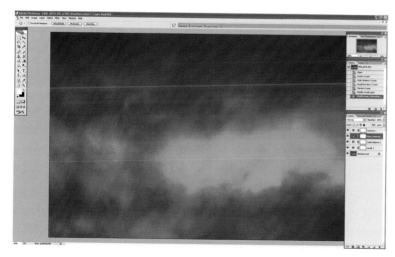

Figure 2.11
Configuring the palettes the way you feel most comfortable will help you work more efficiently in Photoshop.

To start, set the palettes the way you want them. Then select Window > Workspace > Save Workspace from the menu, enter a name for the arrangement you have established, and click Save (as shown in Figure 2.12). Then, any time you want to access or refresh this workspace, select the name of your saved settings from the Window > Workspace menu, and the configuration will be loaded immediately.

Figure 2.12
The Save Workspace dialog box allows you to provide a name for the palette configuration you have established so it can be easily loaded in the future.

Then, when you open an image, you're ready to start using the various navigation tools to evaluate various areas of your image. These methods are also used as you're working on images, making judgments about how much of an adjustment is necessary based on a review of several key areas of the image.

Try It! To practice using the various navigation tools presented here, open the image called Navigate on the accompanying CD and try the methods discussed in this section. Then save a workspace with the palette arrangement you prefer to use when working on your images.

Zoom Tool

The Zoom tool is the most basic of navigation tools, but it does include some hidden features that can be very helpful. To select the Zoom tool, click its icon on the Tools palette [🔍] or press Z on your keyboard.

Note: If you're using any other tool, you can switch to the Zoom tool by pressing Ctrl/⌘.

Try It! ⌘+spacebar. When you let up, your tool switches back.

In the most basic use, after selecting the Zoom tool, click anywhere in your image to zoom in by one preset percentage level. When you do so, not only is the image enlarged on the screen, but the point you clicked becomes the center of the new display. To zoom out, select the minus (–) option on the Options bar or simply hold down the Alt/Option key while you click. When zooming out, the same basic behavior occurs in reverse. The image zooms out by one level, and the point you clicked becomes the center of the new display.

Note: You can also zoom in or out (without changing the center of the view) by pressing Ctrl/⌘.

Try It! ⌘ and the plus (+) or minus (–) key. Also, if your mouse has a scroll wheel, you can use that for zooming in and out.

The Zoom tool also offers one special capability that makes it incredibly powerful. If you click and drag with the Zoom tool, you create a *marquee* (dashed box) on your image. When you release the mouse, the area you dragged the box around is zoomed as much as necessary to fill the document window. This is an excellent way to zoom in on a particular area of your image to give it a closer look.

Another handy hidden feature of the Zoom tool is the ability to quickly go to a 100 percent view of your image, which is an excellent way to evaluate sharpness and look for small problems such as dust spots within the image. To quickly return the zoom percentage to 100 percent, simply double-click the Zoom tool's icon on the Tools palette *or* press Ctrl+Alt+0/⌘+Option+0. You can also access some of these commands when the Zoom tool is active by right-clicking the image and choosing the desired option from the context menu.

Evaluating Sharpness: The Proper Magnification and Practice

Determining whether an image is critically sharp is a major aspect of the image review process that leads up to the actual optimization workflow. Many photographers have a difficult time evaluating the sharpness of a digital image displayed on their monitor, especially those who have spent many years evaluating the sharpness of images on film by utilizing a high-powered loupe.

The first step to evaluating sharpness for a given image is to view it at 100 percent magnification (or Actual Pixels). To do this, you can use the Zoom tool or the keyboard shortcut Ctrl+Alt+0/⌘+Option+0. At this magnification, one image pixel is represented by one monitor pixel. As a result, you're seeing all of the actual pixels within the image for the area that can be seen on the monitor. If you don't have the display set to 100 percent magnification, the monitor is either using more than one pixel to represent each pixel in the image (if the zoom percentage is higher than 100 percent) or is not showing all pixels for a given area within the image (if the zoom percentage is lower than 100 percent).

After you're viewing the image at 100 percent magnification, look to see whether the edges within the subject matter of the image have good contrast. This is the key attribute of an image with crisp focus. Learning to see what a sharp image looks like on a monitor display takes some practice, and the only way to accumulate that practice is to evaluate a large number of images.

Besides simply reviewing the images on your monitor, it can be helpful to first make prints of some of your images and then compare the printed image (where you'll have an easier time evaluating sharpness) to the image on the monitor at 100 percent magnification. Comparing these images gives you a better idea of how the monitor display translates into actual image sharpness.

Hand Tool

The Hand tool provides a way to navigate around your image when the magnification is higher than 100 percent and it spills over the document window. You can think of this tool as behaving the way your own hand would if you were evaluating a large print on a table. Instead of moving your head around to look at different areas of the image, you can simply move the "print" with your hand. You can activate the Hand tool by clicking its icon in the Tools palette or by pressing H on your keyboard.

With the Hand tool active, drag around on the image. The image moves in the direction you drag, with the display being updated in real time so you can watch the image slide around as you move the mouse.

 Note: The Hand tool can't move your image around if the image is zoomed out to the extent that you can see the entire image at once.

Another handy trick is to use the Hand tool to quickly display your image at a magnification that allows it to fit within the space available without being obstructed by the palettes (if they are docked to the side of the screen) or to fill the screen display area (if they are not), resizing the image window if necessary. To do so, double-click the Hand tool in the Tools palette. This is a great way to quickly get an overview of the image for evaluating overall composition, tonality, and color.

Note: If you're using any other tool, you can switch to the Hand tool by pressing the spacebar. When you let up, your tool switches back.

Navigator Palette

The Navigator palette consolidates many of the features of the Zoom and Hand tools into a single package, and provides an efficient method for moving around your image to evaluate various portions of it (see Figure 2.13). If the Navigator palette isn't visible, choose Window > Navigator from the menu to make it active.

Figure 2.13
The Navigator palette provides a convenient way to navigate around your image.

The Navigator palette provides a thumbnail preview of the currently active image. A red box indicates which portion of the image is being viewed in the document window, so you always have a sense of what portion of the image you are looking at. The bottom-left corner of the palette includes a zoom percentage indicator for reference.

The zooming features of the Navigator palette are utilized primarily with the slider in the bottom-right corner of the palette window. The "little mountains" button to the left of the slider allows you to zoom out by one preset percentage level each time you click it, similar to Alt+clicking/Option+clicking your image with the Zoom tool. The "big mountains" button to the right of the slider allows you to zoom in by one preset percentage level. You can exercise greater control over the zooming process by adjusting the slider left (to zoom out) or right (to zoom in).

Within the thumbnail display for your image, the red box serves not only as an indicator of which area of the image is currently being viewed, but also as a way to change the view of the image to look at a different area. If you drag the boxed area around within the thumbnail display, the document display changes in real time to reflect the area defined by the box. This is similar to the use of the Hand tool for navigating around your image.

Note: You can't move the outline in the Navigator palette if the entire image is currently visible.

You can click a particular point in the thumbnail to center the outline on that spot. This is a great method to use when you want to spot-check various portions of the image. For example, if you're trying to evaluate critical sharpness, check various areas of the subject and even areas at various distances from the camera to see the effect of depth of field. By simply clicking those points in the thumbnail of the Navigator palette, you can check multiple areas of the image quickly and easily.

One last trick in the Navigator palette allows you to reproduce the effect of drawing a marquee on your image with the Zoom tool, so you can quickly fill the screen with a particular portion of your image. To do so, hold the Ctrl/⌘ key and click and drag within the thumbnail display of the Navigator palette to draw a box over the area you want to view. When you release the mouse button, the image is automatically zoomed and repositioned so that the area you drew the box around fills the available space.

Navigating by Keyboard Shortcuts

For those of you who love using keyboard shortcuts to speed up their workflow, there are a variety of options for navigating around your images during the evaluation process (as well as during your actual optimization workflow). If you tend to keep one hand on the keyboard as you work, this may be your preferred way to navigate. Even if you prefer to use the mouse as much as possible, remembering a few of these keyboard shortcuts can help improve your workflow by adding to your arsenal of tricks for working with your images. Table 2.1 recaps the most common navigational shortcuts.

Windows Shortcut	Macintosh Shortcut	Action
H	H	Activates the Hand tool.
Z	Z	Activates the Zoom tool.
Ctrl++	⌘++	Zooms in.
Ctrl+-	⌘+-	Zooms out.
Ctrl+Alt+0	⌘+Option+0	Zooms to 100 percent magnification (Actual Pixels).
Ctrl+0	⌘+0	Zooms document window to fit on screen.
Spacebar	Spacebar	Temporarily activates the Hand tool regardless of currently active tool.
Ctrl+spacebar	⌘+spacebar	Temporarily activates the Zoom tool regardless of currently active tool.
Ctrl+Alt+spacebar	⌘+Option+spacebar	Temporarily activates the Zoom tool in zoom out mode regardless of the currently active tool.

Note: In Windows, if you have a check box or other control active in a dialog box while trying to hold the spacebar to access the Hand tool, you may not get the behavior you are expecting. This is because the spacebar can be used to toggle such controls. To avoid this, click an empty area of the dialog box so that no control has the focus before using the spacebar as a shortcut key.

As you've seen in this section, there are many options for navigating around your images during the evaluation and optimization processes. Instead of trying to decide which particular methods work best for your needs, make an effort to become familiar with all of them. Doing so will ensure that you have the maximum number of techniques available for any given situation. What you'll likely find is that although you have your favorite methods for navigating around your images, in certain situations other methods are more convenient. By being comfortable with all of the available methods, you'll have maximum flexibility and control when working on your images.

Try It! To gain familiarity with the Navigator palette, open the image NavPalette from the accompanying CD and zoom in to various areas of the image, deciding on a specific area to view and then navigating to that area so it fills the monitor display.

Downloading Images

We're sure that you, like us, are anxious to get at your images immediately upon returning from a photo shoot. Of course, you need to download the images from your digital media cards before you can really get started. For this task we recommend using an accessory card reader rather than connecting your camera directly to the computer. This is partly because we just find it more convenient to use a card reader, especially when we have a relatively large number of images to download. However, we also prefer to keep the camera safely in the camera bag rather than sitting on the desk with a cord attached, with the risk that cord might accidentally get pulled and the camera might crash to the floor.

Start by inserting your digital media into the card reader (or connecting the external hard drive if you've used that for storage) and copying (not moving) the images into a folder on your hard drive. Which folder you copy them to depends on your own organizational structure. Hopefully, you've set up folders to organize your images based on your preference, such as location, date, or other attributes of the images. If not, now's a good time to start. You can then copy the images into their appropriate folder, or better yet, copy them into a New_Images folder so you can sort and edit all the new images in one place.

Once you've copied the images, the originals are still on your digital media card. Until you need to use that card, it serves as a backup copy just in case something goes wrong in the meantime (though you should still be backing up the images on your hard drive as well). When you're ready to use that digital media card again, reformat it in the camera to both erase the existing images and reinitialize it to give the file system on the card a clean start.

Renaming Your Images

You may have noticed that the names your camera assigns to each file, such as 8F2S9712 .tif, are less than ideal to help you identify the images. Fortunately it's quite easy to rename all or some of the images in a folder. To rename your images, take the following steps:

1. Either select the particular files you want to rename, or select a folder in the Folders panel. In the latter case the renaming will be applied to all the files in the folder.

2. Choose Tools > Batch Rename in the Bridge menu.

3. Select whether you want your renamed files to be in the same folder, copied to another folder, or moved to another folder. If you copy or move them, specify where by clicking Browse.

4. For New Filename we like to create a name that tells us essential identifying features about the images. This could be text that describes the place (i.e., Holland) or the subject (tulips), along with a date and/or a sequence number and an extension. The number of elements you use is your choice.

   - In the first dropdown box under New Filenames that says Current Filename by default, choose Text. The next box to the right will give you a prompt to type text. This is where you type the location, subject, name, etc.

   - To the far right of this row are + and − radio buttons. Click the + button to get another dropdown box to add more parameters to your name. Many people like to include the date here, although it's clearly a personal choice what you use.

   - Again click the + radio button at the right of the row and this time choose sequence number (or letter) from the dropdown menu. Usually we specify a three-digit number, but if you don't use the date in your naming schema you may prefer to use at least a four-digit number.

Note: Bridge will automatically preserve the file extension, so you don't have to use Extension as your final choice.

You'll see a preview of your new name at the lower right.

5. Under Options, you can choose to keep the original filename in the metadata for the file. If you are renaming copies, this can be helpful in the event you ever want to refer back to the original files.

6. Under compatibility, it's a good idea to select both Windows and Mac (your current operating system is selected by default).

Sorting and Editing with Bridge

Getting your digital images onto your computer is certainly a start. But as you've probably noticed, those images seem to accumulate quickly, and keeping them organized can be a bit of a chore, especially if you have a backlog of images stored in many folders. When you download your latest images, chances are you want to get started working with them right away. The first step, of course, is to figure out what you have and which images you'd like to start optimizing first.

 Note: One of the major differences between Bridge and the File Browser before it is that Bridge is a separate application that can be run even if you aren't in Photoshop.

Setting Bridge Preferences

Bridge includes a Preferences dialog box where you can set a wide variety of options to adjust the behavior of Bridge to your liking. The dialog box is accessed by selecting Edit > Preferences from the menu in Bridge (Bridge > Preferences on Macintosh). Because there are so many settings, and most of them are simply a matter of personal preference, we'll simply highlight the major settings:

General   This section (see Figure 2.14) contains general settings related to the display of Bridge. The Thumbnails section includes a slider to adjust the shade of gray used for the background behind the thumbnails. The Show Tooltips check box determines whether information about the image is displayed as a pop-up tooltip when you hold the mouse over a thumbnail. Three check boxes with drop-down menus allow you to specify additional information about the image to be displayed below the thumbnail. The Favorites Items section allows you to choose the image sources to be included on the Favorites tab. Buttons at the bottom of this section allow you to open a folder view where scripts for Bridge are stored and reset the warning dialog boxes so that all are shown as appropriate, even if you have previously checked the box to not show a particular message.

Metadata   This section (shown in Figure 2.15) allows you to specify which fields are displayed in the Metadata palette for each image. This extensive list includes a variety of metadata formats and fields that are not necessarily supported by all image formats. This section can be used both to include fields you're most interested in to maximize the amount of information displayed, as well as to remove those items you're not interested in to keep the display more manageable.

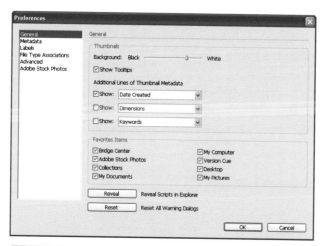

Figure 2.14

The General section of the Bridge Preferences contains settings related to the display of images within Bridge.

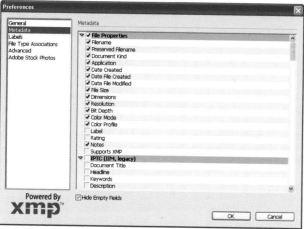

Figure 2.15

The Metadata section of Bridge Preferences allows you to specify which metadata fields should be displayed on the Metadata palette.

Labels This section (see Figure 2.16) allows you to set preferences related to the labels you can use to rate and flag images. The check box at the top determines whether the Ctrl/⌘ key must be held to apply a rating or label to an image. If you clear this check box, you can simply press the appropriate number key rather than holding the Ctrl/⌘ key while pressing that key. The section below allows you to change the description of the colored labels. By default, the name is that of the color, but you can change this to reflect the categories you are using those colors for, if desired.

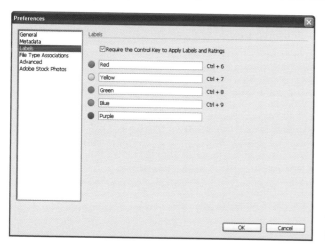

Figure 2.16

The Labels section of Bridge Preferences allows you to adjust the names of the colored labels and determine how keyboard shortcuts for rating and labels behave.

File Type Associations   This section is another long list (see Figure 2.17)—the file types supported by Bridge. By default, most image formats are automatically opened by Photoshop. However, you can change the association so that files open with a different application. For example, PDF documents default to opening with Adobe Reader rather than Photoshop. Similarly, you can set different associations for specific file types within Bridge if you prefer, using the drop-down menu to the right of a given file format to choose an application or browse for the executable for the preferred application.

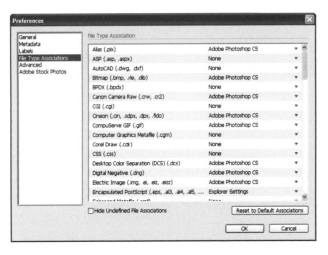

Figure 2.17

The File Type Associations section in Bridge Preferences allows you to specify which application should be used to open each supported file type.

Advanced   This section (shown in Figure 2.18) contains a handful of settings. Some of them are probably best left alone, but a couple can be important. The Do Not Process Files Larger Than option determines the size, in megabytes, above which Bridge will not generate a thumbnail for the image. It can be good to create such a limit (the default is 200MB), because building thumbnails for such large images can be time-consuming, resulting in reduced system performance. However, for photographers who frequently produce such large files, setting such a limit can be a source of frustration, because they aren't able to see thumbnails for many of their images. Consider this setting based on the relative advantages of placing a limit on the building of thumbnails for large files.

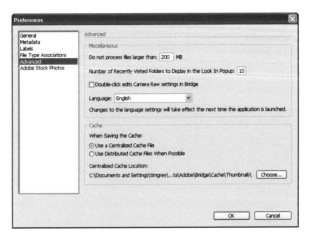

Figure 2.18

The Advanced section of the Bridge Preferences contains a number of advanced settings, with the maximum file size to be processed being the only setting you probably need to consider.

The other setting you should consider is the check box labeled Double-Click Edits Camera Raw Settings in Bridge. When this check box is cleared, raw files open by default in Photoshop, invoking Adobe Camera Raw (unless you've changed the File Type Association for a particular raw format). When you check the box, the Camera Raw dialog box opens without launching Photoshop. This may seem like a subtle distinction, but it enables you to adjust settings more rapidly than you otherwise could for a series of raw captures, as we'll explain later in this chapter.

Adobe Stock Photos   This section (shown in Figure 2.19) provides options related to Adobe's new stock photography service. We suspect most of you won't be using this service, preferring to use your own images for any projects you're working on. However, if you choose to use this service, this section allows you to set various preferences related to the display and downloading of images from the Adobe Stock Photos service.

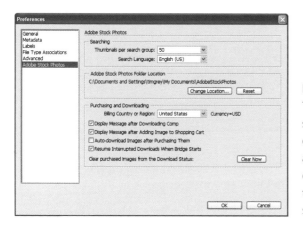

Figure 2.19

The Adobe Stock Photos section of Bridge Preferences allows you to adjust display and download settings for the Adobe Stock Photos service.

Palette Setup

With a plan for sorting through your images, you probably feel much more confident about your ability to sort quickly and efficiently. Bridge makes it easy to perform this task, but the default configuration doesn't provide a very efficient way to work. Making a few changes can greatly improve your experience working with this otherwise excellent tool.

The first step is to make better use of the space consumed by the palettes. The default configuration in Bridge isn't very efficient, so moving palettes around greatly improves your productivity. With each palette effectively having its own portion of the Bridge window, each is limited in space. The Folders palette is difficult to navigate, the Preview palette doesn't provide an image much larger than the default thumbnail size, and the Metadata palette provides only a glimpse of all the data it contains. Because you need to view only one palette at a time in most situations, it makes sense to bring them together into one section, providing more space for whichever you are currently viewing.

To get started, point your mouse at the title tab for the Preview palette, and click and drag that palette up to where the Folders palette is. Release the mouse when you have it hovering to the right of the Folders palette. This causes the Preview palette to be placed in the same pane of the Bridge window, automatically collapsing the pane that once contained the Preview palette. Next, drag the Metadata and Keywords tabs to the same location, so that all of them are in the same pane as the Folders palette. This provides more space for the palettes, so when you're looking at a particular palette, you aren't making a compromise for the available space, as illustrated in Figure 2.20. Simply click the tab of the palette you want to view to bring it to the forefront.

Figure 2.20
By arranging the palettes in Bridge to make better use of space, you can browse your images more effectively.

Lightbox View

For the first pass of sorting, when you want to get an overall look at the images and start deleting the obviously bad ones, Tim recommends using a *lightbox view* of the images in the current folder. Because you've already configured the palettes to make maximum use of the available space, this step requires simply sliding the vertical bar that divides the palettes pane from the thumbnails pane to the left so you can see nothing but thumbnails (see Figure 2.21).

Figure 2.21
Using a lightbox view allows you to see as many of your image thumbnails as possible for an initial sort.

While you're in this view, you can get an overview of the images and a better sense of exactly what you captured. This is a good opportunity to start thinking about which subjects or particular types of images within the current collection seem to have the most potential. This is also an excellent time to rotate your verticals so they appear with the proper orientation, if Bridge didn't automatically rotate them (which requires that your digital camera support this feature). To rotate images, simply select them and click the appropriate rotation button at the top of the Bridge window—these buttons have circular arrows indicating the direction of rotation.

Note: When you rotate an image in Bridge, only the thumbnail preview is rotated. The actual image isn't rotated until you open it.

You'll also notice at this stage that some images stand out as having particularly bad exposures or other problems that make them candidates for immediate deletion. To remove those images, simply select them and do *one* of the following:

- Click the trash can button at the top of the Bridge window.
- Press the Delete or Backspace key on your keyboard.
- Right-click the image and choose Delete from the contextual menu.

If you aren't sure whether an image should be deleted just by looking at the thumbnail, don't delete it yet, because you'll have an opportunity to do a more detailed review later. This first stage is a rough edit designed to clean out the collection of images you don't want to waste time scrutinizing.

Preview View

After you've taken an overall look at the images, rotated them as needed, and deleted those that you can tell shouldn't be kept just by looking at the thumbnails, you're ready to take a closer look and figure out which should be deleted and which should be included in a particular project or otherwise put to use to share with others. For this type of review, we utilize what we call the *preview view* of the images, illustrated in Figure 2.22.

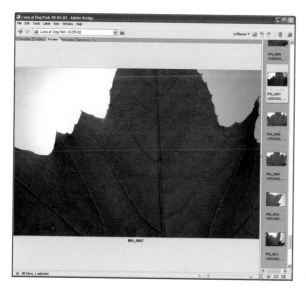

Figure 2.22
A preview view allows you to take a closer look at your images.

To get as large a preview image as possible, drag the vertical divider bar to the right, leaving just enough space at the right side of Bridge for a single column of thumbnail images. This provides a great method for reviewing your images with more scrutiny than your first pass, while still maintaining an easy way to navigate through your images.

Instead of using your mouse to click the images that you want to view in more detail, we recommend taking a close look at all of the images in your collection. Click the first image on the list (scroll to the top of the list if necessary) and then use the up and down arrow keys on your keyboard to navigate through the images. As you move up and down, the preview is updated based on the currently active image. This gives you a much better idea of the overall composition, exposure accuracy, and image quality, so you can decide whether the image should be deleted or kept. You can also start to get a better idea of which images deserve more attention as you sort through them.

Switching Views

As you continue sorting through your images, you may find that you want to switch back and forth between lightbox view and preview view. Now that you have Bridge configured properly, you can switch between the two views by clicking the double arrow button in the bottom-left corner of the Bridge window. You can also achieve this by simply dragging the vertical divider bar left or right as needed.

There are several options for changing the display arrangement for the thumbnails area in Bridge:

- View > As Thumbnails is the default.
- If you choose View > As Filmstrip, you'll see thumbnails in a single row, with a larger preview of one image. This is the method Ellen prefers, with the vertical bar moved to the far left so the preview can be as large as possible.
- The View > As Details option presents considerable additional information about the image to the side of the thumbnail.
- Finally, View > As Versions And Alternates displays the various versions of the image created using Version Cue if you are utilizing that in your workflow.

These options can also be selected by clicking the small buttons at the bottom-right corner of the Bridge window.

 Try It! To get more comfortable with the many options available in Bridge, point it to a folder containing some of your images and adjust the various options we've discussed here for changing the interface.

Sizing Thumbnails

Bridge has replaced the various sizing options for thumbnails in File Browser with a much more efficient resize tool. A slider is located at the bottom of the Bridge window, toward the right side:

A button to the left of the slider allows you to instantly set the thumbnails to their smallest size (as shown in Figure 2.23), which is helpful for getting a broad overview of a huge number of images. Of course, it also requires pretty good eyes since the thumbnails are so small! The button to the right of the slider sets the thumbnails to their largest size, which is quite large, making the image more of a preview than an actual thumbnail (though also severely limiting how many images you can see at once).

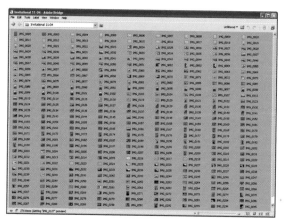 

Figure 2.23 The button on the left of the thumbnail size slider allows you to set the thumbnails to their smallest size; the button on the right allows you to set them to their largest size.

Best of all, the slider between those two buttons allows you to adjust the thumbnail size to your liking very quickly. Simply click your mouse on the slider handle and drag to the left or right to reduce or increase the size of the thumbnails. The thumbnail size and image layout adjust dynamically as you move the slider, making it very easy to decide exactly what setting works best for you. It also makes it quick and easy to adjust the thumbnail size on the fly based on the particular task or images you're working on.

Rating Images

As you sort through your images, deleting those you don't want to keep, you also want to start thinking about which images are your favorites, since those are the ones you'll want to spend the most time optimizing. Adobe Bridge includes a rating capability that allows you to assign a value of one to five stars to your images, much like you might rate a movie. In so doing, you can quickly go through your images and rate them, so that when you're finished with the sorting and editing process you'll know exactly which images are your favorites.

To assign a rank, simply select an image (or images) and move your mouse over the row of five dots below the thumbnail. The dots represent the possible star ratings, so click the first to rate one star, the second to rate two stars, and so on (these dots are only visible if the image is selected, but the star rating you've applied to an image will display regardless of whether it is selected). If you have multiple images selected when you click, the rating will be updated to the same value for all of the selected images. You can also remove a rating by clicking to the left of the row of dots. The star rating display replaces the dots below the image, so you can see at a glance what you rated a given image (Figure 2.24).

Figure 2.24

When you apply a rating to an image, that rating is reflected with stars displayed below the image thumbnail.

For those who prefer keyboard shortcuts, you can hold the Ctrl/⌘ key and press a number from 1 through 5 to assign a star rating. Pressing Ctrl+0/⌘+0 will clear the rating from the selected image(s). Using the keyboard shortcuts can be very efficient as you're reviewing your images, using the arrow keys to move from one image to the next and then pressing the shortcut key for the rating you want to apply to the current image before moving on.

When you have assigned a rank to all images that you are considering for your current project, you can sort the images by rating, from fewest stars to most, by choosing View > Sort > By Rating (Figure 2.25).

Figure 2.25

By selecting View > Sort > By Rating from the menu in Bridge, you can view the images sorted by the number of stars you assigned.

The rating option in Bridge is a helpful tool for sorting and categorizing images based on how much you like them, making it a great way to filter out your favorite images.

Labeling Images

The labeling feature in Bridge allows you to take the rating system a step further by assigning a color code to your images. This is done by applying a colored label to images in a way very similar to rating. You can then filter the display to show only the images that are labeled, or only those labeled with a specific color. The available colors for labels are red, yellow, green, blue, and purple.

To use these effectively, you'll first want to come up with a system that identifies what the colors mean. You might, for example, use the colors to prioritize images, but this becomes very similar to rating. Instead, you might want to use the labels to identify categorizations of images. For example, you might use a red label to mark images for which you have not yet identified the species of animal photographed, and a green label to identify images that have been cleaned up and optimized and are ready to be used in any upcoming projects. However you use them, it is a good idea to document your system so you won't get confused later as you are reviewing images that have been previously labeled, or trying to remember what color specific images should be labeled in a new group of images. Consistency is important to taking full advantage of this capability.

To label an image, you simply select it (or several images) and choose Label and then the desired color from the menu. You can also right-click the image and choose a color from the Label menu option, or use a keyboard shortcut to label images by holding Ctrl/⌘ and then pressing a number: 6 for red, 7 for yellow, 8 for green, and 9 for blue (purple doesn't have a shortcut key). You can turn off the label by selecting No Label from the Label menu (which also doesn't have a shortcut key).

When you label an image, a colored bar appears below the thumbnail (Figure 2.26). This allows you to see at a glance which images were marked for a particular purpose, based on the system you're using for color-coding with labels.

Figure 2.26
When you apply a label to an image, a colored bar appears below the thumbnail in Bridge.

Of course, just seeing a colored bar below the thumbnail image doesn't quite provide you with a powerful way to review your decisions about the images. However, Bridge provides some additional options to make greater use of the labeling feature.

The first is an ability to view only those images that you have labeled. You can do this by choosing an option from the Filtered/Unfiltered drop-down at the far right of the Bridge window. You can select Show Labeled Items Only to show only images that have a label of any color, or you can choose a specific label color to filter by. You can even filter the display to show only those images that are not labeled, which can be handy if you want to move the "rejects" to a separate location, for example.

Choosing one of these options will filter the list of images to include only those you have labeled based on the option you select. This is a great way to review the images you've decided you want to work with, and then scrutinize those images to make sure that there aren't any redundant images or that you don't want to remove some of them after seeing the whole group together. If you clear a label for an image at this point, it will disappear from the current view, because only labeled images are being displayed. When you want to see all the images again, choose Show All Items from the same Filtered/Unfiltered dropdown.

Another option is to sort the images by their label attribute. To utilize this option, choose View > Sort > By Label from the Bridge menu. All labeled images will then be sorted by label color, with unlabeled images first and then the labeled images in order by color.

Note: One of the keys to taking full advantage of your photographs is having a sensible set of standard keywords that you can use to search for related subjects, similar image types, or even that one particular photo you need. Assign keywords every time you import images. In Bridge, you do so by highlighting one or more images, clicking the Keywords tab, and checking the keyword(s) to apply. (To create new keywords or keyword sets, use the pulldown menu at the top-right of the Keywords palette, or the icons at the bottom.) Many third-party image-organizer applications, including BreezeBrowser and ACDSee, have even more extensive search and management functions, such as nested keyword sets, simultaneous filtering by multiple criteria (for example, by keyword and resolution), and the ability to save category settings.

Slide Show Rating and Labeling

Another great way to apply labels and ratings to your images is to do so while viewing a slide show display of your images. This display can be activated by choosing View > Slide Show from the Bridge menu, or by pressing Ctrl+L/⌘+L. This will start a slide show of the selected images, or all images in the current folder if none are selected. By default you move through the images by clicking the mouse or using the arrow keys on the keyboard. However, you can press the spacebar to play or pause the slide show with the images advancing automatically.

Note: In Slideshow view, you can press H to show or hide a display of the various keyboard shortcuts available to you.

While viewing the slide show (Figure 2.27), you can apply a rating or label by simply pressing the numeric key associated with the appropriate value (1 through 5 for one to five stars, and 6 through 9 for the color values discussed above). There is no need to hold the Ctrl/⌘ key to apply the rating or label in Slideshow view.

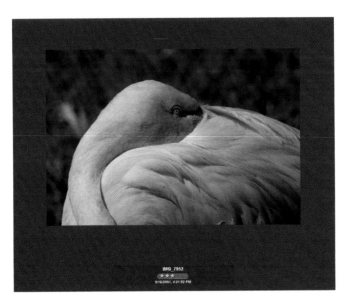

Figure 2.27
You can apply a Rating and Label to images while viewing them in a Slideshow view within Bridge, which can be very efficient.

Reviewing Metadata

Besides reviewing your images based on their aesthetic value, it can be very helpful to review the *metadata*—the technical information that's recorded with and embedded in your digital captures, including details on camera settings. This information can be very helpful for nature photographers who want to know a little more about how they captured a particular image. This can be as simple as providing basic exposure information for an image when submitting it for a contest or for publication. It can also provide a way to learn what is working and what isn't for a particular photographic subject. For example, when reviewing a series of images that you made of flowing water, the metadata can help you get a better feel as to which shutter speeds produce the effect that your prefer.

To review the metadata, simply click the Metadata palette in Bridge (illustrated in Figure 2.28). This provides a long list of metadata values, and you can scroll through all of them for any image. You can also view the same information by choosing File > File Info within Photoshop and clicking the appropriate categories on the left side of the dialog box that appears. For example, the Camera Data 1 and 2 sections contain most of the information you'd be interested in for a given exposure.

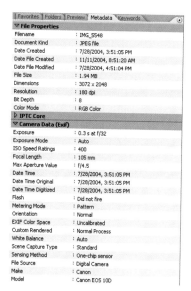

Figure 2.28

Reviewing the Metadata palette in Bridge allows you to get a sense of the settings used to capture an image, for both evaluation and learning for future photography.

Try It! To see how easy it is to evaluate metadata in Bridge, point Bridge to the Chapter 2 folder on the accompanying CD and look at the Metadata tab for the images Metadata1 and Metadata2 to see the differences in exposure settings.

Revising Metadata

As you can well imagine, much of the information contained in metadata is for informational purposes only, and you wouldn't want to be able to revise the values. For example, if you could edit the aperture and shutter speed values in metadata for a given image, that information wouldn't be reliable and therefore wouldn't be very helpful.

However, some fields in metadata are completely user-definable, so you can set the value as desired. These are primarily the fields in the IPTC Core section of the Metadata palette in Bridge. (IPTC stands for International Press Telecommunications Council, the organization that created this metadata standard.)

A good example of a situation where you might want to change the metadata values is to apply a copyright to your images. Granted, not too many people are likely to view the metadata to determine who owns the copyright for a particular image, but having your images marked as your own could certainly provide a benefit in the future.

Fortunately, adjusting metadata values is remarkably easy in Bridge. Start by selecting the image (or images) you want to change the value for. Then simply click one of the user-adjustable fields in the Metadata tab. In this example, click the box to the right of the Copyright Notice label and type in the box with your copyright message, such as your name and website address (see Figure 2.29). When you click a different image or in a blank area of the thumbnail display area, a dialog box asks if you're sure you want to apply the changes. If you don't want this message to display every time you adjust metadata values, select the Don't Show Again check box before clicking Apply to apply your changes.

Figure 2.29
It's easy to quickly adjust metadata values for a group of images using the Metadata palette in Bridge, such as for adding copyright text for a group of images.

This same basic method can be used to adjust any of the fields that allow changes on the Metadata tab, making it fast and easy to apply important information (such as copyright notice) to a large group of images.

Camera Raw and Bridge

As we mentioned in the discussion of Bridge preferences earlier in this chapter, it's possible to have the Camera Raw dialog box appear directly within Bridge rather than launching Photoshop for a raw image when you double-click it. To enable this functionality, select the Double-Click Edits Camera Raw Settings In Bridge check box in the Advanced selection of the Preferences dialog box.

When you then double-click a raw image, especially if Photoshop is already running, this may seem like a minor point. But the big advantage is that you don't need to have Photoshop running in order to adjust the raw settings for your captures. The real benefit is that you can work through a large number of raw captures very quickly, adjusting the settings for each without actually opening the images in Photoshop, and without the potential performance reduction you might otherwise see by having Photoshop running in the background (or launching when you double-click a raw file in Bridge).

As a result, you can select a group of images you want to adjust in Bridge and then double-click any of the selected images to bring up the Camera Raw dialog box. If you select more than one image, you'll be in batch mode for Camera Raw, with a list of thumbnails on the left side of the dialog box, as shown in Figure 2.30. You can then adjust the settings for each image and click Done to apply the settings. This updates the Camera Raw settings for the images without actually opening or converting the raw captures.

Figure 2.30

Using the option to bring up Camera Raw directly from Bridge rather than in Photoshop makes it fast and easy to establish RAW conversion settings for a large group of images during the sort/edit process.

This is a great way to pre-process your raw captures to update the thumbnails to better reflect your intentions for the image, or to even fully process the images during the sort/edit process. With the Camera Raw settings established for these images, you can then simply open them in Photoshop and apply the default Camera Raw settings (which now reflect your changes).

As you read this, you may still be feeling that there isn't much benefit to working in this way to update Camera Raw settings directly within Bridge without opening Photoshop. But once you've actually used this process, you'll see that it helps streamline your work when dealing with a large number of raw captures.

All Set!

With Photoshop configured just the way you want it, and with a good understanding of how to view and navigate your images, you're ready to start using some of the tools in Photoshop on your way toward optimizing your images to perfection.

Basic Tools

3

We know you're anxious to jump right in and start optimizing your beautiful nature photographs in Photoshop, but there's still some groundwork to be laid. Much of the work you'll do in Photoshop, and in fact most of the advanced work, involves using the various tools on the Tools palette. In this chapter we're going to introduce you to some of these tools to help you build a strong foundation for the adjustments we'll cover in later chapters. Think of this as an introduction to the use of tools in Photoshop, and know that in later chapters you'll be putting these tools to use, in some cases extensively.

Chapter Contents

Selection Tools
Saving and Loading Selections
The Brush Tool
The History Brush

Selection Tools

The selection tools are an excellent group to start with, because there are several different tools that enable you to produce the same basic goal: creating a selection. This helps reinforce the general techniques you employ when working with most of the tools in Photoshop. Using several tools that perform the same basic task helps you get more comfortable using Photoshop and the various tools it offers.

Selections can be used extensively for making targeted adjustments and for other tasks, as we'll discuss in later chapters. For example, you can select the sky to apply adjustments that only affect the sky, or select a foreground subject to enhance it so it stands out among the landscape better. So let's look at how you can use some of the selection tools most commonly employed by nature photographers.

The Lasso Tool

The Lasso tool provides maximum flexibility, because it allows you to literally draw a custom shape around the pixels you want to select. This is very helpful for situations where the more automated selection tools don't provide the accuracy you need, requiring you to trace by hand. For example, if you are trying to select a dark bird against a dark background, other tools may not be able to tell the difference between the two. The Lasso tool allows you to define the specific shape and location of the selection edge. Activate the Lasso by choosing it from the Tools palette 🔲 or by pressing L on your keyboard.

The Options bar for the Lasso tool (shown in Figure 3.1) contains some settings that allow you to adjust the behavior of the Lasso tool. These include four modifier options, which we'll discuss in the next section. Also on the Options bar for the Lasso tool are the Feather and Anti-Aliased controls. We recommend leaving Feather set to 0 px (we'll explain what feathering is and how to feather a selection later) and Anti-Aliased selected (to help smooth out portions of the selection lines that are not perfectly horizontal or vertical).

Ⓐ New Selection
Ⓑ Add To Selection
Ⓒ Subtract From Selection
Ⓓ Intersect With Selection

Figure 3.1

The Options bar for the Lasso tool lets you decide how to use the tool.

Zoom in on the area you want to select. (Refer to Chapter 2, "Putting Photoshop to Work for You," for details on zooming in and out.) Creating an accurate selection is easiest to do when you magnify the image to clearly see the edge you're trying to select along. Carefully position your mouse along that edge; then click and hold the mouse button. Drag the mouse along the edge so you're effectively tracing that edge to define your selection, as illustrated in Figure 3.2. Take the time to be as precise as you can so the selection you create is as accurate as possible.

Note: For tools like Lasso that require you to draw on your image, using a tablet such as the Wacom Intuos 3 (www.wacom.com) can be a tremendous help, providing you with greater control and precision.

Figure 3.2
When working with the Lasso tool, you can trace along any shape within your image to define your selection. (Photo by Tim Grey.)

Note: For all of the Lasso selection tools, use the keyboard shortcuts discussed in Chapter 2 to zoom in and out while you are in the process of creating the selection.

When working on a zoomed portion of your image, the area you're trying to select might extend outside the document window. In that case, as you near the edge of the document window, press and hold the spacebar. This temporarily allows you to use the Hand tool, so you can click and drag the image to change the area you're currently looking at. When you're finished moving the image, release the spacebar and continue dragging the mouse to extend the selection you're in the process of creating.

When selecting an area of the image, be sure to define all of it, dragging the mouse all the way back to your original starting point and releasing the mouse button to finish the selection, as shown in Figure 3.3. If you don't finish at the same point you started, Photoshop automatically completes your selection by extending a straight line from the point where you release the mouse button to your original starting point, which is obviously less than ideal in most situations.

Figure 3.3
When you finish tracing the object you wish to select, returning to your starting point, the selection will be completed.

Working with the Lasso tool can require a steady hand and a bit of practice. It isn't always the fastest or easiest way to create a selection, but it does offer exceptional flexibility.

Selection Modes

With the Lasso selection tool under control, you can start making more complicated selections by adding pixels to or subtracting pixels from a selection. Start by using the Lasso tool to create a basic selection. To the right of the Tool Preset drop-down list on the Options bar is a set of four buttons (these are labeled back in Figure 3.1) that allow you to modify the behavior of these (and other) selection tools.

 Note: The options discussed in this section can be applied to any of the selection tools in Photoshop.

The first button, New Selection, causes the current selection tool to behave in the "normal" manner, creating a new selection whenever you use the tool. With this option active, when you click and drag to create a selection, it replaces any existing selections.

The second button is the Add To Selection option. With this option chosen, whenever you use a selection tool to surround pixels, the new selection is added to the existing selection. For example, if you use the Lasso tool to create a selection around a flower, but then realize you left a part of the flower out of the selection, choose the Add To Selection option and then select the area you missed; it is then added to the overall selection (see Figure 3.4). You can also hold the Shift key to access the Add To Selection option regardless of the current state of the tool.

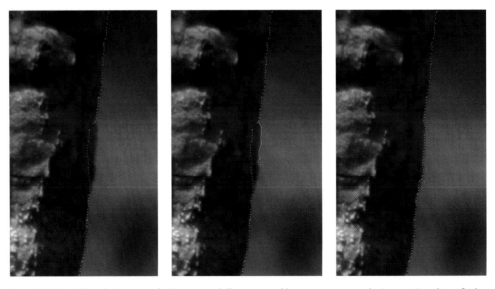

Figure 3.4 The Add To Selection option for the Lasso tool allows you to add a new area to your selection, creating a larger final selection.

The third button in the set is the Subtract From Selection option, which allows you to subtract pixels from an existing selection. When this button is selected, drawing a selection causes the surrounded pixels to be omitted from the existing selection, as shown in Figure 3.5. You access this option by holding the Alt/Option key when using any selection tool. You must still draw a closed shape to define the area of the selection you want to subtract.

Figure 3.5
The Subtract From Selection option for the Lasso tool allows you to remove an area from your selection, creating a smaller final selection.

The Add and Subtract options are helpful, and you'll use them extensively as you build complicated selections that require a fair amount of fine-tuning. The last button of the four, the Intersect With Selection button, is one you'll use less frequently but that can be very helpful in certain situations. When this option is chosen, creating a new selection when you have an existing selection results in a selection of only the pixels in the areas where the two selections overlap (see Figure 3.6). This option can also be accessed by holding the Shift and Alt/Option keys when using a selection tool.

Try It! To get more comfortable revising selections, open the image Lasso from the accompanying CD. Start by creating a quick but not very accurate selection, and then use the Add To Selection and Subtract From Selection options with the Lasso tool to revise the selection.

Figure 3.6 The Intersect With Selection option for the Lasso tool allows you to create a selection that represents the overlap between the existing selection and the new selection you draw. (Photo by Tim Grey.)

The Magnetic Lasso

The Magnetic Lasso is very helpful for selecting objects within your images where reasonably good contrast exists along the edges defining that object. Instead of selecting precisely where you drag, the Magnetic Lasso defines a selection by periodically placing anchor points as you drag the mouse around an object, automatically identifying the locations of highest contrast as you move the mouse around the edge. In other words, this tool simplifies the process of identifying exactly the area that you want, reducing the need to work extremely slowly and carefully, as you must with the Lasso tool.

The Magnetic Lasso is found under the regular Lasso on the Tools palette. Click and hold the mouse (or right-click) on the Lasso tool to bring up the flyout menu, and choose Magnetic Lasso (see Figure 3.7). You can also press L on your keyboard to activate the current Lasso tool, and then press Shift+L to switch tools until activating the Magnetic Lasso.

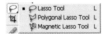

Figure 3.7
The Magnetic Lasso tool is found under the Lasso tool on the Tools palette.

Besides the standard controls found on the Options bar for the other selection tools, and discussed in the prior section on the Lasso tool, the Options bar contains some special controls for the Magnetic Lasso tool. (Figure 3.8 shows the Options bar.) The first is the Width control; as you "paint" with the Magnetic Lasso, the Width determines the size of the area in which you'd like Photoshop to search for contrast. You could enter a value in pixels to determine the size of the edge width for the Magnetic Lasso, but obviously this is a rather arbitrary decision. Instead, simply place your cursor along the edge where you'll start making the selection and use the left or right square bracket key ([and]) to reduce or enlarge the size of the edge width, respectively. You want the Width to be small enough that the strongest area of contrast within the sample area is the edge you're trying to select, but large enough that you don't have to be overly precise in dragging the mouse pointer along that edge.

Figure 3.8 The Options bar for the Magnetic Lasso tool includes some specialized settings in addition to those found with the normal Lasso tool.

The Edge Contrast setting determines how much contrast the Magnetic Lasso should look for. For high-contrast edges, if you use a higher setting, you won't need to be as precise as you move the mouse along that contrast edge. For low-contrast edges, use a lower setting, but be more precise in dragging the mouse along the edge you're trying to select. Frankly, the change in behavior achieved with different settings is very slight, so we recommend keeping the Edge Contrast setting set to the default value of 10%.

The Frequency setting determines how often anchor points are placed as you drag the mouse pointer over the edge. A higher Frequency value causes anchor points to be placed quickly in close proximity to each other; a lower value causes them to be placed farther apart. (Both of these situations are illustrated in Figure 3.9.) Higher settings are best for well-defined edges, whereas lower settings tend to work well for more nebulous edges. A Frequency value of 60 is a good general starting point, and you can then revise that number based on whether the anchor points are being placed at an appropriate rate (the allowed range is 0 to 100). It's generally better to have a higher frequency with more anchor points rather than a lower frequency, so the shape of the selection better matches the edge of the object you're trying to select.

69 ■ SELECTION TOOLS

Note: If you move the mouse fast with the Magnetic Lasso tool, the anchor points are spread farther apart than when you drag slowly.

 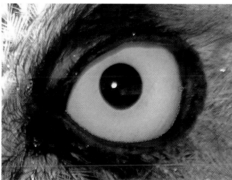

Figure 3.9 A low Frequency setting for the Magnetic Lasso causes anchor points to be spaced out relatively far apart, while a high setting causes them to be placed closer together. (Photo by Tim Grey.)

The final setting on the Options bar is a Pen Pressure check box. This setting applies only if you are using a tablet. With this check box selected, varying the pressure you apply to the stylus (pen) affects the edge width. Pressing harder causes the Width to decrease, as though the pressure is focusing the edge width onto a smaller area. Less pressure causes the edge width to enlarge, so the Magnetic Lasso looks for contrast across a broader area.

With the Options bar settings established, you're ready to start creating a selection with the Magnetic Lasso tool. Position the cursor over the contrast edge you want to select and click the mouse button once to place the initial anchor point. Then drag the mouse along the edge of the object you are trying to select. Photoshop automatically places anchor points at the area of highest contrast within the target area (Width), with spacing based on the Frequency setting. If you get to an area of the image where contrast isn't adequate for the Magnetic Lasso to accurately place an anchor point, click the mouse to manually place an anchor point. For example, if you have a well-defined subject such as a flower against the sky, the Magnetic Lasso will likely do a good job. But where the flower overlaps foliage or other flowers below it, the Magnetic Lasso may not be able to identify the edge, requiring you to place anchor points manually by clicking.

At times you'll find the Magnetic Lasso doesn't do a very good job of placing anchor points where you want them, placing them in inappropriate places. When that happens, you need to delete anchor points before trying again in the problem area of the image. First, move the cursor back to the last place where you want an anchor point. Then press the Backspace/Delete key once for each anchor you want to remove. They are removed starting with the most recently created point. You can then adjust the Width with the square bracket keys, or change other settings on the Options bar, and drag again along the edge. If you can't find settings that work well for a particular area, place the anchor points manually by clicking the mouse.

To access the regular Lasso tool while working with the Magnetic Lasso, press and hold the Alt/Option key as you click and drag the mouse along the edge you want to define by drawing freehand. Click the mouse again without the Alt/Option key to return to the Magnetic Lasso.

If you decide you want to cancel the selection in progress, simply press the Esc key; all anchor points are removed and there is no active selection (unless there was a selection active before you started using the Magnetic Lasso).

Try It! To get more comfortable working with this tool, open the image MagneticLasso on the accompanying CD, zoom in on the eye of the owl, and use the Magnetic Lasso to create a selection of the eye.

The Magnetic Lasso tool is powerful, but it isn't perfect. Although it does a good job of selecting based on contrast in the area you drag the mouse over, in most cases it won't create a perfect selection, as you can see in Figure 3.10. However, it usually creates a very good basic selection, making it an effective tool that can save you tremendous time in creating selections. Think of it as a tool for creating a rough selection, knowing you'll have to modify that selection after creating it. Using the Magnetic Lasso tool saves considerable time in the overall process of creating the perfect selection.

Note: The third Lasso selection tool is the Polygonal Lasso tool. However, for nature photography, this tool tends to be less useful than the tools described in this section because it is designed for creating selections comprised of straight lines.

Figure 3.10
The Magnetic Lasso tool doesn't generally create perfect selections, as you can see here, but it does provide you with a good basic selection with minimal effort.

The Magic Wand

When the Magic Wand tool can create a selection with a single click of the mouse, it seems truly magical. When too many clicks are required, it can be a bit frustrating. The trick is knowing what type of image is best suited for this tool and how to configure the settings for the best result.

The Magic Wand tool functions by sampling the pixel that you click and then comparing other pixels to see whether they are a close-enough match. If they are, they are included in the selection.

Before setting the options for the Magic Wand tool ⚟, it's important to check a setting on the Options bar for the Eyedropper tool 🖋. Although these tools don't seem related, the Magic Wand tool uses the Sample Size setting from the Eyedropper to determine the actual value to use in evaluating pixels for inclusion in the selection. Choose the Eyedropper from the Tools palette and choose an option from the Sample Size drop-down menu on the Options bar, as shown in Figure 3.11.

Figure 3.11
The first step in using the Magic Wand tool is to set an appropriate option from the Sample Size drop-down menu on the Options bar for the Eyedropper tool.

The chief options available when you select the Eyedropper tool are 3 By 3 Average and 5 By 5 Average. As their names indicate, they sample a grid of pixels (a total of 9 or 25 pixels, respectively) surrounding the one you click and average their values. This average value is then used as the basis of the Magic Wand tool selection. Averaging helps to compensate for any local variation among pixels. We recommend using the 3 By 3 Average setting, because it provides a good balance for most images. The 5 By 5 Average setting has a higher risk of averaging the pixel values to the point that the result isn't as accurate based on the pixel area you clicked.

Note: The Point Sample option causes only a single pixel to be used as the basis for pixel comparison by the Magic Wand tool. This can certainly increase precision, but it also introduces potential errors. For example, you could click a dust spot or a pixel with variation caused by grain or noise, and the resulting selection wouldn't match what you were intending to create. For this reason, we don't recommend using the Point Sample option.

After you've established an appropriate Sample Size setting on the Options bar for the Eyedropper tool, choose the Magic Wand tool so you can adjust the settings and create your selection.

The key to using the Magic Wand tool effectively is the Tolerance setting on the Options bar (see Figure 3.12). This setting determines how different the pixel values can be and still be considered a match. With a low setting, pixels must be very similar to the value of the pixel you clicked to be included in the selection. With a high setting, even pixels with very different values can be included in the selection.

Figure 3.12 The Tolerance setting on the Options bar for the Magic Wand tool is key to getting the best results.

The Magic Wand tool is obviously best suited for images with broad areas of similar tone and color that you want to select. An example is an area of open sky with no clouds (see Figure 3.13). Because the pixels already have similar values, a relatively low Tolerance setting should be appropriate. I typically start with a Tolerance value of 16 and work from there.

Figure 3.13
The Magic Wand tool is best suited to images with broad areas of similar tone and color, such as the sky in this image. (Photo by Tim Grey.)

Click the area of the image you want to select and adjust the Tolerance setting based on the result. If too many pixels from areas you don't want to select are selected, Tolerance is too high; cancel the selection (choose Select > Deselect from the menu) and reduce the Tolerance value. If you don't get the complete area you want to select, deselect and increase Tolerance.

A good approach is to double the Tolerance setting when a higher value is needed and halve it when a lower value is needed. Then narrow the value down by working between the established "border" values. For example, if 16 is too low, use 32. If 32 is still too low, use 64. If that is too much, go back to 48 (halfway between 32 and 64), and continue "meeting in the middle" until an appropriate value is found.

Of course, you could spend a lot of time chasing the right Tolerance value. We recommend taking a tempered approach, trying to find a *good* value without spending too much time finding the *perfect* value. If you can't find a good value relatively quickly, opt for a Tolerance setting that is a bit lower than needed. Then use the Add To Selection option to build up the final selection.

> **Note:** It's better to start with a Tolerance value for the Magic Wand that results in a selection that encompasses less than the area you are trying to select and then build up the selection with the Add To Selection option.

It's important to keep in mind that when you add pixels to or subtract pixels from a selection by using the appropriate options with the Magic Wand tool, the selection is modified based on the pixel you click after making your initial selection. The natural tendency when adding to a selection with the Magic Wand tool is to Shift+click an area that isn't selected to add it to the selection. However, this often causes areas you don't want to have selected to be added, based on the new sample point you clicked. You may need to Shift+click inside the existing selection, but at a different location than you originally clicked, to add the appropriate range of pixels to the selection. Also, keep in mind that you can adjust the Tolerance setting between mouse clicks when using the Add and Subtract options, giving you even greater control. Each time you click with the Magic Wand tool, pixels throughout the image are evaluated based on the Tolerance setting, regardless of whether the pixels are already selected.

Although the Tolerance setting is the pivotal setting for the Magic Wand tool, there are other settings on the Options bar you should consider. The Anti-Aliased check box serves the same purpose as it does with the other selection tools discussed earlier in this chapter, and we recommend leaving it selected.

The Contiguous option affects which pixels are evaluated. When you click a pixel with the Magic Wand, Photoshop looks outward from that pixel to find matching pixels. If it meets a pixel that doesn't match closely enough based on the Tolerance setting, that pixel creates a border so that pixels outside the areas defined by that border aren't considered. In other words, all pixels in the final selection are contiguous to each other.

With many images, you need to select similar areas that are noncontiguous. For example, you may need to select a sky in an image where the sky shows between the leaves and branches of a tree. Turning off the Contiguous option causes Photoshop to evaluate every pixel based on the pixel you click with the Magic Wand tool, as shown in Figure 3.14.

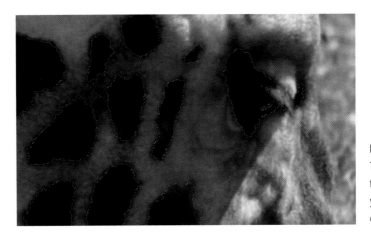

Figure 3.14
Turning off the Contiguous option for the Magic Wand tool allows you to select multiple noncontiguous areas in a single step.

The Use All Layers check box allows you to determine whether Photoshop evaluates pixel values based on all layers in the image or on only the currently active layer. Because you're viewing the image based on all visible layers, it usually makes sense to keep this option turned on. In fact, you can use this setting to make the Magic Wand tool more effective by creating a temporary adjustment layer that accentuates the difference between areas you do want to select and those you don't.

Try It! Open the image MagicWand on the accompanying CD and practice by creating a selection of the sky that doesn't encroach on the clouds.

The Magic Wand tool is best for selecting areas of an image that have similar tone and color. If the area you're trying to select contains too much variation, evaluate the image to see if you can easily select the opposite of what you really want. For example, if you want to select everything in an image except the sky, it might be easier to select the sky and then invert the selection (Select > Inverse).

Feathering Selections

In our discussion of creating selections in this chapter, we recommended keeping the Feather option set to zero pixels. This means that pixels inside the selection are completely selected and pixels outside the selection are completely unselected, with no transition in the degree of selection along that edge. When the selection is actually put to use, as the basis of hiding or revealing pixels in a composite image, for example, or as the basis of a targeted adjustment that only applies to the selected area, a non-feathered selection is generally a bad thing.

Feathering a selection results in a gradual transition along the edge of the selection. For example, if you feathered a selection by 10 pixels, there would be a transition from pixels that are 100 percent selected, to pixels that are 90 percent selected, and so on, until reaching the point where the pixels aren't selected at all. (Yes, that's right—a single pixel can be partially selected.) This creates a soft edge along the selection boundary and results in an equivalent smooth transition along the edge of the adjustment you apply in a targeted fashion using a selection, for example.

You can feather a selection edge as soon as it is created by choosing Select > Feather from the menu. The Feather Selection dialog box appears, where you can enter a value for the number of pixels you'd like to feather by. Of course, as you can imagine, it can be difficult to judge how many pixels you want the selection edge to transition across. For this reason, we generally recommend that you save your feathering for later. In most cases, a selection is used as the basis of a mask for an image or adjustment layer, defining where that particular layer should be visible. You can apply a blur to this mask to produce the same effect as you would achieve by feathering a selection. We'll cover these topics in later chapters.

Combining Tools

We've covered a few of the key selection tools here, primarily to help build a foundation for the use of tools within Photoshop, as well as get you started on creating selections you'll use to apply targeted adjustments to your images. However, we want to stress here that you can mix and match any of the selection tools or methods in Photoshop to create the perfect selection.

In the workshops we teach, we often see participants getting stuck on a single selection tool for a given task. For example, if they're trying to create a selection of the sky, they naturally start with the Magic Wand tool. If that tool isn't providing a very good solution in a particular portion of the sky, we often see the person struggling to find just the right Tolerance setting and just the right pixel to click on in order to get the selection perfect. The result is a lot of frustration as the photographer has to repeatedly undo a step in their selection process and then redo that step with different settings.

This sort of frustration can be avoided (or at least minimized) by combining various selection tools to create a selection. For example, when selecting a sky, you might start with the Magic Wand tool to create a basic selection and then employ the Lasso tool to clean up that selection and areas the Magic Wand tool wasn't able to select effectively. Always keep in mind that every tool or method for creating a selection in Photoshop can be utilized in building a selection, adding to or subtracting from the selection as appropriate, using the means most appropriate for each given area of a selection as you work to create the final result.

> **Note:** Of course, selections by themselves don't do anything for your images. But in later chapters we'll show you exactly how to put selections to use for creating targeted adjustments.

Combining selection tools can be a tremendous help when trying to build a very specific selection that can't be created all by itself. For example, if you have a group of flowers set against the sky and you want to select only the primary grouping, the steps might go like this:

1. Use the Magic Wand tool with an appropriate Tolerance setting to select the sky. After the initial mouse click on the sky, hold the Shift key and click in additional areas to build up a selection of the entire sky. Be sure to uncheck the Contiguous

option on the Options bar if there are areas of sky isolated by other elements in the image.

2. Inverse the selection so that everything except the sky (the flowers in our example) is selected, choosing Select > Inverse from the menu.

3. Choose the Lasso tool. Hold the Alt/Option key for the Subtract From Selection option and draw a loop around the area you want to exclude from the selection (in this example, flowers other than the principal ones you're concerned with).

4. Zoom in on the edge of the selection and use the Add To Selection (hold the Shift key) and Subtract From Selection (hold the Alt/Option key) options to clean up the edge of the selection so that it matches the edge of the object you're trying to select.

 Try It! To gain a better understanding of how you can combine various selection tools on an image, open the image CombineSelection on the accompanying CD and perform the steps described in this section.

Saving and Loading Selections

After you've created a selection, you probably want to save it for future use, just in case. Once you save a selection and then save the image file in an appropriate format (such as Photoshop PSD or TIFF), the selection is then saved as part of the image file, so you can always reload the selection in the future if needed.

 Note: Selections are saved as alpha channels. As you may know, RGB images are comprised of individual channels that describe the amount of red, green, and blue light that should be combined to produce the color value for each pixel. An alpha channel is a special channel in addition to these RGB channels, and it is generally used to describe selection shapes for an image.

To save a selection, choose Select > Save Selection from the menu, bringing up the dialog shown in Figure 3.15.

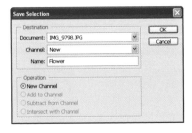

Figure 3.15
The Save Selection dialog box allows you to specify a name (as well as other settings) for the selection you are saving.

Although you can save selections in different documents with the same dimensions, it's generally best to save your selections within the image you've created the selection for. Therefore, leave the Document setting to the default value, which is the name of the current document.

The Channel drop-down list should be set to New so the selection is saved as it is. If an existing selection has been saved, you can also choose that selection from the Channel drop-down list and merge the current selection with the previously saved selection. We don't recommend this option, because it merges two separate selections together so they can't be used separately in the future.

The Name is the key setting (and generally the only one you need to change) in the Save Selection dialog box. Be sure to save the selection with a descriptive name that will make sense to you in the future when you need to load a selection, since you'll typically be choosing a selection from a list of names when you load it.

If you're using the New option from the Channel drop-down list, the Operation section of the dialog has only a single option to create a new channel. Otherwise, you'll have the same options as you have for each selection tool to create a new saved selection: Add To Channel, Subtract From Channel, or Intersect With Channel. When you click OK, the selection is saved as an alpha channel, which you can view on the Channels palette.

> **Note:** Saved selections aren't truly saved until you save the image that you stored them in. If you save a selection but then close the image without saving it, the selection isn't saved.

In the future, you can "load" the selection—that is, select the same pixels once again—by choosing Select > Load Selection from the menu and choosing the name from the Channel drop-down list, as shown in Figure 3.16.

Figure 3.16

The Load Selection dialog box allows you to recall previously saved selections.

> **Note:** Not all image file formats allow you to save selections, because they don't all allow you to save alpha channels, which is how a selection actually gets stored. If you're going to save a selection, it should be part of your master image file saved as a Photoshop PSD or TIFF image file.

The Brush Tool

As a nature photographer, using a camera to produce artistic images, you may not think you'd have a need to utilize the Brush tool in Photoshop. After all, if you capture an image with a camera, you certainly don't need to draw an image from scratch. However, there are actually many situations where you'll use the Brush tool while optimizing your photos. For example, we use the Brush tool extensively for dodging and burning on the image and for painting on masks to identify areas where we want targeted adjustments to apply. (Both of these topics are covered in later chapters.)

Note: The Clone Stamp and Healing Brush tools are advanced types of Brush tools that allow you to clean up your images; we'll cover those in Chapter 4, "First Steps."

The Brush tool allows you to paint pixels with great flexibility. This comes in handy for a number of different adjustments you can make by painting on a layer with special properties, or to paint on a mask (which you'll learn about in later chapters) to change where adjustments will apply to your image, for example. By learning how to work with the Brush tool, you open up many opportunities for making more advanced adjustments and taking full control of your images.

To get started, create an empty document by choosing File > New from the menu. The New dialog appears. Choose 5× 7 from the Preset drop-down list, make sure the Color Mode is set to RGB, and click OK. Then select the Brush tool by either clicking the paintbrush icon on the Tools palette ![paintbrush icon] or by pressing the B key.

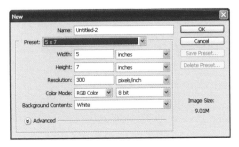

Figure 3.17
To practice with the Brush tool, create a new document to serve as your blank canvas.

Next, look at the color swatches on the Tools palette (see Figure 3.18). The large squares indicate the current foreground and background colors (represented by their relative positions). For painting, think of the foreground color as the color you'll actually be painting with and the background color as an alternative color you have quick access to when you need it. If you want to change either of the colors, simply click the corresponding box to bring up the Color Picker dialog box (shown in Figure 3.19). Click (or click and drag) the vertical color bar to define the basic color you want, click in the large area to select a specific color to paint with, and then click OK.

Figure 3.18
The color picker area on the Tools palette shows you the current status of your foreground and background colors.

Figure 3.19
The Color Picker dialog box allows you to select a specific color value you wish to paint with.

To set the colors back to the default values of black and white, just click the smaller thumbnail at the bottom-left corner of the color swatches on the Tools palette. You can also set these defaults by pressing D on your keyboard.

Since the foreground and background color options are mostly a way to have two colors readily available when working with the Brush tool, you often want to be able to switch back and forth between them. At the top-right corner of the color swatches is a double-headed curved arrow icon. Click this icon to switch the foreground and background colors, or perform the same action by pressing X.

The Options bar contains several settings that allow you to modify the behavior of the Brush tool (see Figure 3.20). Near the far left is a Brush drop-down list where you can select the type of brush you'd like to use. Click the drop-down list to see the available options, shown in Figure 3.21. The Master Diameter setting controls the size of the brush you're using in pixels. It's much more effective to adjust the size of the brush based on its relative size in your image, so we'll set the size in a moment. The Hardness setting determines whether your brush will have a hard edge or a soft and "fuzzy" edge, or somewhere in between. We'll discuss specific settings for various situations in later chapters, but for now, experiment with different settings to get a sense of how this setting affects the brush.

Figure 3.20 The Options bar for the Brush tool contains a number of options that allow you to adjust the behavior of this tool.

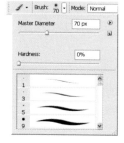

Figure 3.21

The Brush drop-down list contains several settings for adjusting the type of brush you'll paint with.

At the bottom of the Brush drop-down list is a scrollable list containing a variety of brush shapes. The first group contains hard-edged brushes of various sizes, and the second group contains soft-edged brushes of various sizes. Below that are a variety of brushes with more artistic shapes, which can be used in a variety of applications.

Note: You can also access the options from the Brush drop-down list by right-clicking the image when the Brush tool is active.

Once you've set the basic properties of the brush, adjust the remaining settings on the Options bar. The Mode drop-down list allows you to adjust the blending mode for the brush, which affects how the "paint" you are drawing with interacts with the underlying image. We recommend leaving this set to Normal; generally, if you need a different behavior, we recommend changing the blending mode of the layer you're painting on instead.

The Opacity setting controls how opaque or transparent the paint you're drawing with appears. At full opacity, the paint completely covers the underlying pixels, effectively replacing them. At a reduced opacity, the underlying pixels show through. (Figure 3.22 illustrates both of these situations.) We'll use the Opacity setting to vary the strength of the painting in several adjustments we'll discuss in later chapters, but for now, play with various settings to get a sense of how they affect the behavior of the Brush tool.

Figure 3.22 The Opacity setting allows you to determine whether your paint strokes completely cover up the pixels below them, or allow them to partially show through.

The Flow setting and Airbrush option control the variability of the Brush tool, causing it to behave like an airbrush or can of spray paint, where the longer you hover over an area, the more the paint spreads out. Because this creates a somewhat unpredictable response from the Brush tool, we recommend leaving the Airbrush setting off, which means the Flow setting is ignored.

You're just about ready to take the Brush tool for a test drive, but you still want to adjust the size of the brush. So, bring the mouse pointer out over the new document you created and evaluate the size of the brush. Then, press the left and right square bracket keys ([and]) to reduce or enlarge the size of the brush, respectively.

 Note: The Caps Lock key toggles the mouse pointer display between precise and brush size settings. If you're not able to see the circle that defines the shape of your brush, check the status of Caps Lock.

Now comes the fun part. You have an empty canvas before you, and you know how to adjust the behavior of the Brush tool. So start painting away! Get comfortable working with the Brush tool, using the mouse (or a stylus) to paint strokes on the canvas. Be sure to adjust all the various settings for the Brush tool, including color, Hardness, Opacity, and the size of the brush, so you get comfortable adjusting those various parameters. You can then use the Brush tool with confidence in a wide variety of situations, including many we'll describe in later chapters.

The Color Replacement Tool

The Color Replacement tool is a specialized Brush tool, with properties that allow you to alter the color of specific areas within your image. It actually produces very similar behavior in most cases to what you could achieve with the Brush tool in conjunction with specific settings, but it provides extended capability above and beyond what the Brush is capable of. The Color Replacement tool is very useful for fixing small areas of color problems within an image, where you need to change the color without changing the tonality or texture of the area.

For this type of use, we typically work with the Color Replacement tool with the following options set:

Mode set to Color, so we're changing the color in the image.

Sampling set to Continuous (the first of the three option buttons), which causes the tool to change color anywhere we paint, not just based on an initial sampling point, for example.

Limits set to Contiguous, to only adjust colors that are contiguous to those we paint over.

Tolerance at 100%, so all areas we paint on are adjusted.

When you paint with the Color Replacement tool with the settings recommended here, it changes the color of the pixels under the brush, preserving tonality and texture. For example, if you have some color contamination on a flower because a flower of a different color was very close to the lens and resulted in a wash of color that is completely out of focus, you could use this tool to paint an appropriate color to fix the flower. Painting with a neutral color (such as black) changes the color to a shade of gray.

If you want to paint a color correction, you naturally need to find an appropriate color to paint with using the Color Replacement tool. To do so, simply hold the Alt/Option key and click an appropriate color within the image to make that color the foreground color. You can then paint with that color in appropriate areas of the image using the Color Replacement tool to change the color as needed.

Try It! To practice using a Brush tool, open the image ColorReplacement on the accompanying CD, select the Color Replacement tool, set the foreground color to a muted orange, and paint on the red flower on the left to change its color. Be careful to paint only the red flower, zooming in and using a small brush as needed when painting near the foreground flower.

The History Brush

The History Brush tool is unique—it allows you to selectively paint certain areas of your image to take them "back in time," reflecting what they looked like before certain tasks were performed. This allows you to perform actions on the entire image, and then undo those actions in specific areas as desired.

As its name implies, the History Brush is a brush tool, allowing you to paint on the image. The difference is that instead of painting pixels, you're painting an area to change it back to the way it looked at an earlier time. Let's take a look at an example to help you understand this concept.

Start by opening an image and applying an artistic filter to that image. For example, you might select Filter > Distort > Glass, adjust the settings for this filter, and click OK. Then select the History Brush from the Tools palette 🖌. (You can also access it by pressing Y on your keyboard.)

By default, when you paint with the History Brush, it changes the areas you paint on to what they looked like when you first opened the image. However, you can change the *source* for the History Brush to any history state on the History palette. To do so, click the box to the left of the name of the history state (which defines the action performed at that step) on the History palette. This places a small History Brush icon in that box, as shown in Figure 3.23, so you know it is the source for this tool.

Figure 3.23

On the History palette, click in the box to the left of the state you want to paint back to, defining the source for the History Brush tool.

For example, in your new, blank practice document, you've only opened an image and applied the Glass filter to it, so there aren't too many options. However, you can set the source to the Open step (the last step done before the application of the Glass filter) to specifically select that history state as the definition of how you want to change the pixels or what steps you want undone for them as you paint.

With the source set, you're ready to paint. Note that you have the same options on the Options bar for the History Brush as you do for the normal Brush tool. In most cases, you want to use a soft-edged brush of an appropriate size, the Normal blend mode, and a 100 percent opacity. Wherever you paint, the effect of the Glass filter in this example is removed, returning those areas of the image to their original appearance, as shown in Figure 3.24. However, at times you might want to paint at a reduced Opacity setting, for example when you want to "tone down" an adjustment in certain areas of the image rather than eliminating the effect altogether.

Think of the History Brush tool as a "selective undo" tool. Any time you've changed pixel values in an image and would like to tone down or eliminate the effect in certain areas, this tool allows you to do exactly that with very good control.

Figure 3.24
With the History Brush, you can selectively paint areas back to the way they looked before making a particular adjustment.

Building Tool Knowledge

In this chapter we've explained how to use a handful of the tools you're most likely to use in Photoshop, providing you with an introduction to the use of these tools. Because so many of the tools in Photoshop behave similarly in a general sense, you can apply your knowledge of one tool to using another. Of course, in later chapters we'll describe additional tools and techniques for optimizing your images.

First Steps

Now that you have Photoshop set up the way you want it, it's time to start working on your images. If you get in the habit of following a routine approach for optimizing your images, ultimately you'll find you're working much more efficiently. Of course, different people follow slightly different workflows. We're going to suggest an overall workflow that you may want to modify to suit your particular needs.

The most important element in your workflow is to make it nondestructive. This means that you avoid working directly on pixels as much as possible because every time you modify a pixel you run the risk of degrading your image. We'll show you how to improve your images while being as nondestructive as possible.

4

Chapter Contents

Our Typical Workflow

Every time we initially choose an image in Bridge for further work, we follow a similar series of steps. First, we double-click the image and take a good hard look at it. (Note: If it's a raw image, it will open in the Adobe Camera Raw converter, whereas if it's a TIFF or JPEG, it opens directly into Photoshop.) We think about what we like about the image and those aspects we want to emphasize, and decide what things we want to modify. It's important to have an overall game plan in your head to keep you on track. Otherwise, it's easy not to know what to do next and even not to know when you're done! It sounds silly until it happens to you—suddenly you realize you've been working on an image for a long time and start wondering if you're done. Having a game plan in mind makes it easier to know where we're going. So our first step is to look at the image and decide what we want to do.

If we're dealing with a raw file, we make a series of preliminary adjustments in the converter to help us begin with the best file possible. (We'll explain this in more detail later in this chapter.) By making adjustments before doing the actual conversion, we're essentially able to choose the best mathematical algorithms to have Photoshop apply to the information that has been captured by the photosites on the camera's sensor. We're choosing how to present the information—lighter, darker, more or less contrast, different color casts, etc.—*with no damage to the pixels*. This is why many pros prefer to do as much of their adjustments as possible in the conversion process.

However, the downside to trying to complete as much of our image optimization in the raw converter as possible is that if we make an adjustment that is too extreme (for instance, we've maximized the contrast or cropped tightly), then to undo it, we need to return to the original raw file and start from scratch. Our preference is to get the image close to what we think we want in the converter, but allow some leeway for final tweaking within Photoshop.

With a TIFF or JPEG, the next step is to do any initial cropping and straightening that may be needed. Sometimes we prefer to wait until we're in Photoshop itself to do these steps with a file converted from raw format as well. This is not a final artistic tight crop, but rather a rough, loose crop to eliminate areas that there's absolutely no chance of us wanting in our final image. At the same time it's a good idea to straighten the image if our horizon is crooked. We do this using the Crop tool or the Measure tool. There's no sense in taking the time to correct pixels that you aren't going to be using.

The next step is to remove any dust spots by using the cloning and healing tools. We'll talk more about how to do this later in this chapter. This is a good time to remove any objects we don't want from the picture.

At this point we have the basic image. The next step is to make whatever adjustments are necessary to the exposure. This may involve using the Shadow/Highlight tool on a copy of the background layer if there are blocked-up shadows or extremely light (but not completely blown out) areas, or using Levels and possibly Curves adjustment layers to bring out the details in our image. We'll explain how to do this in detail in Chapter 5, "Exposure Adjustments."

After we're satisfied with the exposure, it's time to work on the color within the picture. Most images benefit from a slight boost in the saturation of the color, and sometimes we need to modify the hue or color casts within the image. We'll be using adjustment layers for this, of course, and we'll talk about how to do it in detail in Chapter 6, "Color Adjustments." (Using adjustment layers will become second nature to you, and we'll talk more about them and why they're so important later in this chapter.)

With most images we've now created the master file—the optimized version that we save *without resizing it and without sharpening it.* We save the master file as a TIFF or a PSD file, since both allow us to save the file with the layers intact.

One pro we know prefers to save a flattened version of his master files for space reasons, since saving the layers increases the file size. However, flattening the master file means we're unable to go back and tweak our adjustments without having to start all over.

It's not uncommon to go back to an image that was previously optimized and realize that perhaps we prefer the color to be slightly different or we like more or less contrast in a particular part of the image, etc. If the adjustment layers are there, these minor modifications are quick and easy. If we have to make them on a flattened file, then we're risking some slight image degradation by changing and therefore damaging the pixels again. In reality, such damage is likely to be slight, but since we're after the best finished product we can make, we want to save with our layers intact.

The reason we save our file without sharpening it is because sharpening must be done according to the final output size. If we resize the image—either interpolating to increase or decrease its size—different sharpening values will be needed. We want our master file to be at the native resolution without any interpolation since interpolation also inherently slightly degrades the image quality. We'll talk more about resizing and sharpening in Chapter 9, "Output."

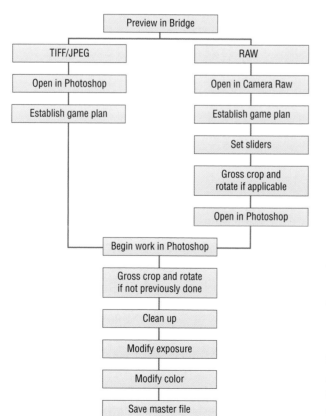

Following this same basic series of steps with each image allows us to work efficiently and without needless repetitive steps that might in reality conflict with one another. Of course there are times when some of the steps in the basic workflow aren't necessary, and those steps are omitted. You'll have to decide what your image needs and how much you want to fine tune the exposure and color within your image. Figure 4.1 diagrams our basic overall workflow.

Figure 4.1
Following this workflow, and customizing it according to the needs of individual pictures, will enable you to efficiently optimize your images.

Using Adobe Camera Raw

Adobe Camera Raw (CR) has been significantly improved in Photoshop CS2 and is part of our regular workflow. It's worth mentioning that this converter is different than the one supplied by your camera manufacturer. The one that came with your camera may be able to take advantage of some proprietary information captured by your camera, and this can, in a small percentage of cases, result in better image quality in the conversion. However, there is a huge convenience factor in using the very user-friendly and generally faster converter included within Photoshop. You'll rarely, if ever, encounter a problem by using CR.

Note: At the time this book is being written, some Nikon cameras, notably the D2X, have an encrypted white balance that results in a color cast when the files are opened in CR. D2X owners can either buy the Nikon proprietary software or make adjustments using the sliders in CR to correct the white balance.

Setting the CR Workflow Options

The user interface with Camera Raw is intuitive and easy to use. You can choose to make only basic corrections to your image or perform some quite sophisticated adjustments. We'll begin by looking at the various settings available at the bottom left of the dialog box if you check Show Workflow Options (see Figure 4.2).

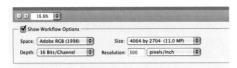

Figure 4.2
Check Show Workflow Options to reveal these settings.

Choosing the Space

After opening an image in CR, check the Show Workflow Options box to reveal several additional settings. First, you have the option to set the Space. This refers to the color working space; you have four choices:

• Adobe RGB (1998)

• ProPhoto RGB

• sRGB IEC61966-1

• ColorMatch RGB

Only the first three options are useful for nature photographers.

As mentioned in Chapter 2, "Making Photoshop Work for You," Adobe RGB 1998 has been the most frequently used color space for nature photographers seeking to make prints and archive their files, because it is a reasonably wide color space and corresponds fairly well to the color spaces available in most inkjet printers. Many people still prefer to use this space as their default color working space.

If you're planning to work with images in 16-bit color (and we recommend you do), you may want to use the ProPhoto RGB workspace. It's a wider space than the commonly used Adobe RGB 1998 and will allow you to use some colors that your camera may have captured but that may be outside the gamut of Adobe RGB 1998. Some of these colors can be printed by some inkjet printers. Further, if you have some clipping—that is, pixels that are at the extremes of the tonal values—in one or more channels, you may want to see if changing to the ProPhoto RGB space allows you to capture more detail in those channels. The disadvantage is that if you are converting back to an 8-bit image, you may have more colors that need to be converted than if you had limited yourself to Adobe RGB 1998; this may lead to some posterization or banding.

Occasionally, some people might want to use sRGB IEC61966-1. This is a narrower color space, but it's useful if your intended output is limited to projection and/or web usage. If you think that there's any chance you might want to print the file, we recommend you use one of the other two spaces mentioned in this section (Adobe RGB or ProPhoto RGB) and convert to sRGB for the specific use. (See Chapter 2 for a more complete discussion of color spaces.)

ColorMatch RGB is a space that is wider than sRGB and narrower than Adobe RGB. This means that it may have more colors than you can use for web use or projection, but fewer than your inkjet printer is capable of printing. Therefore, one of the other spaces is usually a better choice.

Choosing the Depth

You have the choice of converting your image into a file with 256 possible tonal values (8 bits/channel) or a file with 32,768 possible values (16 bits/channel). The clear advantage to 16-bit is accurate and smooth reproduction of tonal variations. Prior to Photoshop CS, working in 16-bit was difficult, but if you have CS or later, the workflow is as easy for a 16-bit file as for an 8-bit file. The only slight disadvantages are that since the file is larger, your computer may process adjustments a little more slowly, you may need more RAM to process the files, and the files will take up more space in memory.

> **Note:** Although it would seem logical that "16-bit" implies 2^{16} or 65,536 tonal values, in fact Photoshop uses 2^{15} or 32,768 when dealing with 16-bit files. Since most high-bit scans and digital captures currently range from 10-bit to 14-bit, this isn't an issue.

Choosing the File Size

Camera Raw provides a drop-down menu, found under the Size option, listing various file sizes specific to the camera used to take the image. Some of the sizes are marked with a plus sign (+) and some by a minus sign (−). One size has neither; it refers to the native resolution of the image with no interpolation. Most of the time this is the choice you'll want. However, if you know ahead of time that your intended usage needs a huge file, select one of the sizes marked with a +.

Many people find that the interpolation done in the converter is slightly superior to that which can be done later. The disadvantage is that the file will be much larger from the start and therefore slower to process on your computer. It'll also take up more space on your hard drive. Rarely does it make sense to convert the images to be smaller since you're trying to create master files. But conceivably you may be preparing a slide-show to give a talk and only need your images to be of the size that matches your projector resolution. If that's the only use you will ever make of the image, you may want to choose a small size so your files will process faster and take up less room on your hard drive. Otherwise, convert a larger file at the outset and resize it as needed later.

Setting the Resolution

As discussed in Chapter 2, the resolution, expressed in ppi (pixels per inch), merely refers to how tightly or loosely packed the pixels are; it doesn't change anything about the total number of pixels. The actual number of pixels is controlled by the file size that you choose. The resolution you set determines whether pixels are distributed 72 to an inch, 300 to an inch, etc. Since one of the most common outputs is for print, we recommend setting your resolution to your print resolution setting (usually 300 ppi). This way, when your image opens in Photoshop, it is sized according to an output resolution of 300 ppi. We'll cover resizing images for print further in Chapter 9.

Seeing Your Image within CR

By default when CR opens, the image is set to Fit In View, so you see your entire image within the workspace. As shown in Figure 4.3, the small box in the lower left of the dialog box gives the current magnification of your image. To zoom in or out, click the – or + boxes there, or click the arrows next to the number to get a drop-down menu revealing a variety of common magnifications. To check for critical sharpness within your image, you may want to zoom to 100 percent. To return to the original view, select Fit In View from the drop-down menu or use the keyboard shortcut of Ctrl+0/⌘+0.

Figure 4.3
You have the option of seeing your entire image or zooming in to closely examine parts of the image. (Photo by Ellen Anon.)

Note: To change the default view, zoom, and other settings for *all* images you open, see the section "Controlling the Default Appearance of Your Image" later in this chapter.

When you are zoomed in beyond the Fit In View size, you can click the hand icon in the strip of icons at the top left of the CR window, as shown in Figure 4.4, then click within the preview and drag to inspect various parts of the image. Alternatively, you can simply hold down the space bar while clicking and dragging within the preview. Note that you can also click the magnifying glass icon in that same strip of icons to zoom into your image and hold down the Alt/Option key while clicking to zoom out.

(A) Zoom tool
(B) Hand tool (Scroll in preview)
(C) White Balance tool
(D) Color Sampler tool
(E) Crop tool
(F) Straighten tool
(G) Rotate Image 90°
   Counterclockwise
(H) Rotate Image 90° Clockwise

Figure 4.4 This strip of icons allows you easy, one-click access to a number of important features in CR, including zooming, navigating, taking a reading of a point, selecting a point, cropping, straightening horizons, and rotating the canvas.

If your image needs to be rotated, click one of the circle arrows [○][○], or press the letter R to rotate the image 90 degrees to the right (clockwise) or L to rotate it 90 degrees to the left (counterclockwise).

As you can see in Figure 4.5, there are three check boxes to the top right of the image preview: Preview, Shadows, and Highlights. Check all three of them. Checking Preview enables the preview to be continuously updated with the changes you are making. To toggle back and view the original settings used in-camera with the image, uncheck this option.

Figure 4.5

Checking the Preview, Shadows, and Highlights boxes allows you to see if there is any clipping in your image either from the way it was captured or due to the changes you make within CR.

Placing checkmarks in the Shadows and Highlights boxes enables Photoshop to show you any highlights that you may be clipping by making those areas appear bright, solid red, and any clipped shadow areas appear as a solid vivid blue. This way you can readily see when you may have made an adjustment that will lead to accidentally throwing away detail in your highlights or shadows. With this obvious warning enabled, it's easy to modify your settings to retain as much detail as possible within your image.

Note: *Clipping* means forcing pixels above or below a certain value to become pure black or pure white, thus losing detail in either your highlights or shadows.

Camera Raw Shortcuts

This list presents some of the keyboard shortcuts available while working in Camera Raw. Some of these can be extremely helpful in making your workflow within CR more efficient.

Windows	Macintosh	Action
Delete	Backspace	When Crop tool is active: Clear crop In Curve tab: Delete selected points on curve In Text field: Delete selected text In Filmstrip mode: Toggles "mark for delete"
Escape	Escape	Exit Camera Raw (same as Cancel) When Crop tool is active: Clear crop
Alt+Cancel button	Opt+Cancel button	Reset
Tab	Tab	Move to next control
Shift+Tab	Shift+Tab	Move to previous control
Ctrl++	⌘++	Zoom in preview
Ctrl+-	⌘+-	Zoom out preview
Ctrl+Alt+0	⌘+Opt+0	Zoom to 100%
Ctrl+0	⌘+0	Fit preview to window
Ctrl+Z	⌘+Z	Undo/redo last
Ctrl+Alt+Z	⌘+Opt+Z	Undo multiple
Ctrl+Shift+Z	⌘+Shift+Z	Redo multiple
Ctrl+Shift+A or Ctrl+D	⌘+Shift+A or ⌘+D	Select primary image
Ctrl+O	⌘+O	Open
Ctrl+Alt+O or Alt+Open button	⌘+Opt+O or Alt+Open button	Open a copy
Ctrl+S	⌘+S	Save
Ctrl+Alt+S or Alt+Save button	⌘+Opt+S or Opt+Save button	Save with previous settings (no dialog)
I	I	White Balance tool
Z	Z	Zoom tool
H	H	Hand tool
C	C	Crop tool
A	A	Straighten tool
S	S	Color Sampler tool
R or Ctrl+]	R or ⌘+]	Rotate right
L or Ctrl+[	L or ⌘+[	Rotate left

Windows	Macintosh	Action
Arrow keys	Arrow keys	Adjust selected slider In Curve tab: Adjust selected curve point In Filmstrip mode: Select image
P	P	Toggle Preview check box
Alt+Shadows slider	Opt+Shadows slider	Show Shadows clipping in preview
Alt+Exposure slider	Opt+Exposure slider	Show Highlights clipping in preview
Ctrl+Tab	Control+Tab	Select next point in curve
Ctrl+Shift+Tab	Control+Shift+Tab	Select preview point in curve
D	D	Deselect point in curve
Ctrl+U	⌘+U	Toggle all Auto check boxes
Ctrl+K	⌘+K	Preferences
Ctrl+A	⌘+A	In text field: Select all text In Filmstrip mode: Select all images
Ctrl+Alt+A or Alt+ Select All button	⌘+Alt+A or Opt+Select All button	In Filmstrip mode: Select all rated images
Alt+Synchronize button	Opt+Synchronize button	In Filmstrip mode: Synchronize selected with previous settings (no dialog)

Cropping and Rotating within CR

Photoshop CS2 offers the ability to crop and rotate within CR. You may not want to do a final tight artistic crop here since if you change your mind later and find you want a looser crop, you'll have to start all over with your raw file. But if there is a portion of your image that you are certain you could not possibly want to include within your image, it makes good sense to crop it out immediately

To use the Crop tool, simply click its icon 🄴 or press C on your keyboard, then click a beginning point in the image preview, and drag diagonally across the image. You can refine your selection by clicking any one of the small boxes appearing on the boundaries of the image and dragging them inwards or outwards as desired. You can move the crop around on the image by placing the cursor within the center of the area to be cropped and then clicking and dragging.

If you click and hold on the Crop tool, you'll see a drop-down menu listing various preset cropping options, so you can crop the image to a particular aspect ratio of your choosing (see Figure 4.6). You can even create Custom settings for other aspect ratios that you frequently use such as 8×10. To do this, simply click the Custom option to reveal a Custom Crop dialog box. Fill in the boxes with the appropriate numbers and click OK. To remove a crop, press Esc while the Crop tool is still selected or choose Clear Crop from the Crop drop-down menu.

Figure 4.6

You can crop to a preset size or to a custom size within CR. The Size menu will reflect the cropped file size. (Photo by Ellen Anon.)

As you set the crop to the desired size, notice that the Size menu on the bottom left has changed and now reads Crop Size, and the sizes reflect the number of pixels you have selected. This is quite helpful because if you realize you'll need a larger file size, you can select it now and have the interpolation done within the converter.

Photoshop CS2 also enables you to easily straighten horizons within CR. To do so, simply choose the Straighten icon ⬣ or press the letter A. Now click at the beginning of your horizon, or area that should be straight, and drag across to the opposite side. You are telling CR what part of your image should be a straight horizontal or vertical line. When you release the click, you will see the preview rotated and automatic crop lines will have been set as illustrated in Figure. 4.7. The Crop tool icon will automatically be highlighted or selected. To quickly reset your image back to its original position, click Ctrl+Z/⌘+Z or select Clear Crop from the Crop tool drop-down menu.

Figure 4.7

The straighten tool automatically crops and straightens your image. (Photo by Ellen Anon.)

One potential drawback to cropping and rotating within the converter is that CR limits your crop to the boundaries of the image, meaning you cannot rotate and crop in such a way that the boundaries extend beyond the pixel information at any point. If the placement of your subject matter dictates that you need to clone in additional background area after straightening the image, wait to crop and straighten the image within Photoshop.

Try It! Open the raw image named ConvertRaw.dng on the accompanying CD or one of your own and practice cropping and rotating it.

Controlling the Default Appearance of Your Image

Bridge generates thumbnails and initial previews of your images to help you edit your images based on the CR settings. These previews also serve as a starting place for your CR adjustments. By default, they are set to use Auto settings and to apply some sharpening to generate these previews. You may decide that you would rather edit your images in Bridge, viewing the file previews with the settings you used to shoot them or some other combination of settings. CR allows you to specify what settings it should use to generate the thumbnails and previews.

Using the Default Auto Settings

CR now includes an option to preview your images using auto-corrections for exposure, shadows, contrast, and brightness. For images from some cameras, these auto-corrections work fairly well and give you a good start on optimizing your images. With images from other cameras, the settings can be too extreme and result in clipped data or other less than ideal presentations. By default, CS2 ships with the Auto setting functionality turned on. This means that when you view your images in Bridge, you're seeing the raw files with the Auto settings applied. In reality, your raw file is still a raw data file; the settings are only applied to the previews, not to the raw files themselves. *When you open the image in CR, you not only can, but should, modify any and all settings to customize the conversion as you desire.* The Auto settings are useful primarily as starting points.

You may prefer to set CR so that Auto is not applied to your RAW files, and that way when you edit them in Bridge you'll be seeing them as you shot them. To disable Auto, take the following steps:

1. Open CR. To do this, simply select a raw image in Bridge and double-click it or press Ctrl+O or ⌘+O to open it within Photoshop.

Note: Alternatively, you can press Ctrl+R or ⌘+R to open CR within Bridge, but without Photoshop opening. This can be useful if you want to convert multiple images but not work on them within Photoshop at that time.

2. Open the fly-out menu accessible via the triangle button shown in Figure 4.8. By default, it will say Camera Raw Defaults.

Figure 4.8
Clicking the right-facing triangle reveals options to set different defaults for CR. Note that the auto settings are clipping some important areas.

3. Click the triangle and then click Use Auto Adjustments to toggle the adjustments off. You can then save this as your default view by clicking Save New Camera Raw Defaults. When you open another raw file, the Camera Raw Defaults will appear without the Auto Adjustments.

4. You can also save the settings in CR to a default of your own preference by choosing Save Settings from the same fly-out menu. You are prompted to give these settings a name. CR uses these settings as the default until you direct it otherwise.

These settings are saved and available to use with other images. This way you can create settings that are useful for a particular situation and then apply them with a single click to other images when you open them in CR.

Note: In addition to setting the New Camera Raw Default to not use the Auto settings, you can also set the workspace, resolution, and other preferences to the default you want CR to open with each time. Lock in these preferences by setting up an image exactly the way you want them to open in CR and then clicking Save New Camera Raw Defaults from the fly-out menu.

Adjusting the Default Sharpening in CR

By default, CR applies some sharpening to each image. This is to balance the slight bit of softening that is inherent within digital capture. Although using this sharpening may make your images look better initially, you have very little control over this sharpening. If it happens that the sharpening is too much for part of your image and results in halos or other artifacts, there's no way to undo it later within Photoshop. To prevent that scenario, we recommend setting the sharpening in CR to apply to the preview only. This way it gives you an idea of what your final image may look like, but you don't run the risk of oversharpening the image from the beginning.

To set CR to apply sharpening only to the previews, open the fly out menu shown in Figure 4.8 and choose Preferences. From the Apply Sharpening To menu shown in Figure 4.9, choose Preview Images Only and then click OK. Now you can have the best of both worlds: seeing your images with some sharpening within Bridge as well as CR, while running no risk that they may be oversharpened.

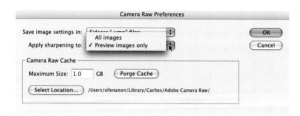

Figure 4.9

By instructing CR to apply the sharpening to Preview Images Only, you'll
have the best of both worlds and
you won't risk oversharpening your
images

Modifying Tonalities and Color: The Adjust Tab

Whether or not you choose to use the Auto settings as your default, the chances are
that you will often want to make some tonal and color adjustments to your image. The
ability to easily make subtle tweaks, as well as major corrections, to your exposure is
one of the many advantages of working with raw files. The main way to make such
exposure changes in CR is with the sliders on the Adjust tab.

Adjusting Exposure

The Exposure slider is similar to using Levels in Photoshop to set your white point. In
plain English this means you are selecting what tonal value (pure white, almost but not
quite pure white, etc.) to give the lightest pixels within your image, and all pixels in the
image are remapped accordingly. In many ways it's similar to modifying your in-camera
exposure, but instead of being limited to a half or a third of a stop, or multiples thereof,
you can choose from continuous values using tiny increments, up to four stops over or
under the in-camera exposure. However, remember that if you overexposed your image in-
camera to the point that no details were captured in the brightest highlights, using the
Exposure slider does not restore the details. CR cannot produce detail that was never captured in either highlight *or* shadow areas. However, it may make those blown out areas a
little less obvious by making them a very light shade of gray instead of bright white.

   The Shadows slider is used to set the black point. You are telling CR how close
to pure black you want the darkest pixels within your image to be. Simply drag the
Shadows slider to the desired value. Usually you won't have to drag the slider very far,
because you're working on the linear-gamma data, that is, preconverted information.

   We normally set the Exposure slider first, followed by the Shadows slider. Then
we use the Brightness slider, finishing up with the Contrast slider. (Often we prefer to
wait to adjust the contrast as an adjustment layer in Photoshop.)

   To easily set your Exposure and Shadows sliders without accidentally clipping
any pixels, do the following:

- Hold down the Alt/Option key and drag the Exposure slider; the preview box
  turns completely black. Drag it to the right until you see colored pixels appearing. These are the first pixels that start to become pure white with no detail.
  Back off the slider slightly so there is no clipping and release the mouse button.

- Hold down the Alt/Option key while sliding the Shadows slider to set the black
  point with no clipping. With the Shadows slider, the preview becomes totally
  white. When you see colored pixels begin to appear, back off slightly. By doing
  this you have distributed the pixels in your image over the maximum tonal range
  using clipping previews.

Although you could just rely on the clipping warnings in the preview, holding down the Alt/Option key makes it easier to see clipping in small areas.

It's tempting for some photographers to assume that all pictures should have as wide a range of tonal values as possible. Indeed, many images look their best utilizing the full range of tonal values—which is what you're doing if you set the white and black points using the Exposure and Shadows sliders while utilizing the clipping previews. However, especially within nature photography, not all images are suited to using the full range of tonal values. For example, if you take a moody picture of a lovely foggy scene, as shown in Figure 4.10, you most assuredly don't want maximum contrast. You want a limited tonal range reflecting the limited tonalities visible through the fog. You need to look at each image and decide whether or not it should utilize the full range of tonalities.

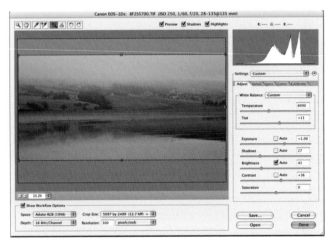

Figure 4.10
Some pictures like this foggy scene must, by their nature, not use the full range of tonal values. Note that the histogram does not extend all the way to each end, but rather is limited to more of the middle tonalities. (Photo by Ellen Anon.)

The Brightness slider is used to shift the majority of the pixels lighter or darker to make the overall image appear lighter or darker. Watch how the bulk of the histogram shifts as you move this slider each way. It's similar to moving the center slider within Levels in Photoshop. The more extreme the adjustments you make with the Exposure slider, the more likely it is you'll need to make adjustments using the Brightness slider. Don't forget to keep an eye out for any clipping you may introduce by increasing or decreasing the Brightness.

The Contrast slider is similar to applying an "S" curve within Curves in Photoshop to increase or decrease the contrast within the bulk of the pixel values. Contrast is primarily modified to those pixels in the middle tonalities with the lightest and darkest tonalities being left alone. Increasing the amount above the default of +25 lightens values above the midtones and darkens values below the midtones. Similarly, reducing the value darkens values above the midtones and lightens values below the midtones to reduce the overall contrast. If you have made only small adjustments via the Exposure and Shadows sliders, you may prefer to wait to make final tweaks to the image contrast using Curves within Photoshop. If you decide to adjust the contrast in CR, make certain to check that you have not introduced any clipping to your highlights or shadows. You may have to readjust the Exposure and Shadow sliders.

Modifying Color and Setting White Balance

One of the major advantages of shooting in RAW is the ability to fine-tune the white balance, or color cast. If you decide that you want to make your picture as neutral as possible, then including a card such as the Whi-Bal card available at www.rawworkflow.com within one frame of your pictures makes it easy to determine the correct white balance. Just use the White Balance tool and click the gray tone in the card in your image. In fact, you can use this eyedropper to click any pixel within any image that you want to define as neutral, that is to say, any shade of gray from the lightest to the darkest gray, and the tonalities within the entire image are remapped accordingly.

However, for most nature photographers, pure neutral is not our goal for every image. We nature photographers tend to like the warm color casts of early morning and late day light. Sometimes we even like the cool colors of shadows and/or the harsh blue light on winter snow. And sometimes we like to pretend those color casts were present even when they weren't! In such cases, the white balance you ultimately select may be correct, but perhaps not accurate. Fortunately, there are no "white balance police" running around demanding that your choice of white balance must be true to life! However, if you're trying to depict your images more documentarily, then you'll want to make your white balance choices as accurate as possible.

There are two sliders found within the Adjust tab that control the white balance or color cast of your image:

- The Temperature slider refers to the temperature of the light (in degrees Kelvin). What you really need to know is that moving the slider to the left adds a blue cast to your image, similar to using an 80 A, B, or C filter. Moving the Temperature slider to the right adds a warm yellow cast, similar to using an 81 A, B, or C filter. The major advantage this has over using a filter is that the adjustments are continual and gradual so you can choose the exact amount of warming or cooling to make your image convey the mood you have in mind.

- The Tint slider controls the green/magenta color cast. Moving this slider to the left increases the greenish cast; moving it to the right increases the magenta cast.

Unless you are color-blind (and we're being serious here, not sarcastic, having had several color-blind students), it's well worth getting into the habit of spending a little time adjusting the white balance, because the changes you can make to the colors of your image here are subtly different than what you can do within Photoshop (see Figure 4.11). And if you are color-blind, you may want to get into the habit of setting the cursor on a specific point in the image and noting the RGB values that appear above the histogram. You can learn to interpret the values so you know when your image is slightly warm or cool.

Figure 4.11
Adjusting the temperature and tint sliders allows you to make finer adjustments to the color cast in your image than would be possible using traditional filters. (Photo by Ellen Anon.)

Lastly, the Saturation slider is useful for increasing color saturation, although we suggest limiting any adjustment here to small amounts, since large changes can lead to unexpected clipping within the different color channels. Some images may benefit from reduced saturation as well. Watch the histogram as you make any changes. It's questionable whether there is any benefit to making saturation changes with the raw converter or waiting and doing them on an adjustment layer in Photoshop.

Sharpening Preview and Reducing Noise: The Detail Tab

There are three sliders available on the Detail tab. The first, Sharpness should be followed by "(Preview Only)" if you've set your preferences to have CR apply the sharpening only to the previews, as discussed earlier in this chapter. You can drag the Sharpness slider to preview the effects of more sharpening, but the controls here are less sophisticated than what are available within Photoshop. We rarely use this slider at all.

The remaining two sliders help you control noise. Noise is a by-product of digital captures, more problematic when using higher ISOs and/or correcting underexposed images and a bigger problem with some cameras than with others. Noise may be seen primarily in areas of darker tonalities, although it can extend into the midtones as well. As you can see in Figure 4.12, noise appears as variations in tones and colors in areas that should be smooth such as skies or skin tones.

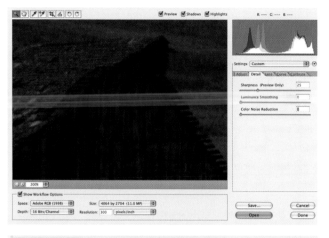

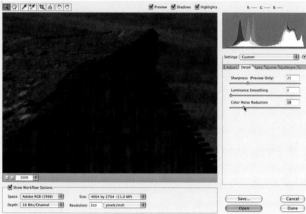

Figure 4.12

Noise appears as random variations in tones and colors in areas that should be smooth. Using the noise reduction sliders is an easy way to eliminate it. (Photo by Ellen Anon.)

CR offers two sliders to deal with noise:

- The Luminance Smoothing slider deals with grayscale noise, the unexpected and unwanted variations in tonal values that appear. This type of noise is similar in appearance in many ways to film grain. By reducing these tonal variations, this type of smoothing may reduce the overall sharpness of your image, so keep these corrections to a minimum. It's a good idea to zoom into various critical areas of your image to 100 percent or even 200 percent to see how they're being affected as you make adjustments.

- The Color Noise Reduction slider is used to reduce color noise, the unexpected color variations that often appear. While this noise is most common in the darker tonalities, it can also sometimes be seen as green and magenta blobs in areas that should be neutral gray and as rainbow artifacts in the highlights. Again, zoom to a 100 percent or 200 percent view of the areas demonstrating problems with noise and move the slider to reduce the color variations. Make the minimum amount of adjustment necessary to decrease the noise.

Although you can also reduce noise within Photoshop after conversion, and there are a variety of post-processing software programs that also deal with noise, controlling it before converting the image is usually best. This is because CR is doing this processing still on the linear data. The bottom line is, it's less destructive to do your noise reduction in CR.

Practicing with Adjust and Detail Sliders

Now that we've covered the basics of using CR, it's time for you to try it. Open the raw file ConvertRaw.dng from the CD that accompanies this book or one of your own. Once you have the Workflow Options set, you can essentially forget about them and concentrate on optimizing your specific image.

Take the following steps:

1. Begin by dragging the Exposure slider and then the other sliders. Don't forget to hold down the Alt/Option key while setting the Exposure and Shadows sliders to avoid clipping any pixels. Move the Brightness and Contrast sliders as needed.

2. Next, adjust the white balance. Try clicking the eyedropper in various areas to see how it affects the image. Fine-tune your results with the Temperature and Tint sliders.

Note: Make certain to keep an eye on the histogram to ensure you don't accidentally clip any pixels!

3. Click the Detail tab and do any noise reduction that you need.

4. When you're finished, click one of the buttons at the bottom right:

    Done   The Done button applies the changes but does not open the image. The image is still a raw file, and the changes are still tags. The thumbnail preview in Bridge will reflect the settings you chose in CR, and those settings will reappear when you reopen the image in CR.

    Open   The Open button applies the changes to the selected image and opens it in Photoshop. The image is now converted, and the changes are set as a permanent part of the file.

    Open Copy   The Open Copy button is available if you are using CR hosted by Photoshop and hold down the Alt/Option key. (This is not available if CR is being hosted by Bridge.) This allows you to apply the current changes and open another copy of the same raw file within Photoshop using different settings. This is useful when you are trying some of the creative techniques covered in Chapter 8, "Creative Effects."

Note: To open CR hosted by Photoshop use Ctrl+O/⌘+O from within Bridge. To open CR *without* Photoshop use Ctrl+R/⌘+R.

    Save   The Save button converts the image and saves it; another dialog appears, prompting you to choose a location, name, and format (such as DNG, JPEG, TIFF, or PSD) for your converted image. (If you don't want this dialog to appear, hold down the Alt/Option key when you click Save.)

    Cancel   The Cancel button closes CR, and the settings you chose are not retained.

Fixing Aberration and Vignetting: The Lens Tab

The Lens tab offers solutions to some issues—specifically vignetting and fringing (chromatic aberrations)—that may result when using particular lenses with digital cameras. Some photographers never have and/or notice these problems, and that's fine. Others perceive them readily and are quite bothered by them.

Vignetting is darkening in the corners of your images and can typically occur when a lens originally designed for 35mm photography, and not optimized for digital cameras' sensors, is used with a digital camera having a sensor that is smaller than the film area would have been. However, vignetting also sometimes results when using a lens hood with wide angle lenses or even from using filters with wide angle lenses. The Vignetting controls enable you to reduce or eliminate the darkening in the corners:

- The Amount slider controls the amount of lightening or darkening that is applied to the corners.

- The Midpoint Slider controls where the adjustment gets applied. Larger values on the Midpoint slider increase the area that is affected, while smaller numbers reduce it.

Make adjustments in small increments while closely watching the effect on your image.

Chromatic aberration, also known as *fringing*, occurs when the lens fails to focus the red, green, and blue wavelengths of light on exactly the same plane (the camera's image sensor); this causes color fringes along high-contrast edges. Chromatic aberration seems to be more of a problem with wider angle shots, especially those made with lenses not optimized for digital cameras; it may be more noticeable towards the corners of the image, as seen in Figure 4.13. These sliders will help you correct this effect.

- The Fix Red/Cyan Fringe slider helps you to reduce or remove red/cyan fringing.
- The Fix Blue/Yellow Fringe slider addresses any blue/yellow fringing.

Before using these sliders it's a good idea to zoom in to 200 percent or more to easily see the fringing and the results of moving the sliders. Holding down Alt/Option while dragging these sliders limits which color channels are visible and makes it significantly easier to locate the best setting for each slider.

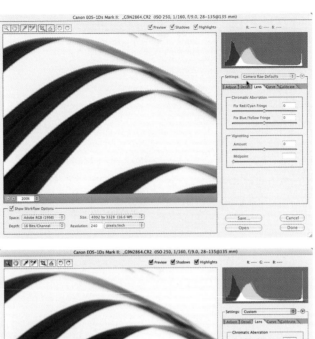

Figure 4.13

Chromatic aberrations (fringing) result when the lens fails to focus the red, green, and blue wavelengths of light to exactly the same spot. By using the Fix Red/Cyan Fringe and Fix Blue/Yellow Fringe sliders, you can significantly improve or eliminate any fringing. (Photo by Ellen Anon.)

Applying a Contrast Curve: The Curve Tab

Many photographers are more than happy with the results they get simply by adjusting the sliders on the Adjust tab. However, if you want to have even more control, you should venture into the Curve tab after you've made your initial corrections on the Adjust tab.

A *tone curve* is an algorithm or set of instructions for how to process the raw linear data to make the image more visually accurate and/or pleasing. It's plotted in a gamma 2.2 space in order to make it easier to make the adjustments.

When you click the Curve tab (illustrated in Figure 4.14) you'll see a drop-down menu for the Tone Curve, which by default is set to Medium Contrast. You'll also see a graph showing the actual tone curve superimposed over a graph showing the distribution of pixels. By clicking within the drop-down menu you can choose the Linear curve option, which causes no additional contrast to be added to your image, or the Strong Contrast option to use a preset tone curve that adds more contrast to your image.

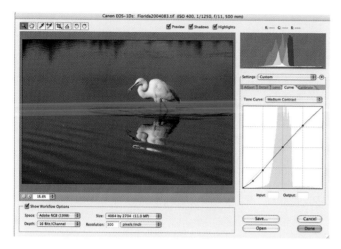

Figure 4.14
By using the Curve tab, you can access various tone curves, including the ability to make a custom curve to further refine your image.

However, the really useful part of the Curve tab is that you can begin with any of the Tone Curve presets and modify the curve, using the preset points as well as any points you wish to add, to create a custom curve for each image. The advantage of doing this here in CR rather than later in Photoshop is that the curve is still operating on the linear data. As long as you have the Highlights and Shadows boxes checked in the main window of CR, you can see if the changes you make are causing any clipping. If you're comfortable using curves, you may wish to experiment with tone curves within CR. If curves are new to you, you may want to wait until you are more familiar with them to use them in CR, so you don't have to reconvert your raw file if you decide later you've made a mistake.

Accounting for Camera Variation: The Calibrate Tab

The Calibrate tab is one that most nature photographers never touch; those of you who do will need to use it only rarely. The purpose of the Calibrate tab is to tweak the performance of the built-in camera profiles to account for any variations between your camera and the one they actually used to build the profiles in CR for that specific camera model.

If you notice that your images routinely have a slight color cast, rather than removing it in the Adjust tab, you can use the sliders here to set a correction. To do this accurately, you need to shoot a color checker chart, such as those available from Gretag-Macbeth (www.gretagmacbeth.com), and then compare it to a downloaded version with known values. You then move the sliders to match up the colors. In reality, this is more difficult than it sounds since each change affects all the other values. For a complete explanation of how to go about this, see *Real World Camera Raw with Adobe Photoshop CS2*, by Bruce Fraser (Peachpit/Adobe Press, 2005).

Batch Converting Multiple Images

If you have a series of images that you want to convert, you can select them all in Bridge and then open them in CR by either clicking Ctrl+R/⌘+R to open the CR dialog while remaining in Bridge, Ctrl+O/⌘+O to open the CR dialog hosted by Photoshop, or by double-clicking one of the selected thumbnails. (You can set an option within Preferences in Bridge to indicate whether double-clicking opens the Camera Raw dialog in Bridge or in Photoshop.) When CR opens, it opens in Filmstrip mode, as shown in Figure 4.15. The images to be converted appear in a vertical column on the left.

Figure 4.15

When selecting multiple images to convert, CR opens in Filmstrip mode. (Photo by Ellen Anon.)

Selecting a number of images that you wish to convert and having them open within a single CR dialog box can save time. You can choose settings for them individually or select a group to have the same settings. Although you are most likely to want to customize the CR settings for each image, if you have a series of images, shot under the same conditions, that need the same settings, batch converting can be a huge time saver. To batch convert a group of images in CR, take these steps:

1. Click one of the images to select it and then make all the adjustments you want to perform in CR.

2. In the left pane, click the image to which you want to apply these same settings. To assign the settings to more than one image at a time, Ctrl+click/⌘+click all the desired files.

3. Next, click the Synchronize button. A dialog appears (Figure 4.16) where you choose the parameters you want to copy from the file you just optimized to the other selected files. Sometimes you may want to copy all the changes you made; other times you may only want to select a few, such as white balance.

Figure 4.16

You can choose which parameters to apply to all the highlighted images in CR by checking them in the Synchronize dialog box.

4. Mark images to delete by pressing the Delete key. Those thumbnails now have a large red X on them.

5. When you are finished, click one of the buttons at the bottom right:

   Save   The Save button converts the images and saves them; another dialog appears, prompting you to choose naming and a location for your images. (If you don't want this dialog to appear, hold down the Alt/Option key when you click Save.)

   Open   The Open button applies the changes to the selected images and opens them as converted files in Photoshop.

   Done   The Done button applies the changes but does not open the images.

   One of the time-saving improvements in CS2 is that you can have CR converting images in the background while you continue to edit other images.

Initial Cropping and Straightening in Photoshop

At last we're in Photoshop itself! The goal of all the adjustments in CR was to create the best possible file from the data collected on the camera sensor when you took the picture. Although by now the image may look pretty good, there are some things you can't do within CR such as removing dust, fine color adjustments, specific resizing and sharpening. And it's likely you'll want to tweak some of the exposure settings as well. We do these things in a routine order to continue optimizing the file to make the best final image possible.

Let's begin by assuming you've opened an image in Photoshop that you converted using one of the many converters that don't allow you to crop or rotate your images, or that you shot the image as a JPEG, or that this image is a scan from film. We're going to begin our routine Photoshop workflow.

Initial Cropping

If there is some portion of your image that you're absolutely positive you would never want to be included in your final image, now's a good time to crop it out. This includes cropping those black edges that often appear when scanning slides. Those black edges can throw off the histograms as well as the levels and curves adjustments you'll be making. We recommend that you don't do a final tight artistic crop at this point because it's quite possible that by the time you're done optimizing the image, you may change your mind and want a tad bit less cropped out. If you did a tight crop at the beginning, this means you'll have to start all over again.

To crop an image, take the following steps:

1. Select the Crop tool ⊒ by clicking it.

2. To crop your image to a particular aspect ratio—for example, 8×10—you can set these values in the Options bar at the top of your screen, as shown in Figure 4.17, and then click and drag within the image. To clear these settings, click the Clear button.

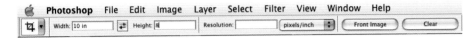

Figure 4.17 You can enter specific dimensions to crop your image to any desired size.

Note: If you want to size your image for final output, you can also enter the resolution here. However, because we're just doing an initial crop at this stage, not a final artistic crop, we generally leave the resolution blank and wait to do our final resizing until near the end of our workflow.

3. To mark out a crop manually—without constraints on height, width, or resolution—place your cursor in any corner of the image approximately where you want to begin the crop, click, and drag diagonally, releasing the cursor after you are close to where you want the crop to end. The area to be cropped out darkens so you can preview how image will look.

The Options bar changes, adding a Shield check box, which controls how, and whether, the area to be cropped away is darkened. Select the color and opacity of the shield by clicking the color swatch. We recommend leaving the Shield box checked and the color set to black at 75 percent opacity. This way you get an effective preview of your crop for most images. If the outer edges of your image are quite dark, you may wish to use a different color for the Shield. We leave the Delete box checked rather than Hide. Although it's not often needed in nature photographs, if you check the Perspective box, you can transform the crop by pulling out the corners as desired.

4. Fine-tune the crop boundary. You can change the size and proportion of the crop by dragging the handles at the sides and corners of the boundary. To reposition the crop within your image, place your cursor within the remaining image area, click, and drag. If you entered both Height and Width values before you started, you can change the size of the crop area but not its proportion. If you added a resolution as well as height and width, you can change the overall location of the crop but not the size.

5. Once the crop boundary is where you want it to be, to make Photoshop perform the crop do one of the following: press Enter and double-click within the image area, or click the check mark on the Options bar.

Note: To crop an image to match the dimensions of another image, open both images. Click the one that has the correct dimensions, click Front Image, and then click the other image. Notice that the dimensions of the first image are specified in the height, width, and resolution boxes. You can now readily crop your second image to match the size of the first.

Straightening Horizons

There's a very easy way to straighten a horizon while using the Crop tool:

1. Begin by using the tool to draw a crop on the image. Don't worry about placing it precisely yet.

2. Click the small square box in the middle of the horizontal line closest to the horizon and drag it to be nearly on top of the horizon.

3. Now place your cursor outside the crop area and notice it changes from an arrowhead to a double arrowed icon. Click and drag it up or down to rotate the crop and make the horizontal line follow your horizon, as shown in Figure 4.18. When you are satisfied that the crop line parallels the horizon line, let go.

Figure 4.18
Drag one edge of the crop close to the horizon and then rotate it until it parallels the horizon line. (Photo by Ellen Anon.)

4. Now click the center box on that crop line to drag it back to an appropriate place in your image. The rotation of the crop should remain as you reset all the outside edges, as you can see in Figure 4.19.

Figure 4.19
Carefully drag the edges of the crop where you want them while leaving the rotation alone. (Photo by Ellen Anon.)

5. Be careful not to drag the corners of the crop beyond your image, or you'll have empty areas in the cropped version that you'll need to create background for or recrop. However, in some instances it might actually be better to go too far than not far enough.

6. Now when you click Enter or double-click the image to perform the crop, it rotates the image as well to straighten it in one step, as illustrated in Figure 4.20. Pretty cool and very convenient!

Figure 4.20
Cropping and rotating the image in one step is easy and saves time. (Photo by Ellen Anon.)

Note: An alternative method for straightening an image, one that is particularly effective with reflections, is to use the Measure tool, located with the Eyedropper tools. Click the subject's eyes or other identifiable point and then drag to the same point in the reflection. Choose Image > Rotate Canvas > Arbitrary. A dialog box will appear that has the precise angle and direction needed to rotate the canvas. Click OK, and the image will be straightened. You'll need to crop the image after straightening it.

Try It! Open the image called Straighten from the accompanying CD, or one of your own, and use the Crop tool to straighten the horizon.

Understanding Layers

Before proceeding any farther with the workflow, you have to understand layers—what they are, why they're so important, and how to make them. Most Photoshop novices are initially intimidated by the concept of layers. But in reality, they're quite simple and easy to understand.

Let's begin by thinking of a couple of prints that are the same size. If you took one print and placed it on top of the other print, you would no longer be able to see the print that's on the bottom. You know it's there, and you know if you remove the top print or make a hole in the top print that you would see the print that's underneath. But when one print is simply on top of the other, you only see the top print. Those prints are actually two layers. Agreed? In Photoshop each of these prints is called a *pixel layer*. Pixel layers contain pixels, which are the building blocks of your image. Pixel layers work much the same way as stacking prints on top of one another. Whatever pixel layer is on top is what you see.

Note: Right now we are discussing how pixel layers behave in the Normal blending mode. Later in this book we'll discuss some more advanced behaviors of layers using different blending modes. For now, we'll keep it simple.

But wait, there are actually two types of layers: layers that have pixels, and adjustment layers, which don't have any pixels at all! *Adjustment layers are simply instructions for changing the appearance of the pixel layers.* For example, they may contain instructions to make the pixels lighter or darker, more or less contrasty, more or less saturated, or bluer, or redder. In other words, adjustment layers modify the appearance of your image but not the content. It would be similar to putting a filter over your top print in our analogy, and viewing the print through the filter. Your print would look warmer if it was a slightly yellow filter, bluer if it was a blue filter, etc. The filter would change the appearance of your print but not the content.

Note: Adjustment layers modify the appearance of every pixel layer below them.

All of the modifications you make in adjustment layers could be performed directly on your pixels by choosing Image > Adjustments and selecting the type of adjustment you want to make. *But that's exactly what we want you to avoid doing!* Every time you work directly on a pixel, you damage it and you risk losing some quality in your final output. By using *adjustment layers,* you can see the changes you have made, but they are not applied to the pixels until you either print the file or flatten it. This way you can make multiple changes and only affect the pixels once.

Even better is the flexibility that working in layers gives you. You can return to your image at any time in the future, even after closing it, as long as you have saved the image file with the layers intact, and you'll be able to modify the adjustments you made. You can increase them, decrease them, eliminate them, etc.—all without damaging your pixels.

And the best part is that it's so easy to actually select the adjustment layers. You simply click the New Adjustment Layer icon at the bottom of the Layers palette, as shown in Figure 4.21, and choose from the menu. Almost all the adjustments that are available from the Images > Adjustments in the menu bar are available from this list. By selecting them here, the adjustment is automatically performed as an adjustment layer.

Figure 4.21

To make an adjustment layer, click this icon and choose the type of adjustment you want.

We have a couple more thoughts for now about layers. If you place a pixel layer on top of one or more adjustment layers, the adjustment layers don't have any effect on that pixel layer because the adjustment layers are below it rather than above it. It's like taking another print and putting it on top of the stack—you're going to see what's on top, and what's underneath is not going to affect it.

Now imagine you have a print with a great sunset, and you have another print with a silhouette of a group of birds flying by. If you took the print with the silhouette of the birds flying and placed it on top of the sunset picture, you'd only see the silhouette picture. But you could cut the birds out of that print and lay them on top of the print below. Now you'd see the sunset with the silhouetted birds flying through it. In Photoshop this is akin to having a pixel layer that is partially transparent (the part that you removed from the print is the transparent part) and partially filled with pixels (the silhouetted birds) resting on top of the original pixel layer—the sunset. The sunset is the background layer, and the layer with the birds is only partially filled with pixels. In other words, pixel layers can be partially transparent and partially filled with pixels.

This is enough theory for now about layers, but we'll be talking more about them later in this book. Take the time to reread this section again slowly if you're feeling a little shaky about layers.

Doing Cleanup in Photoshop

Digital cameras seem to include a dust magnet on the sensors (not really, but it seems so!). Therefore you have to carefully go through your images and remove these blobs. Scanned images also often have dust and/or scratches on them that need to be removed. First, you're going to learn about the three tools you can use, and then you'll go through the actual steps to use on an image.

The Photoshop Cleanup Tools

The Clone Stamp tool, the Healing Brush, and now in CS2, the Spot Healing Brush are all useful in removing dust spots, removing unwanted objects from your image, and even filling in areas when you need to enlarge your canvas. They're very similar tools, but they're also different in some important ways.

The Clone Stamp tool 🔲 may be the easiest to understand. It simply copies the pixels that you specify from one place to another place using the following steps:

1. Place the cursor over the area you want to sample from.

2. Hold down the Alt/Option key and click.

3. Then let go of the Alt/Option key and position the cursor over the area that you want to replace and click. It's that simple!

The thing is that if you just keep clicking to sample an area and then clicking to put it somewhere else, you're likely to end up with a series of circular replacements that are easy to spot. On the other hand, if you click and drag for long distances, you're likely to get repeated patterns that are a telltale sign of a poorly optimized image as well. The trick is to just drag a little around the replacement area, and make certain not to have an identifiable repeated pattern. Most of the time you should make sure to use a soft brush and adjust the size of the brush, using the bracket shortcut keys as explained in Chapter 3, "Basic Tools," so that the brush is just slightly larger than the smaller dimension of the dust you're trying to remove. If you are cloning out a large area, then you'll have to use a small enough brush to be able to convincingly re-create the background. You'll become an artist at borrowing pixels to recreate that area of the picture.

It's important to remember to have Sample All Layers checked in the Options bar at the top of your screen. If it seems like nothing is happening, it's probably because this isn't checked. Most of the time you also want Aligned checked. This means that the source you are sampling from moves in keeping with the movement of the cursor at the destination. Otherwise, every time you unclick and then click to continue cloning, the source resets to where you initially began sampling. Therefore, you'll be creating repeated patterns.

The Healing Brush tool operates very similarly to the Clone Stamp tool. Press Alt/Option+click to define the source area and then release the Alt/Option key and click the area you want to change (the destination). However, the Healing Brush copies the *texture* of the source area and blends the colors so that a natural-looking correction results in which texture has been added and color has been blended from the source and destination. This can be quite useful to create very natural-looking corrections, especially in areas of sky and clouds. Its behavior initially seems less predictable when used near edges with strongly contrasting tonalities. In the tool bar, make sure that Proximity Match is checked and that Texture is unchecked. As with the Clone Stamp tool, you usually want Aligned and Use All Layers checked as well. Adjust the brush size and hardness as with the Clone Tool. Let the Source remain at the default of Sampled.

The Spot Healing Brush , new to CS2, operates like a "smart" Healing Brush. You don't have to define a source; instead, you simply click the tool and then click and drag your cursor over the area that needs fixing. This can work extremely quickly and efficiently in areas of low detail such as sky and clouds, but at other times you may prefer the additional control of being able to specify the precise source that the Healing Brush uses. Usually the Spot Healing Brush works best if it's a little larger than the narrowest dimension of the area to replaced, but just one click of the bracket keys larger than what you would use with the regular Healing Brush. We've found that the Spot Healing Brush can be a huge time saver.

> **N o t e :** If intitially the Spot Healing Brush gives you an unacceptable result, adjust the size with the bracket key to slightly larger or smaller, and try again. Often a slight adjustment to the brush size enables Spot Healing to work effectively.

To use these tools well takes some practice. Be careful not to create repeated patterns that make it obvious you "fixed" something. Taking the time to do a careful job in removing unwanted areas and recreating background areas is well worth it if you want the image to look natural.

Try It! To get familiar with the behavior of these three tools, open the image called Cloning on the accompanying CD and play with each tool, noting what happens when you sample in one colored or textured area and than try to heal or clone to the same or a different area. See how each tool behaves in each situation and near edges.

Darrell Gulin offers the following cleanup suggestion based on his workflow creating dramatic images of butterflies and moths.

114

Repairing Wings Using the Patch Tool

by Darrell Gulin

When I am working with raising and photographing moths and butterflies, they can damage their wings and scales so easily. The Patch tool has been a life saver for me to fix minor—and sometimes not so minor—damage to their wings.

The Patch tool, located under the Healing Brush in the Tool palette, is on my tool bar at all times. I use the Patch tool with the Source Mode selected on the Options bar. This means I select the area to be cloned out and move the selected area to an adjacent area that looks good, or what I want in the image. The sample of the Io Moth's wing tips was almost 95 percent corrected with the Patch tool.

© Darrell Gulin

Zooming, Navigating, and Layering for Cleanup

To remove those dust bunnies, you first need to zoom into the picture to a 100 percent view by double-clicking the Zoom tool. You need to check your image in a systematic way to ensure you don't miss any areas. We recommend beginning in the upper-right corner. Make sure the blue scroll bars are as far to the right as they go and at the top, as shown in Figure 4.22. To navigate through the image you can drag one of the scroll bars. When you reach the other side, take the cursor and place it in the white area next to the other scroll bar and click. This advances that scroll bar to the next unit so that you don't miss anything. Continue this process throughout the image.

Figure 4.22
Begin navigating through your image in a systematic way by placing the blue scroll bars at the top of the vertical axis and to the right on the horizontal axis. (Photo by Ellen Anon.)

Next, put some of your knowledge about layers to work. Rather than doing any cleanup directly on the background layer, you're going to make a new pixel layer to do your cloning and healing. To make a new pixel layer that initially has no pixels in it, click the New Layer icon next to the trash can icon at the bottom of the Layers palette. Notice in the palette that a new layer has appeared. To name this layer—so you know what you were doing in it if you return to the file later—double-click the words Layer One and then type the new name. You want a short but clearly identifiable name, such as Cleanup or Dust and Scratches, as shown in Figure 4.23.

Figure 4.23
Make a new layer to do your cleaning up on and be sure to label the layer.

> **Note:** Naming your layers is a good habit to develop. Initially while you're working, it may seem unnecessary, but the more layers you create, the more likely it is that you'll forget exactly what you were doing in any one layer.

Once you're familiar with the tools, you've examined your photo, and you have a layer available, you're ready to clean up your image.

Removing Dust

In most cases, removing the spots created by dust and dirt on your camera's imaging sensor is a relatively easy job. Create a new layer as described in the previous section, zoom in, and begin carefully navigating throughout your image checking for dust (see Figure 4.24). Our first choice tools for removing these spots, particularly in sky areas, are the Spot Healing Brush or the Healing Brush. Often they blend the corrections seamlessly into the image with little effort. However, sometimes you'll find that the Clone Stamp tool is a better choice, particular when working in areas of high detail. You'll know quickly whether one of the Healing Brushes is going to work.

Figure 4.24
Carefully navigate through your picture at 100 percent magnification to find the dark blobs resulting from dust on your camera's sensor. (Photo by Ellen Anon.)

Whether you're using the Clone tool or one of the Healing Brushes to remove dust spots, select a brush size just barely larger than the smallest dimension of the offending spot. For example, if it's a hair, the brush should be just wider than the width of the hair. Click and drag the tool along the length of the hair to remove it. The brush doesn't need to be large enough to cover the whole thing in one click. In fact, more often than not, you'll run into trouble if you try to do that. Sometimes you need to zoom in even further and use a very tiny brush.

The single most important trick to remember to successfully use these tools is to click and then drag the cursor just a smidge. This avoids the appearance of "correction circles."

Try It! Open the image named Dust from the accompanying CD or one of your own and practice removing the dust spots.

Removing an Undesirable Object

The procedure to eliminate an object—whether it be a branch, a bird, an animal part, or whatever that has crept uninvited into your image—is very similar to doing dust removal. But to do a good job requires finesse, patience, and practice. In fact, careful cloning is actually an advanced technique!

Note: Sloppy cloning is one of the telltale signs of a poorly optimized image. If you've done your job well, no one should have a clue that anything was removed from the image.

When you decide to remove an object from your image, you need to think even more like an artist. Imagine what the background would look like if you could see through the offending object and then work to create that background by using the existing pixels in the rest of the picture or by borrowing pixels from another picture.

Often you'll need to begin by using the Clone Stamp tool. Click and drag the cursor a small distance to "paint" over the offending object and then sample another spot and continue working. Balance dragging the cursor with resampling. After you have hidden an object, you need to look at the area even more carefully. If you are creating something with distinct patterns or textures, such as grasses or ocean waves, you should probably work with the Healing Brush on top of the cloned area. Sample from a variety of different areas where the lighting, size, and direction of the textures match what you need to fill the spot. You can also vary the opacity of the Clone Stamp tool or the Healing Brush, along with their sizes, by changing the Opacity setting in the Options bar. By combining these different approaches and tools, you can create a very natural-looking replacement area.

Cloning from a Separate Image

You can use an entirely different image as the source for your cloning! Open both images, making certain they are the same size, resolution, and color space. Place your cursor on the image you want to copy from and click while holding the Alt/Option key; then release the Alt/Option key and place the cursor on the other image where you'd like to replace the pixels and click and drag.

Here's a trick to make it easy to remove an object that comes right up to your subject, for example, a stick that comes right up to a bird's body. Before you do any cloning or healing, use the Lasso tool to carefully outline the part of the subject that you need to protect and then make a loose selection into the area where you'll be working, as shown in Figure 4.25. When you do your cloning and healing, Photoshop does not allow the effects to extend beyond the boundaries of the selection you just made. That way you don't have to worry about accidentally affecting your subject.

Figure 4.25
By making a selection before you do your cloning or healing, you can protect your subject matter so you don't accidentally damage it while fixing another part of your image. (Photo by Ellen Anon.)

Try It! Open the image named Extra Pelicans from the accompanying CD and remove the background pelicans while creating natural-looking water. Don't worry if it takes you more than one try. It takes many people more practice than they think at first, but once you get the hang of it, it'll be an invaluable skill to have.

Creating New Background on Empty Canvas

Sometimes you may find that your subject is too tight in the frame, whether because you framed it poorly, or the subject moved, or you cropped the image, or you had too long a lens for the subject. No matter what the cause, you can add canvas to remedy the situation by following a similar procedure as described previously after expanding the canvas size.

To increase the canvas size to allow more space around your subject, choose Image > Canvas Size. The dialog tells you the current size of your image. In that dialog, take the following actions:

- Check the Relative box. This tells Photoshop that the number you put in the box is the number of inches or pixels (depending on the unit you choose) to *add* to your image.

- Fill in the desired increase in pixels or inches.

- To specify where to add the additional canvas (top, bottom, right, or left), click in the Anchor area to anchor the image on one or two sides. In this way you can choose to add canvas to one, two, three, or four sides of your image, depending where you anchor it.

- You can also specify what color to make this new canvas:
  1. To get a jumpstart on creating a new background, choose Other from the drop-down menu. This opens the Color Picker.
  2. The cursor turns into an eyedropper icon; click a similar background color in the image.
  3. Click OK in the Color Picker dialog.

- Now click OK in the Canvas Size dialog. Your newly added canvas starts out in a similar color to what will be needed.

At this point you can use the Healing Brush along with the Clone Stamp tool to create the patterns and tonalities that one would naturally expect to see there. Don't forget to alternate between the tools as necessary. Again, you're going to have to use some artistic imagination to visualize how this additional background might have looked and then create it from pixels in other places in this image, or by sampling pixels from similar images.

Note: An alternate quick way to expand your canvas is to use the Crop tool to draw around your image. Increase the size of the window around your image by dragging the bottom-right corner of the image window if you are not in Full Screen mode. Drag one or more of the side boundaries of the crop out beyond the image. Click OK, and your image will be cropped (which means expanded in this case) using the background color in your Tool palette.

Try It! Open the image named Add Canvas from the accompanying CD and try adding canvas while making the background appear natural.

We've covered a lot of territory in this chapter beginning with creating the best file possible in CR followed by the first steps we routinely take in optimizing our images. Each step is a building block to make your final image the best it can be. In the next chapter we'll cover ways to improve the exposure to maximize the detail and impact of your image.

Exposure Adjustments

Nature photography—and all photography for that matter—is about light and creating a proper exposure that records that light. Once you've captured the optimal exposure, you can use Photoshop to make the most of the information you've captured to produce the best final image possible. In this chapter, we'll guide you through the methods you can use to fine-tune the exposure for your images in Photoshop.

5

Chapter Contents
Shooting for Optimal Exposure
Tonal Adjustments with Levels
Dodge and Burn Layer
Curves
Shadow/Highlight Adjustment

Shooting for Optimal Exposure

The ability to perform exposure adjustments in imaging software leads some photographers to feel they can be a little less careful during the original capture. We strongly advise you against believing that. Creating the very best images in a digital workflow requires that you start with the very best quality. Therefore, focus on creating the best exposures in the field, and select only your very best exposures to work on in Photoshop (see Figure 5.1). By ensuring you have achieved an appropriate exposure in the original capture, you'll achieve maximum detail in the image. Your adjustments can then focus on revealing the maximum amount of detail possible and emphasizing particular areas of your image, as we'll discuss in this chapter.

Figure 5.1
Achieving optimal exposure is an important first step for any photograph. It is especially important when you need to preserve detail in highlight areas, such as in the feather detail of this bald eagle. (Photo courtesy Arthur Morris, www.birdsasart.com.)

Note: When considering the best exposure, keep in mind Michael Reichmann's advice back in Chapter 1, "Thinking Digitally in the Field," to "expose right" in the camera.

Tonal Adjustments with Levels

The Levels adjustment provides excellent control over tonal adjustments for your images, with the capability to adjust contrast by independently controlling shadows and highlights within your image.

The primary component of the Levels dialog box is a histogram display (shown in Figure 5.2) that charts the distribution of tonal values within your image. Those values

are represented from black at the extreme left to white at the extreme right. This gradation of tonal values is shown as a gradient bar along the bottom of the histogram chart.
The shape of the histogram chart tells you about the distribution of tonal values within
the image. For example, histogram data that is shifted toward the left indicates that the
image is generally dark. However, that doesn't necessarily tell you anything about the
quality of the image; it may simply be a dark scene. Similarly, a brighter image has a histogram shifted toward the right.

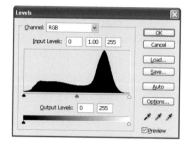

Figure 5.2
The Levels adjustment revolves
around a histogram display that
charts the distribution of pixels
among the available tonal values within your image.

The key things to watch out for on the Levels histogram are clipping and gapping. *Clipping* is an indication that information has been lost in the highlights or shadows of your image. *Gapping* is represented by gaps in the histogram, and indicates
tonal values that are not represented in your image.

Clipping is indicated on the histogram display by data running off the end of the
chart. There are two ways clipping might be displayed. One is as a spike at one end of
the chart. This is most commonly seen at the highlight end and is often caused by specular highlights within your image such as reflections from water, glass, or metal. In
other words, it isn't necessarily a major problem within the image, as you don't expect
to see detail in such highlights.

The other type of clipping is more likely to represent a problem within your
image, especially if it occurs in the highlights where it is important to retain detail. In
this type of clipping, the data of the histogram gets cut off abruptly at the end of the
chart (see Figure 5.3), rather than ending gracefully before the chart ends. If you think
of the histogram as representing a mountain range, ideally the mountains should gradually drop down to the flatland before the chart ends. If instead the mountains end suddenly in a steep cliff, detail is lost in the area that would have gradually lowered to the
base of the chart. All pixels within the "missing" tonal values have been clipped to the
minimum (pure black without detail) or maximum (pure white without detail) value at
that end of the histogram chart.

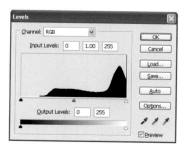

Figure 5.3
Clipping of data in your image
is exhibited by a histogram
chart that appears "cut off" at
one end, as with the highlights
in this histogram.

Ideally, your image shouldn't exhibit any clipping when you get started with your adjustments. If it does, it is generally preferable that the clipping occur in the shadows rather than in the highlights, as you're usually more forgiving of lost shadow detail in a photographic image than blown highlights. However, be careful not to *produce* excessive clipping through excessive contrast as a result of your adjustments in Levels.

Another problem to be aware of is gapping in the histogram. Think of the histogram chart as a bar chart made up of many narrow bars, so that the final result typically looks like a curving data display rather than one composed of individual bars. However, when gapping occurs, you start to see the individual bars that create the data display, as shown in Figure 5.4. Gapping indicates that certain tonal values are not represented by any pixels in the image (or are represented, but only by very few pixels).

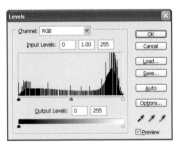

Figure 5.4
Gaps in the histogram indicate tonal values that are not represented within the image.

Note: Gaps in the histogram rarely occur for 16-bit files, because many more values are available than the 256 represented by the histogram display. 16-bit files have 65,536 tonal values per color channel available, compared to 256 values per channel for an 8-bit file. As a result, 16-bit files can lose a significant number of tonal values without obvious gapping or the posterization it can be indicative of.

Gaps in the tonal values indicate that smooth and subtle transitions between tones and colors within the image may be compromised. Instead of making a gradual change from one value to another with 10 values in between, for example, the transition may be from one value to another without any transition values between them. This lack of smooth gradations is referred to as *posterization* and is illustrated in Figure 5.5. This sort of flaw won't be seen out of the camera, only by making strong adjustments in Photoshop.

Figure 5.5
Posterization is represented by a lack of smooth gradations within an image.

However, gaps in a histogram are not an immediate indication of a serious problem with your image. Minor gaps of only a few pixels wide, representing just a few tonal values, aren't likely to be visible with the human eye. In fact, it isn't until the gaps become relatively extreme (at least 10 tonal values) that they are likely to be visible in the final output. Although gaps certainly indicate a potential problem, they don't define image quality by themselves. If you have significant gapping in an image, use caution not to make extreme adjustments that may worsen the situation, and closely evaluate the final image to ensure there isn't visible posterization.

Revealing Detail

Nature photographers are often focused on the detail within the image, and so tonal adjustments often revolve around revealing and enhancing detail and texture in the photo. Levels allows you to do exactly that by enhancing contrast and adjusting brightness to reveal the desired level of detail while maintaining an appropriate tonality within the image.

Let's make a Levels adjustment so you can see this in action. Create a new adjustment layer for Levels by clicking the Create New Fill Or Adjustment Layer button on the Layers palette. This adds a new Levels adjustment layer on the Layers palette, and the Levels dialog box appears. For most adjustments with Levels, there are only three controls you need to adjust; all three are found directly below the histogram display in the Levels dialog box:

- The black point slider (for shadows) is at the far left.
- The white point slider (for highlights) is at the far right.
- The midtones slider is in between the two.

Together, these controls allow you to adjust the overall contrast (by shifting the black point and white point sliders) and brightness (with the midtones slider) of your image with excellent control.

As with the Brightness/Contrast control, we recommend establishing overall contrast before fine-tuning brightness. Therefore, start with the black point and white point sliders. These provide contrast adjustment by allowing you to vary the amount of adjustment being applied to the shadow and highlight areas of your image. As a result, you can, for example, sacrifice more detail in the shadows to improve overall contrast without losing significant highlight detail.

As a general rule, most nature images benefit from having the brightest pixel value set to white and the darkest pixel value set to black, to maximize contrast and tonal range within the image and to ensure that as much detail as possible is visible. In other words, after making adjustments, your histogram should resemble a mountain range that stretches (in most cases) nearly the full width of the chart, with no gaps in that range. There are obviously plenty of exceptions to this, but it is a good basic rule. Because you know that the last data point at either end of the histogram chart represents the darkest and brightest pixels, a very basic adjustment could be made by dragging the black point and white point sliders inward to the point where the data begins at each end of the histogram (see the example in Figure 5.6).

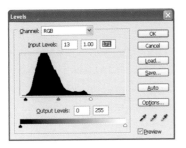

Figure 5.6
A basic start with Levels involves bringing the black and white point sliders in to where the data begins on the histogram.

Of course, this is a somewhat arbitrary way to approach an image. Although it indeed produces good results for most images, it isn't an ideal solution for everyone. Photography is very much a visual pursuit, so it makes sense to perform a visual review of the image and decide whether you're happy with the results of the adjustment you've made. You may want to back off the adjustments slightly in some situations to minimize the risk of introducing excessive contrast. In other situations, you may want to bring the sliders in just a bit farther to produce stronger contrast. It's up to you to determine the best adjustment for a particular image.

Note: If you're having trouble making appropriate adjustments, hold the Alt/Option key to change the Cancel button to a Reset button in most dialog boxes in Photoshop. If you then click the Reset button, all settings in the dialog box return to their default values.

After you've established the black and white points for the image, effectively performing a well-controlled contrast adjustment, you're ready to adjust the midtone slider. Think of this slider as a brightness control. Moving the slider changes which pixel value within the image should be mapped to a middle-gray tonal value, but the result is a brightness shift. This adjustment doesn't have any rule of thumb you can follow in terms of positioning the slider at a particular point along the histogram chart, so you need to make a decision based on a visual review of the image.

When you've adjusted all three sliders, you've finished the basic tonal adjustment with Levels. Click OK, and the Levels dialog box closes. As with any other adjustment layer, if you change your mind about the adjustment at a later time, you can simply double-click the thumbnail icon for the Levels adjustment layer on the Layers palette and the dialog box appears, with the sliders positioned exactly as you left them the last time you clicked OK.

Note: The Levels dialog box also includes eyedroppers that allow you to click areas of your image to automatically set the black, white, and neutral values. However, these tools tend to require a hunt-and-peck approach that doesn't allow you to make very accurate adjustments, so we prefer not to use them.

The Clipping Preview

Although a basic visual evaluation of your image while making adjustments with Levels is certainly effective, it can be even more helpful to use the clipping preview display available in Levels. This display allows you to see exactly where you are losing detail within your image as you adjust the black point and white point sliders. As a result, you can make a much more informed decision about the settings you'd like to use for these sliders.

When you start with an image that lacks strong contrast, and want to maximize the contrast without sacrificing detail in highlights or shadows, the clipping preview display allows you to see exactly where you'll lose detail based on your specific adjustment of the black point and white point sliders.

We recommend adjusting the white point first, simply because highlight detail tends to be the more critical adjustment. If you've already created a Levels adjustment layer for the image you're working on, double-click the thumbnail icon for that layer on the Layers palette. Otherwise, create a new Levels adjustment layer.

To enable the clipping preview display, hold the Alt/Option key while you adjust the white point. Your image display initially changes to a completely (or almost completely) black display. This indicates that no pixel values (or very few) are clipped to white without making any adjustment. As you continue to hold the Alt/Option key, slide the white point slider to the left. You'll see more pixels showing up as you move the slider, as shown in Figure 5.7. As a general rule, we recommend adjusting the white point until pixels just start showing up in the clipping preview. This is the point where you've maximized contrast and tonal range within the image, while sacrificing minimal highlight detail. Of course, the benefit of the clipping preview display is that you're able to make an informed decision about the amount of detail you're sacrificing to achieve the level of contrast you'd like to see and about that detail's location within the image to achieve the level of contrast you'd like to see in the image.

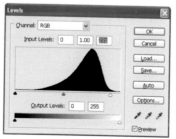

Figure 5.7 Holding the Alt/Option key gives you a clipping preview as you adjust the white point slider in Levels, so you can see where you start losing highlight detail and in which areas of the image.

Note: The colors of the pixels that show up in the clipping preview display indicate the color channels that are losing detail within the image. The pixels won't appear as pure white or black in the image until the clipping preview shows those values. However, even if they aren't pure white or black, they are probably very close if any channels are clipping, so you can generally treat such values as though they were indeed white or black.

The process for setting the black point is nearly identical: hold the Alt/Option key while adjusting the black point slider, and a similar clipping preview appears, except that now it starts completely (or almost completely) white, with pixels showing up to indicate where you're losing shadow detail (see Figure 5.8). As discussed previously, you are generally willing to sacrifice more shadow detail as opposed to highlight detail to maximize contrast. The clipping preview allows you to make an informed decision about how much detail you're giving up with a particular adjustment and the location of that detail, so you can better determine the extent to which you can push the black point to produce the desired contrast level.

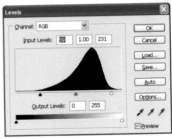

Figure 5.8 The clipping preview while adjusting the black point slider shows you where you're losing shadow detail in the image.

After you've adjusted the black and white points by using the clipping preview, you're ready to adjust the midtone slider for overall brightness. Because this doesn't affect the extreme tonal values within the image, there isn't a clipping preview for the midtone slider. You need to rely on a visual evaluation of the image for this adjustment.

Try It! To practice utilizing the clipping preview in Levels, open the image Levels on the accompanying CD and use the clipping preview to adjust the white point and black point, and adjust the midtone slider visually.

When you're finished with all three of these adjustments, using the clipping preview for the black and white points, you've produced an image with optimal contrast based on your willingness to sacrifice detail to achieve your goals for the image.

Emphasizing the Subject

Making overall adjustments to bring out the maximum amount of detail in your images is a common goal, but at other times you'll want to focus on emphasizing a particular subject within the image. This type of adjustment isn't exclusive of revealing detail. Rather, we tend to focus on revealing detail first, and then direct our attention at emphasizing the key subject in the image. Doing so requires the use of a layer mask to target the adjustment to a particular area of the image.

Masking from Selection

Creating an adjustment layer that is masked based on a selection is easy, especially since you've already seen some of the methods you can use to create selections, as described in Chapter 3, "Basic Tools." This is the method Tim prefers in most cases, working to create the best selection possible before making an adjustment to apply to that area.

To mask an adjustment layer, start by creating a selection that defines the subject you'd like to emphasize, as shown in Figure 5.9. Then create a new adjustment layer of the desired type (in this case using Levels). Because a selection is active when the adjustment layer is created, Photoshop assumes you want to mask the adjustment layer based on the selection. Therefore, the adjustment layer applies only to the areas that were selected when you created the adjustment layer.

Figure 5.9
The first step in emphasizing a particular area of your image with a targeted tonal adjustment is to create a selection defining that area. (Photo by Tim Grey.)

When you make adjustments to the Levels dialog box, as in this example, the adjustment only affects the area that had been selected when the adjustment layer was created. On the Layers palette, notice there's a black-and-white thumbnail (to the right of the adjustment layer icon) that matches the shape of the selection you originally created (see Figure 5.10). This is the layer mask, which controls which areas of the image are affected by the adjustment and which are not. Black on the layer mask blocks the adjustment from taking effect in the corresponding area of the image, and white reveals the adjustment.

Figure 5.10
When you create an adjustment layer with an active selection, the mask for that adjustment layer reflects the shape of the selection so the adjustment only applies to that area of the image.

Note: On a layer mask, black blocks and white reveals the layer's effect.

Using this concept, it's very easy to see how you could create a selection to define the area you want to emphasize and then create a Levels adjustment (or a different type of adjustment as appropriate) to adjust that area and draw more attention to it.

Painting on a Mask

In some situations you don't want to create the adjustment layer mask based on a selection. For example, when you're going to adjust an image area that is defined by relatively nebulous edges, or when you need to modify a mask after creating it from a selection, creating a selection to start from can be a challenge. When the edge of the area you want to adjust isn't well-defined, this is often the better approach. This is actually Ellen's preferred method whenever possible, so she can skip the sometimes laborious process of creating a selection before making a targeted adjustment based on that selection. In those situations, painting to define the mask provides a solution. In fact, adjustment layers are always created with a layer mask attached, so you don't even need to create a layer mask if you've created an adjustment layer when there wasn't an active selection. In that case, the mask is simply filled with white.

Start by creating an adjustment layer; make an adjustment so you can see an effect in the image. We recommend making an exaggerated adjustment so it's easier to see exactly where in the image the adjustment layer applies. To modify the mask for an adjustment layer, select the Brush tool, press D to set the colors to their defaults of black and white, and then press X as needed to switch foreground and background colors. Paint with black to block the effect of the adjustment in specific areas of the image or paint with white to reveal the adjustment.

Note: You can Alt/Option+click the adjustment layer mask to see what the mask looks like and clean up small areas that may have been missed in painting.

If you later decide you need to further revise the adjustment layer mask, simply click the adjustment layer to make it active and paint as needed to change the areas where the adjustment is blocked or revealed.

At times, you'll want the adjustment layer to apply to a very small area of your image, but that area won't be conducive to making a selection. In such situations, it may seem that the only solution is to paint with black throughout most of the image. However, you can also fill the initially white adjustment layer mask with black so it doesn't apply to any of the image, and then paint with white in the areas where you want the adjustment to be revealed. After creating the new adjustment layer, choose Edit > Fill from the menu, select Black from the Use drop-down list, and click OK (see Figure 5.11). This fills the layer mask with black, blocking the effect of the adjustment from the entire image. You can then use the Brush tool with the foreground color set to white to paint the adjustment in the areas where you'd like it to be applied.

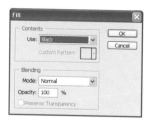

Figure 5.11

You can use the Fill command to fill a layer mask with black and then paint with white to apply the adjustment to specific areas of the image.

Note: You can also use Alt/Option+Delete to fill a layer mask with the foreground color and use Ctrl/⌘+Delete to fill a layer mask with the background color.

So far you've seen how you can paint with black or white on an adjustment layer mask to target specific areas where the adjustment should be blocked or revealed. However, keep in mind that you can use any method at all to place pixels onto a layer mask.

For example, if you'd like to only partially block or reveal the effects of an adjustment layer, paint on the layer mask with a shade of gray. This causes the effect of the adjustment to be blocked or revealed to the extent that the shade of gray you use is nearly black or white, respectively, as shown in Figure 5.12. You could also paint at a reduced opacity to produce a similar effect. And, as mentioned previously, paint with a soft-edged brush if necessary to produce a gradual transition between the areas that are and are not affected by the adjustment layer.

Figure 5.12

You can use shades of gray on an adjustment layer mask to have the effect partially revealed within the image.

Note: Any method or tool that allows you to place pixels on a layer can be used to place pixels onto a layer mask, so be creative when you're trying to solve a particular problem with a mask.

Of course, you can also combine the two approaches. Start by creating a selection that defines the area you want to adjust, and then paint on the layer mask to fine-tune the area you want to have affected by the adjustment. This allows you to utilize the best of both techniques to achieve the best results possible in your images.

Try It! Open the image SelectiveLevels on the accompanying CD and create a rough selection of the interior of the flower using the Lasso tool. Then create a Levels adjustment, lighten the interior of the flower, and click OK. Finally, use the Brush tool to refine the initial selection edge, painting with white where you want the selection to apply and painting with black where you don't want it to apply.

Blurring the Layer Mask

If you used a selection that wasn't feathered (as we generally do since you'd then be guessing at how much feathering you want) or if you used a hard-edged brush to adjust the layer mask for an adjustment layer, the transition between the areas you adjusted and those you didn't will be relatively harsh, as you can see in Figure 5.13.

Figure 5.13
When you use a non-feathered selection or a hard-edged brush with a layer mask, the transition between adjusted and non-adjusted areas will be relatively harsh.

Note: We described the selection tools' Feather option back in Chapter 3, but we still don't recommend using it!

To create a more natural effect, we recommend applying a blur to the layer mask when you've finished defining its shape to create a smooth transition between adjusted and non-adjusted areas. By using this method, you can see the actual effect in the image rather than, for example, guessing how many pixels you should feather a selection by.

Make sure the appropriate layer mask is selected first and then select Filter > Blur > Gaussian Blur from the menu to bring up the Gaussian Blur dialog box (shown in Figure 5.14). With the Preview check box selected, start with a value of 1 pixel and adjust the slider up or down to achieve the desired effect in the image. You want to produce a gradual transition between the areas you're adjusting versus not adjusting (see Figure 5.15), but not softening the effect so much that the adjustment blends across too large a distance. When you've found the appropriate value, click OK to apply the blur to the mask.

Figure 5.14

Applying the Gaussian Blur filter on the mask for your adjustment layer allows you to soften the edge of the mask.

Figure 5.15

After blurring the adjustment layer mask, the result is a more gradual transition between adjusted and non-adjusted areas of the image.

Try It! Open the image BlurMask on the accompanying CD, select the layer mask for the Levels adjustment layer, and apply a Gaussian blur to the mask to soften the vignette effect in the image and help you gain a better understanding of the process for blurring a layer mask.

Applying a Gradient to a Mask

One particularly helpful example of a tool that can be used to place pixels onto an adjustment layer mask is the Gradient tool. This allows you to place a gradient on a layer mask, resulting in an adjustment that affects one side of the image completely but gradually tapers off in a given direction until it has no effect at the other side of the image. The most common example of using such a gradient is in a composition where you would otherwise shoot with a graduated split neutral density filter, such as when you need to darken the sky without darkening the foreground of an image.

To create an adjustment layer with a gradient mask, follow these steps:

1. Start by creating a new adjustment layer that produces the desired effect in the area of the image you want it to apply to. For example, you might create a Levels adjustment layer that darkens the sky in an image by moving the midtone slider to the right. After you've made the adjustment, click OK in the dialog box for the adjustment to apply the settings on the layer.

2. Select the Gradient tool from the Tools palette (the shortcut key is G). On the Options bar, click the drop-down list for the gradient editor and choose the first gradient thumbnail on the list, which is the Foreground To Background gradient. Next, select the Linear option for the Gradient tool on the Options bar (shown in Figure 5.16), which is the first in the set of five buttons allowing you to choose a style for your gradient.

Figure 5.16 To use a gradient on a layer mask, select the Foreground To Background gradient with the Linear option from the Options bar.

3. Press D to set the colors to the defaults of black and white, and set white to the foreground color (pressing X to switch foreground and background colors if necessary). You're now ready to create a gradient that transitions from white to black.

4. You want to create the gradient on the layer mask for the adjustment layer you just created, so make sure that is the active layer on the Layers palette. Then click and drag on the image to create a gradient: the foreground color starts where you first click, with a smooth gradation to the background color where you release the mouse, as shown in Figure 5.17. The length of the line you drag determines the distance over which the gradient transitions, and the direction determines the angle of that gradient. To lock the gradient to 45-degree increments, simply hold the Shift key as you drag.

Figure 5.17
Draw the gradient on the layer mask so the adjustment tapers from adjusted to non-adjusted areas.

5. In the example of darkening the sky, click in the area of sky that represents the lowest area you still want the adjustment to affect completely and drag downward to the point where you don't want any effect at all. If you're not happy with the initial gradient you created, simply click and drag again to replace the gradient with a new one. The result is an adjustment that blends smoothly, from applying completely in one area of the image to having no effect on another area (see Figure 5.18).

Figure 5.18 By applying a gradient mask to the adjustment, you're able to produce an adjustment that gradually blends, as with the sky darkened in this example. (Photo by Tim Grey.)

Dodge and Burn Layer

Dodging and burning is a technique borrowed from the wet darkroom, where you can use your hands or various instruments to block light from specific areas of an image. The longer the light from the enlarger strikes any given area, the darker that area will be. Blocking light to small areas during exposure is referred to as *dodging,* and results in the blocked areas being lighter in a print than they otherwise would have been. *Burning* is the opposite: blocking light from *most* of the image so you can concentrate light for a portion of the exposure on one particular area, darkening that area of the print.

In Photoshop you can produce similar effects. In fact, Photoshop includes Dodge and Burn tools on the Tools palette, but we don't recommend using them because they must be applied directly to an image layer, and they don't offer quite the flexibility of the method we'll present here.

Setting Up

As you know very well by now, any adjustment you apply to an image should be done on a separate layer, so the first step here is to create a new layer to paint on so you can apply selective lightening and darkening to the image. However, you want the layer you create for dodging and burning to have certain special properties. Therefore, Alt/Option+click the New Layer button on the Layers palette. The New Layer dialog box (see Figure 5.19) appears so you can adjust the settings for the layer as it is created.

Figure 5.19

The New Layer dialog box allows you to establish the necessary settings for the dodge and burn layer.

To help stay organized, we recommend giving the layer a name. *Dodge & Burn* seems a good candidate. However, you can enter any name you like that will help you remember why this layer was added.

The most important setting here, and the key to the whole technique, is the Mode setting. This sets the blending mode for this layer, which affects how the pixels on this layer interact with underlying pixels to produce the final effect. We recommend using the Overlay blending mode, because it results in a relatively strong effect and slightly increases contrast. However, you could also use Soft Light if you prefer, which produces a more subtle effect.

After you've set the blending mode, the Fill With Overlay-Neutral Color (50% Gray) check box is enabled. We recommend selecting this box so the layer is filled with 50 percent gray, which is the neutral color for the Overlay and Soft Light blending modes. Having the layer filled with 50 percent gray doesn't cause any change in the image, but it makes it easier to see where you've applied dodging and burning.

Note: The Color option in the New Layer dialog box relates to the ability to apply color-coding to layers on the Layers palette, not to the content of the layer itself or the effect on the image.

Click the OK button on the New Layer dialog box (see Figure 5.20), and the layer is created based on the settings you've established.

Figure 5.20
With the appropriate settings established for your dodge and burn layer, click OK to create the actual layer.

Now you're ready to configure the Brush tool, which is used to paint with light and apply selective lightening and darkening to the image. Start by selecting the Brush tool from the Tools palette or by pressing the B on your keyboard. Then press D to set the colors on the color boxes in the Tools palette to their default values of black foreground and white background. Click the small icon below the bottom-left corner of the color boxes to set these defaults. Note that you can switch the foreground and background colors by pressing X as you're working, allowing you to easily switch between black and white.

On the Options bar (see Figure 5.21), select a soft-edged brush with 0 percent Hardness. The Mode on the Options bar should be set to Normal, because you want the brush itself to behave normally and changes to be applied only by the layer itself.

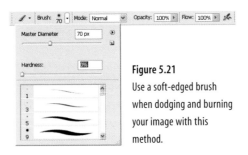

Figure 5.21
Use a soft-edged brush when dodging and burning your image with this method.

Note: It is important that the Brush be set to Normal blending mode, and the layer you're painting on be set to Overlay or Soft Light mode.

The tool's Opacity option should be set to between 10 percent and 20 percent. You can set this value quickly by using keyboard shortcuts: press 1 for 10 percent, 2 for 20 percent, and so on. If you want to set the value to something in between, such as 15 percent, just press 1 and 5 in relatively rapid succession. You'll likely want to adjust the Opacity setting, which controls the strength of the dodging and burning as you're working on the image. The Flow setting can be left at any value; it doesn't apply unless you use the Airbrush setting, which we recommend leaving turned off because it introduces variability in the behavior of the brush.

Note: If you're using a tablet, you can also use pen pressure of the stylus to determine the Opacity setting when dodging and burning with this method.

Painting with Light

With your new layer and the Brush tool properly configured, you're ready to start painting with light. Paint with black to darken portions of your image, and paint with white to lighten your image. Because you're painting at a reduced opacity, the result is relatively modest. If necessary, you can paint over areas multiple times to build up an effect. However, the best effect is usually subtle. When someone looks at the final image, they shouldn't get the impression that you were using dodging and burning techniques. However, when you toggle the visibility of the Dodge & Burn layer off and on, you'll see a difference between the images.

It's important to understand the behavior of the Brush tool when working at a reduced opacity for this technique. As long as you hold down the mouse button, the effect does not accumulate no matter how many times the mouse passes over a particular area. However, if you release the mouse and start painting again, the effect is uneven if you partially overlap areas you've previously painted. Therefore, it's important that you click and hold the mouse button while painting until you've covered the entire area you want to adjust. Then, release the mouse and start painting again in additional areas you'd like to change.

Try It! To practice dodging and burning, open the image DodgeBurn from the accompanying CD and use the method presented here to add drama to the rock formation, enhancing texture and contrast.

Dodging and burning is one of our favorite techniques in Photoshop. We think this has a lot to do with the capability to paint with light, bringing out details in various areas of the image or simply emphasizing particular features (see Figure 5.22). So much of the image-optimization process seems very mathematical, adjusting sliders and other controls to apply formulas to an image. The process of dodging and burning is different, allowing you to work directly on the image. As a result, it feels more artistic than other methods and enables you to take great control over tonal adjustments.

Figure 5.22
Dodging and burning allows you to enhance detail or add drama to various areas of your image with tremendous flexibility, producing an image that has been adjusted in a subtle way but with a big difference in the final result. (Photo by Tim Grey.)

Correcting Mistakes

Of course, now and then you may be less than satisfied with an adjustment you've made when using this technique. Fortunately, because it was applied on a separate layer, it is easy to fix mistakes even if it is too late to simply undo a step on the History palette.

There are two basic ways to correct your mistakes. The easiest is to select the Eraser tool and a soft-edged brush and then erase the areas you don't like (see Figure 5.23). Because you're working on a separate layer, all you're erasing are the pixels you painted onto your Dodge & Burn layer.

Figure 5.23 When you feel you've made a mistake with dodging and burning, simply use the Eraser tool to remove the adjustment you're not happy with.

Using the Eraser works well, but the disadvantage is that the middle gray pixels that fill the layer are also erased. This isn't a major problem, but it does make it more difficult to see where you've painted at a reduced opacity if you look at the layer by itself. The checkerboard pattern representing transparent pixels left after erasing doesn't provide good contrast for viewing the partially transparent pixels painted for the dodging and burning effect.

To avoid this problem, though with a slightly more complicated process, you can instead paint with 50 percent gray to remove the effect of any dodging and burning in particular areas of your image. To start, click the foreground color from the Tools palette to access the Color Picker. Set the Hue (labeled H) and Saturation (labeled S) to 0, and set the Brightness to 50 (see Figure 5.24). Click OK, change the Opacity for the Brush tool on the Options bar to 100 percent, and paint over the image in areas where you want to remove the dodging and burning effect. When you're finished, you can reset the colors to the defaults and adjust the Opacity as desired to continue dodging and burning in other areas of your image.

Figure 5.24

If you don't want to erase on your dodging and burning layer, simply set the foreground color to 50 percent gray in the Color Picker and use that to paint at full opacity in the areas you want to remove the effect from.

Curves

The Curves adjustment in Photoshop has a reputation as one of the most difficult controls to master. Although becoming comfortable with it can certainly be a challenge, it also provides an incredible level of control over your images. In fact, we tend not to use Shadow/Highlight (covered later in this chapter) simply because we can achieve the same results with even greater control (though with greater effort as well) by using the Curves adjustment. It enables you to change the brightness values within your images, but allows you to accomplish this by applying varying degrees of adjustments to pixels of different tonal values.

As with all controls that are available as an adjustment layer, the first step in utilizing Curves is to create a new adjustment layer.

The key to understanding the Curves adjustment is the concept of before and after values. All adjustments in Curves are based on shifting the value of all pixels at (or near) a particular tonal value. Therefore, think in terms of brightening the midtones or darkening the highlights, for example, when working with Curves.

The Curves dialog box shows a "curve" overlaid on a grid (see Figure 5.25). Of course, at first the curve isn't a curve at all, but a straight line at a 45-degree angle. As you learn to "read" the curve, you'll see that this 45-degree line represents no change in the image. The gradient along the bottom of the grid represents the "before" tonal values, and the gradient at the left shows the "after" values. If you follow a vertical line up from a specific tonal value on the gradient below the grid to the point that intersects the curve line, and then follow in a straight line to the left until reaching the after gradient, at this point the before and after values are exactly the same. Changing the shape of the curve alters the relationship between the before and after values, resulting in a change in the appearance in your image.

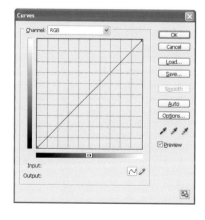

Figure 5.25
The Curves dialog box shows a "curve" that by default is actually a straight line at a 45-degree angle.

In the bottom-right corner of the Curves dialog box is a button that allows you to toggle between large and small versions of the dialog (Figure 5.26). We recommend using the large version whenever possible so you're able to make a better distinction between the tonal values represented within the grid area. However, if you're working with a single monitor, you may want to use the smaller version so you can see more of your image while making adjustments.

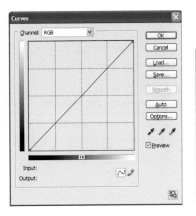
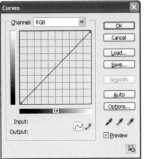

Figure 5.26
The button at the bottom-right corner of the Curves dialog box allows you to toggle between large and small versions of the dialog box. The grid behind the curve line is divided into 25 percent or 10 percent increments (Alt/Option+click in the grid).

The grid behind the curve line is provided simply for reference, and you can set it to either 25 percent or 10 percent increments. In general, the 25 percent increments are preferred by those working in prepress, because they tend to think about quarter tones, midtones, and three-quarter tones. However, most photographers seem to prefer the 10 percent increments, and that is the setting we recommend. To change the setting, hold the Alt/Option key and click the mouse within the grid. Keep in mind that changing the increments has absolutely no effect on the actual adjustment being applied.

The gradients at the bottom and left side of the grid can also be toggled. Having black in the top and right of the gradients appeals to those in prepress because they think of an increased value as more ink on paper, which produces a darker result. However, for photographers we recommend configuring the gradients with white at the top and right so that an increase represents more light and a brighter image. You can toggle this setting by clicking anywhere on the gradient at the bottom of the grid. Changing the gradient configuration doesn't have any impact on the image, and any adjustments you've made with Curves are automatically mapped accordingly, as shown in Figure 5.27.

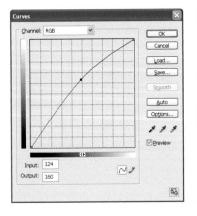
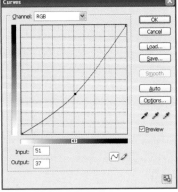

Figure 5.27
Changing the gradient configuration changes the location of the white point or black point in the dialog box, but the curve shape is automatically adjusted, so the adjustment doesn't change.

Note: The adjustments discussed in this section assume you have the gradients set with white at the top and right. If you're using them with black at the top and right, you need to reverse the direction of anchor point movement, discussed in the next section.

Anchor Points

You generally want to use anchor points for changing relationships between the before and after values in your image, which in turn creates the actual tonal adjustment. Anchor points allow you to place a handle on a particular point on the curve and adjust its position. When you do so, Photoshop automatically smooths out the curve to connect all the anchor points, providing a seamless transition in your adjustments.

The curve always starts off with anchor points at the extreme ends, allowing you to adjust the black point and white point within your image. However, because there is no clipping preview available with Curves, we prefer to use the Levels adjustment for establishing the black and white points, and use Curves for fine-tuning the tonal values throughout the rest of the tonal range.

To see the basic functionality of anchor points, position your mouse at about the middle of the curve and click. This places an anchor point at that position, which you can move around to change the shape of the curve, as you can see in Figure 5.28. Move the anchor point upward to lighten the image and downward to darken the image. The result is very similar to adjusting the midtone slider in Levels.

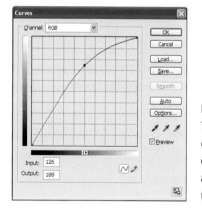

Figure 5.28

To get a sense of the basic control in Curves, click at about the middle of the curve line to create an anchor point and then drag it around to see the effect in your image. (Photo by Tim Grey.)

Of course, this hints at the incredible power of Curves. You can place up to 14 anchor points on the curve to perform adjustments on pixels at various tonal values within the image—but you'll usually only need a handful (typically three to six) to accomplish your goals with the image. By carefully positioning and adjusting these anchor points, you can exercise tremendous control over the tonal adjustments applied to the image.

Clicking the curve to place anchor points is sort of like working blind, because you don't get any feedback about which area of the image you're going to adjust. Also, you're usually thinking in terms of a specific area within the image, and you want to find the position on the curve that represents the tonal value for that area. Fortunately, there's a way to make an informed decision about where to place anchor points.

For one thing, if you point the mouse at your image and click, a small circle appears on the curve showing you where the tonal value for the pixel under the mouse falls (see Figure 5.29). If you drag the mouse around on the image, the circle bounces around as it updates its position based on the tonal value under the mouse. This display allows you to see exactly where particular areas of your image fall on the curve.

Figure 5.29 If you click on your image, a small circle appears on the curve line representing where the tonal value you're pointing at with your mouse falls on the curve. (Photo by Tim Grey.)

Even better, if you hold the Ctrl/⌘ key when you click the image, an anchor point is created on the curve for the tonal value of the pixel under your mouse. You can even drag around the image to review the range on the curve before releasing the mouse to place the anchor point. This allows you to place anchor points very precisely based on the area of the image you'd like to focus your adjustments on.

Note: The Curves dialog box includes eyedroppers with which you can select black, midtone, and white points in the image, but we don't recommend using these because they don't offer the precision you can achieve by directly adjusting the curve.

Adjusting Anchor Points

After you've created one or more anchor points, you can adjust them to change the relationship between the before and after values on the curve. You lighten or darken specific values by raising or lowering an anchor point, respectively.

The anchor points can be moved by dragging them with the mouse, but you can apply a more precise adjustment by clicking an anchor point to select it and then using the arrow keys to adjust its position. You are typically thinking in terms of lightening or darkening, and therefore would adjust the anchor points up or down to change the after value, but you can also move the anchor point left or right. Although this is actually changing which before value you are adjusting, we prefer to think of this as simply fine-tuning the relationship between the before and after values by taking greater control over the specific shape of the curve.

As you're adjusting the anchor points, you'll begin to see the relationship between the shape of the curve and the effect on the image. Raising or lowering the curve in a particular area affects the brightness of the pixels within the tonal range represented by that portion of the curve. Making a portion of the curve steeper than the original 45-degree line represents an increase in contrast; areas that are shallower represent reduced contrast. As you understand these relationships, you'll be better able to read the curve as well as apply the desired adjustments with minimal effort.

Creating the S Curve

One of the most common adjustments recommended for Curves is the S curve. This curve shape applies an increase in contrast to the midtones of your image, while preserving detail in highlight and shadow areas. Because we tend to respond better to photographs with higher contrast, this adjustment can be applied with good results to almost any photographic image.

To create an S curve, we recommend placing anchor points about 20 percent in from the black and white endpoints on the curve (see Figure 5.30). Then move the upper of these anchor points to the left slightly, and the lower anchor point to the right (see Figure 5.31). You don't need to move them much to produce a nice boost of contrast in your image.

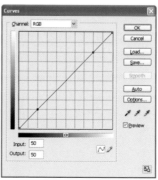

Figure 5.30 To create an S curve, start by placing anchor points about 20 percent in from the white and black endpoints of the curve. (Photo by Tim Grey.)

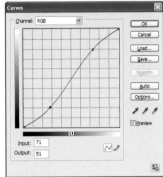

Figure 5.31 To complete the S curve, move the anchor points inward to achieve the desired increase in midtone contrast.

Another great thing about using Curves for such an adjustment is that you can focus your S curve on either the highlights or shadows within your image. If you want to boost the brighter tones more than the darker ones, move the anchor point that's closer to the white endpoint farther inward than the anchor point you added near the black point.

If you're also applying more sophisticated adjustments with Curves, you may want to make one Curves adjustment layer specifically for the S curve, and another for adjustments that apply to various tonal values within the image. Renaming each of these adjustment layers helps you stay organized as you move through your workflow and when you return to the image later.

Locking Down the Curve to Limit Changes

When you move anchor points on the curve, Photoshop automatically adjusts the shape of the curve to provide a smooth transition between all anchor points. Although this is a good thing, sometimes it causes adjustments in areas where you don't want any applied. When this happens, you must prevent changes—"normalize" the shape of the curve—in the areas you don't want altered.

Note: If your Curves adjustment is causing undesirable color shifts in your image, change the blending mode for the Curves adjustment layer to Luminosity (using the drop-down list at the top of the Layers palette) after closing the Curves dialog box. This ensures that the Curves adjustment layer affects only tonal values, not color values, within the image.

For example, if you're trying to focus some adjustments to the brighter areas of your image, you'll find that adjusting the anchor points causes a bend in the curve that also affects the darker areas (see Figure 5.32). To lock the curve, place a new anchor point near the existing anchor point on the side representing the tonal values you want to limit changes to. Drag this new anchor point to finding a position that will result in the rest of the curve being as close as possible to the original 45-degree angle (see Figure 5.33).

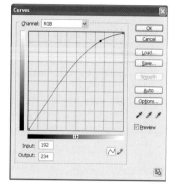

Figure 5.32 At times you will adjust a portion of the curve that you want to affect, only to find that the entire image is being adjusted because of the shape the curve takes on. (Photo by Tim Grey.)

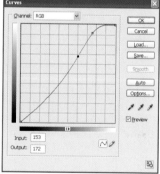

Figure 5.33 Using an additional anchor point, you can lock down the area of the curve you don't want to have affected, bringing it back near the original starting point.

You can also place anchor points outside those you placed for adjustment, producing something of a barrier outside the range you're adjusting. This won't always prevent adjustments from applying to the rest of the curve, but it helps when the adjustments you're making are relatively minor.

The bottom line is that you can use anchor points not just for producing desired changes within the image, but also to adjust the shape of the curve to compensate for unintended consequences of your adjustments. Think of these anchor points as handles that allow you to control the shape of the curve and use them to produce exactly the result you have in mind.

> **Note:** The best advice we can offer for working with Curves is to use very small adjustments. It doesn't take much to cause a significant change in the image, and frustration with Curves is most often caused by adjustments that are simply too strong.

The Curves Pencil Tool

At times, it's challenging to get the curve to do exactly what you want it to by using only anchor points to apply your adjustments. As you adjust one anchor point, the curve moves on both sides, producing an effect that might not be exactly what you intended. In those situations, take full control over the precise path of the curve. The Pencil tool within the Curves dialog box provides exactly this control.

Click the Pencil button near the bottom-right corner of the curve grid, and the anchor points disappears, leaving only the curve. You can then drag with the Pencil tool directly on the curve grid, defining a new curve shape (see the example in Figure 5.34). It's possible to redraw the entire curve if you know exactly what it should look like, but we recommend using this tool to apply spot corrections to specific, small areas of the curve.

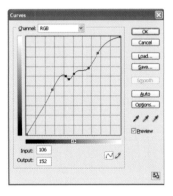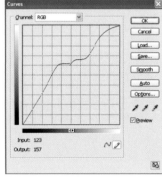

Figure 5.34

The Pencil tool in the Curves dialog box can be used to fine-tune the shape of the curve to fix small problem areas.

We like to use the Pencil tool to manually smooth out small portions of the curve, where the position of anchor points has caused small but radical "bumps." By drawing a smoother curve in that area, you avoid the problem of abrupt changes within the image and bring the adjustment under control.

When you're finished drawing with the Pencil tool, if your hand wasn't as steady as you'd have liked, click the Smooth button to further smooth out the bumps in the curve. After refining the shape of the curve, click the Anchor Points button to the left of the Pencil button to return to a curve with defined anchor points, as shown in Figure 5.35. The position and quantity of the anchor points are updated based on the new shape of the curve.

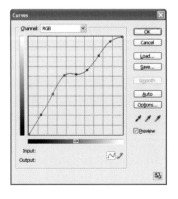

Figure 5.35

Once you've used the Pencil tool to clean up the shape of your curve, you can return to the anchor points mode and Photoshop re-creates or repositions the anchor points based on the shape you produced for the curve.

Note: Avoid repeatedly clicking the Smooth button; doing so reduces the effect of the adjustments you've made using Curves.

Try It! To start getting more comfortable with Curves, open the image Curves on the accompanying CD and make some adjustments, starting with a simple S curve adjustment and then working to fine-tune the overall tonality to your liking.

The Shadow/Highlight Adjustment

While Curves provides tremendous control, it can also be very challenging to use until you gain some experience with it. The Shadow/Highlight adjustment allows you to achieve many of the benefits you would otherwise gain with Curves (or Levels) in a user-friendly control. While Tim still tends to prefer working with Curves, Ellen has found more and more situations where Shadow/Highlight saves her time and effort, and she's grown more fond of this tool.

Note: The Shadow/Highlight adjustment is an excellent way to reveal subtle detail in the shadow and highlight areas of your images.

An improper exposure can result in an image with shadow or highlight detail that has been permanently lost. The Shadow/Highlight control allows you to recover detail that has been lost in shadow or highlight areas because of excessive contrast.

Because the Shadow/Highlight adjustment can't be applied as an adjustment layer, we recommend duplicating your background layer as the first step. To do so, click the thumbnail for the background layer and drag it to the New Layer button at the bottom of the Layers palette. With the duplicate image layer active, choose Image > Adjustments > Shadow/Highlight from the menu. The image changes in appearance based on the default values for Shadow/Highlight.

The default dialog box for Shadow/Highlight in Photoshop includes only the Amount sliders for Shadows and Highlights (see Figure 5.36), so you should rarely use it in this abbreviated form. (We'll talk about Show More Options in just a second.) In effect, think of the Amount slider for Shadows as allowing you to decide how much to lighten the darkest areas of your image, and the Amount slider for Highlights provides a similar ability to darken the brightest areas. Your first reaction may be that doing so simply reduces contrast and produces a muddy image. However, keep in mind that this adjustment is designed for situations where contrast is too high or when you want to extract more detail from the darkest and brightest areas of your image. When used with modest settings, the result is an effective increase in detail without a problematic loss of contrast.

Figure 5.36

The default Shadow/Highlight dialog box includes only basic controls for adjusting your image.

Using the basic Shadow/Highlight control is a simple matter of adjusting the sliders to extract the desired level of detail in the image. As you make these adjustments, use care not to overcorrect, which can create an image that is excessively flat or that has an artificial appearance.

The real power of the Shadow/Highlight control is enabled when you select the Show More Options check box. This enlarges the dialog box to include many additional controls for fine-tuning the adjustment (see Figure 5.37). The controls are divided into three sections. The Shadows and Highlights sections provide similar controls for adjusting areas of your image based on tonal value; the Adjustments section provides additional controls for improving specific aspects of the image.

Figure 5.37

When you select the Show More Options check box, the Shadow/Highlight dialog box expands to include more controls.

The controls in both the Shadows and Highlights sections are the same, although they obviously target different areas of the image based on tonal value:

Amount   The Amount slider affects the strength of the adjustment you're making to the area.

Tonal Width   To adjust the range of tonal values that will be affected by this adjustment, use the Tonal Width slider. A low value causes only a limited range of tonal values within the image to be affected, whereas a high value allows the adjustment to apply to a wider range. In other words, you expand or contract the area to be adjusted by defining a tonal range.

Radius   The Radius slider determines how far outward from pixels that fit within the defined tonal range the adjustment will spread. This provides the ability to blend the adjustment to produce a more realistic effect.

After you've adjusted the controls in the Shadows and Highlights sections, use the Adjustments section to fine-tune the final result. The Color Correction slider is really a saturation adjustment that affects the darkest areas of your image. This control allows you to compensate for shadow areas that often have reduced saturation compared to other areas of the image because there isn't adequate light to enhance the colors. After you've brightened up shadow areas, you'll likely want to increase the saturation slightly so those areas match the rest of the image.

Similarly, brightening shadows and darkening highlights helps to extract more detail but results in an overall reduction in contrast. The Midtone Contrast slider allows you to apply compensation by adjusting contrast for just the midtone values within the image, leaving the shadow and highlight areas you've already adjusted relatively unchanged.

The Black Clip and White Clip settings allow you to specify how much detail can be sacrificed in the image when making adjustments by using Shadow/Highlight. We recommend leaving these values to their default of 0.01 percent to minimize the loss of detail.

Once you've established the optimal settings in the Shadow/Highlight dialog box, click OK to apply the adjustment to your image, as you can see in the examples in Figure 5.38.

Figure 5.38 The Shadow/Highlight adjustment allows you to extract detail in your image with relative ease. (Photo by Tim Grey.)

Try It! Open the image ShadowHighlight on the accompanying CD and work with the Shadow/ Highlight adjustment to extract as much detail as possible while maintaining appropriate overall contrast.

Greg Downing has been an avid birder and nature lover for over 30 years. His connection with nature and interest in avian subjects evolved naturally into a career of photographing birds, selling prints, and teaching photography. He gives us tips on using the Shadow/Highlight tool.

Shadow/Highlight Tips

By Greg Downing

While there are other, more complicated, methods for targeted tonal adjustments, the Shadow/ Highlight (S/H) tool is all the rage with some nature photographers because it is relatively easy to use. The tool permits independent tonal adjustments over the darks and lights, allowing photographers to make precise corrections to high-contrast images or images captured in difficult lighting conditions. Shadow/Highlight can revive an image and even save the day when used correctly. Following are some tips for making the most of this tool.

Make S/H Adjustments in a Layer

As with all tonal adjustments, I recommend using adjustment layers in order to allow additional refinements either later in your workflow or even at a later date if the image is saved with the layers intact. Unfortunately, the S/H tool does not work as an adjustment layer, but here's an easy tip to overcome this limitation: Create a duplicate background layer and run a fairly strong S/H correction on this new layer; then fine-tune the effect by adjusting the overall opacity for the layer.

As I mentioned, unlike actual adjustment layers, you cannot change the amount of S/H adjustment should you later desire to do so. However, you can always go back and adjust the opacity of the layer, apply a mask, or trash the layer altogether or start over should you change your mind.

Add a Layer Mask

The S/H tool is a global tool, meaning it affects the whole image based on the settings used. This is not always desirable, and more often, smaller local adjustments are preferred. For these precise local adjustments, you can apply the S/H adjustment to a duplicate layer as described in this section, focusing only on the areas of importance. Next, apply a layer mask set to Hide All (Layer > Add Layer Mask > Hide All) and brush the adjustment into only those areas needing correction. Again, you can make the initial S/H adjustments fairly strong and then fine-tune them by adjusting the opacity, size, and softness of the brush you use for the mask, as well as the opacity of the entire duplicate layer. This also lets you to make stronger adjustments in one area of the image and more mild adjustments in another area, allowing ultimate control.

Shown here are before and after examples of an image that was corrected using these tips. Notice the additional detail extracted from the light and dark areas of the image using these methods.

Before   After

Becoming adept with the Shadow/Highlight tool and using it in combination with a duplicate background layer and a layer mask opens your images to new possibilities, perhaps even bringing some old photos back to life.

© Greg Downing, www.gdphotography.com

Exposure Optimized

Exposure is everything in photography, and for nature photographers it can be even more critical. Being able to reveal detail hidden within your images, and to emphasize key areas of those images, can be a tremendous advantage for the final result. By practicing the adjustments covered in this chapter, you'll be able to exercise tremendous control over your images, taking them far beyond what you'd be able to achieve if you only used the camera to control your exposure.

Color Adjustments

Nature photographers have more choices to make about the colors in their images than do most photographers. Portrait photographers need to have natural-looking skin tones, and product photographers usually need their photos to have extremely accurate colors. We nature photographers have to make sure our colors are somewhat believable—because in most cases, pink grass or lavender cardinals won't do—and often we're after as natural-looking an image as possible. But we have a great deal of latitude to modify the colors to make our images more expressive, not just of what we recall seeing, but also of how we felt. Photoshop offers us a variety of ways to make subtle color adjustments to make pictures neutral or to stir emotions and create reactions within our viewers.

Chapter Contents
Recognizing Color Casts
Removing Color Casts
Adding Color Casts
Modify Colors to Match Nature or Add Impact
Layer Masks and Color Adjustments

Recognizing Color Casts

Sometimes you may look at your image and decide that the colors just aren't quite right, but you may or may not be able to identify which color is the culprit. At other times you may not even be aware there is a color cast until you do some checking. There are several ways to detect a color cast.

Using Hue/Saturation to Reveal a Color Cast

An easy way to identify a color cast is to open a temporary Hue/Saturation adjustment layer—click the adjustment layer icon at the bottom of the Layers palette, choose Hue/Saturation, and drag the Saturation slider all the way to +100. Although your picture will look weird, this will show you where there are colors that don't belong. Think for a minute about what colors you'd expect to see versus what you do see, since the colors are supersaturated. Pay attention to the hues to determine if there are unexpected colors appearing.

Note: Although it's possible to create any adjustment layer from the main menu bar—by choosing Layer > New Adjustment Layer—we recommend opening all adjustment layers from the icon at the bottom of the Layers palette. By using the icon, you won't accidentally find yourself choosing Image > Adjustments on the main menu and working directly on your pixels.

As an example, Figure 6.1 shows a picture of a snowy egret with no obvious color cast and the same image with the Hue/Saturation slider pulled all the way to +100. Although you expect the water to turn blue or blue/cyan and the sand to turn yellowish, you do not expect the egret to be magenta. Clearly there is at least a partial magenta cast to this image.

Figure 6.1 (left) At first glance, there is not an obvious color cast in this picture. (right) Boosting the saturation to +100 reveals an unexpected magenta cast in the snowy egret. (Photo by Ellen Anon.)

It may be difficult to determine whether the cast is a single color such as cyan, or a combination such as blue and cyan (Figure 6.2 shows an example of this). Note that early morning outdoor pictures on what will be a sunny day often have a cyan cast to them. Pictures taken in shade often have bluish casts. Magenta casts are also common, particularly with landscape pictures or images that include a partly cloudy sky.

Figure 6.2 (left) Initially you may not be certain whether there is a color cast in the lava. (right) Increasing the saturation to +100 reveals a definite cyan cast. (Photo by Ellen Anon.)

If pulling the Hue/Saturation slider has revealed an obviously problematic color, it can be tempting to just go to the channel containing that color and reduce the saturation. Occasionally that approach will work, but the problem is that it reduces the saturation of that color throughout the entire image, even in areas that should be that color. There are several more useful approaches to removing the color cast that we will describe shortly.

After using the Hue/Saturation adjustment dialog to identify a color cast, click the Cancel button to remove this layer. You only need it temporarily to give you an idea of whether you must consider doing something to remove a color cast.

Using the Info Palette to Reveal a Color Cast

When we talk about "neutral" in a digital picture, we're referring to the relationship of the red, green, and blue values for any tone, from pure white (where the RGB values are 255,255,255) to pure black (RGB values 0,0,0), as well as all tonalities of gray in between in which the red, green, and blue values are all nearly identical. Neutral also means that pixels that should be pure red will have an RGB reading of 255,0,0, pure green will be 0,255,0, and blue will be 0,0,255. The farther away from these readings any pixel is that should be neutral gray or pure red, green, or blue, the more of a color cast there is. We nature photographers rarely, if ever, need to be concerned with *total* neutrality. In fact, outdoor lighting almost always imparts a color cast—sometimes warm, sometimes cool. Nonetheless, it's important to understand what neutral would be.

Understanding the values that neutral pixels should have enables you to check for a color cast by using the Info palette. If there are any areas of the picture that you know should be neutral (pure white, gray, or black), zoom in and place your cursor over that area. Take a look at the Info palette to see the red, green, and blue values of that point.

If the pixel is neutral, the values should be all the same (or very close). If one value is higher than the others, then there will be a cast in that direction. For example, if an area that should be neutral has roughly equal blue and green values but a higher red value, there is a reddish cast to the picture. Conversely, if the number for one channel reads lower than the other two channels, then the cast is toward the opposite color of that channel. Table 6.1 lists all the ways that one RGB channel might differ from the other two, creating a color cast.

▶ **Table 6.1** Identifying a Color Cast via the Info Palette

If This Value Is Off	This Cast Will Be Seen
Red high	Red
Red low	Cyan
Green high	Green
Green low	Magenta
Blue high	Blue
Blue low	Yellow

In Figure 6.3, a reading taken from the wing of the white pelican should be close to neutral. Instead, it shows markedly lower red values, reflecting a cyan cast throughout the image.

Figure 6.3
You know this image has a cyan color cast, because the RGB values of a sample from the white wing (point #1 in the Info palette) are 139,152,150. (Photo by Ellen Anon.)

Note: Remembering the basic RGB colors (red, green, and blue) and their opposites (cyan, magenta, and yellow) will make your color adjustments much easier and predictable. Red and cyan are opposites, green and magenta are opposites, as are blue and yellow. Once you appreciate this fact, you'll know to add cyan to reduce a red cast, add green to reduce a magenta cast, add blue to reduce a yellow cast, and so on.

If you have determined that there is a color cast in your image, you'll have to decide whether to eliminate it. Not all color casts are bad! Remember that part of the reason many nature photographers prefer early morning and late afternoon light is for the lovely warm (yellow/red) quality it imparts to their subjects as opposed to the more neutral light that may occur in the middle of the day.

Removing Color Casts

There are a number of different approaches to removing color casts, and depending upon the individual circumstances, one approach is likely to be superior in one situation, whereas another approach may be more effective in another. For that reason we're going to present several ways to deal with color casts, some of which are objective and some subjective.

Subjective Methods for Removing a Color Cast

First we'll look at the subjective ways to remove a color cast from your image. Some of these approaches allow Photoshop to do most of the work for you, while others offer considerable individual control over the process and invite a great deal of personal preference.

Using the Gray Eyedropper

If there's an area that you know should be neutral—it can be any tonality from almost white to almost black and any shade of gray in between—there is a very simple way to eliminate the color cast in your picture:

1. Create a new Levels adjustment by clicking the Create New Adjustment Or Fill Layer icon at the bottom of the Layers palette and selecting Levels.

2. Make sure to take the time to double-click the word Levels and rename the layer; we use the name "color cast." That way, if you return to this file later, assuming you save it with your layers intact, you'll know exactly what you did in each layer.

3. Click the gray (middle) eyedropper to select it and then click the area of your image that should be neutral. Photoshop will automatically define the point you click as "neutral" (that is, having equal red, green, and blue values) and will remap the rest of the image accordingly.

You can also do the same thing using the gray (middle) eyedropper in the Curves Adjustment Layer box; the results will be just slightly different, since Levels uses a linear algorithm to do the remapping whereas Curves naturally uses a tone curve. Practically speaking, the results will be very similar in most cases.

Using Individual Channels within Levels

When you made a Levels adjustment layer in Chapter 5, "Exposure Adjustments," to make tonal adjustments, you used the composite RGB channel (named Master in the Levels dialog). This means that the adjustments you made affected all the channels. Now, instead of working in the composite channel, you'll modify one channel at a time. This is another subjective way to achieve the desired color balance within an image. You will need to use the drop-down menu, as shown in Figure 6.4.

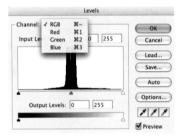

Figure 6.4

To adjust a color cast within Levels, use the individual color channels.

To modify the color cast one channel at a time, take the following steps:

1. Create a new Levels adjustment layer and rename it "color cast."

2. Select the Red channel and adjust the midpoint slider to achieve the desired balance between red and cyan. Don't move the endpoint sliders in the individual channels because this will increase the contrast within that channel and could lead to lost data.

3. Open the Green channel and move the midpoint slider to modify the balance between green and magenta.

4. Finally, repeat the process with the Blue channel until you're satisfied with the balance between the blue and yellow.

In the image shown in Figure 6.5, you've removed the warm yellow cast and made the picture closer to neutral by moving the midpoint slider in the blue channel.

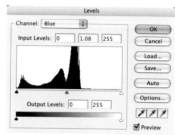

Figure 6.5
By adjusting the midpoint sliders within the individual color channels in Levels, you remove or introduce a color cast as desired. (Photo by Ellen Anon.)

Using Individual Channels within Curves

You can also remove a color cast within a Curves adjustment layer by using the individual RGB channels one at a time. You need to set a point usually that's close to the middle and gently raise the curve upwards or downwards. If, however, you wish to affect the colors primarily in the highlights or shadows, then set a point closer to the ends of the curve—perhaps one-quarter to one-third of the way up or down the curve, as shown in Figure 6.6.

> **Note:** When making a Curves adjustment layer to adjust tonalities and exposure, you may want to set the blending mode of the layer to Luminosity to avoid unwanted color shifts. However, when using a Curves layer to adjust color, you need to leave it in Normal mode.

Just as when you used Curves in Chapter 5 to adjust tonalities, you could choose to only affect a segment of the tonal range—such as the highlights or shadows—by placing three points on the curve to "lock it down" and prevent the remaining tonalities from being affected. It's important to realize that only slight adjustments are necessary. You'll be surprised how a seemingly tiny adjustment can have a huge impact on your image.

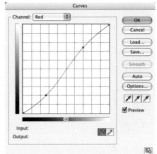

Figure 6.6
Slight changes in the individual color
channels of Curves can have a dramatic
impact on the color within your image.
(Photo by Ellen Anon.)

Try It! Open Colorcast2 from the accompanying CD (or one of your own images) and try adjusting
the color balance within the image, first using the individual color channels within a Levels adjustment
layer. Hide the visibility of the Levels layer and create a Curves adjustment layer. Adjust the curve individually within each color channel and compare the results of the two techniques. See which you prefer; initially,
it's likely that Levels will seem easier, although Curves allows for finer control.

Using a Color Balance Adjustment Layer

A Color Balance adjustment layer may be the most generally useful approach to correcting color casts. In essence, it presents the sliders from each of the individual color
channels within Levels in one interface, along with the ability to set the sliders to affect
primarily the midtones, shadows, and/or highlights. As you pull the sliders, you are
shifting the color values in your image towards the basic colors (red, green, and blue)
or towards their opposites (cyan, magenta, and yellow), as shown in Figure 6.7.

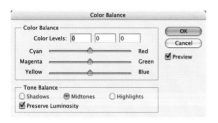

Figure 6.7
Color Balance provides an easy interface to adjust the balance within each color channel as well as to make those changes to the midtones, highlights, and/or shadows.

The Tone Balance section is set by default to affect the midtones when you first open a Color Balance adjustment layer. When Midtones is checked, the changes you make on the sliders affect the majority of the pixels and tones in your image, excluding only the brightest and darkest values. Selecting the Highlights or Shadows option instead allows you to primarily adjust the most extreme tonalities in your image. You may wish to adjust them slightly differently than the midtones.

This can be quite useful in some situations common to nature photography. For example, if you have a white bird photographed in early morning light on water, you may want to emphasize the warm light on the bird, but not make the water appear too discolored. To do this, click Highlights and adjust the sliders to allow for more yellow and red and possibly magenta than in the midtones and shadows, where you might be attempting to limit the color cast, as shown in Figure 6.8.

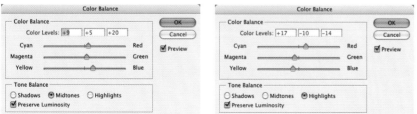

Figure 6.8 Adjusting the Color Balance sliders differently for the highlights than for the midtones enables you to leave more of a color cast on the white bird, while limiting the color cast on the water. (Photo by Ellen Anon.)

Setting the best position for the sliders can be challenging and is a subjective decision. If there is a strong color cast in your image, it's often easiest to begin by working with the corresponding slider in the midtones. For example, if there is a strong cyan cast in your image, start by adjusting the Cyan/Red slider for Midtones. Then, if necessary, adjust the other sliders for midtone values; after that, click Highlights and adjust, and then click Shadows to set those sliders. You may be happy with the color balance after adjusting only the midtone sliders since they affect the majority of the pixels within most pictures.

On the other hand, you may find it necessary to adjust each slider several times, and you may even discover that you can't decide which setting you like best. At that point, there are two suggestions we offer:

- Pull the slider that's creating a problem for you to an extreme position and start again. You might even pull it all the way to the right, then reset it and note the setting, and then pull it all the way to the left and readjust it to where it looks best. Hopefully you'll be able to find a position that looks good to you.

- If you're still not sure, it's time to get up and walk away from your computer for a couple of minutes. When you come back, note your gut-level reaction to the picture. Are the colors good, or are they too much towards a specific color cast? Trust your immediate reaction, don't overthink it, and then make any necessary changes.

Objective Method for Removing a Color Cast

At times, even nature photographers prefer to make their images as neutral as possible, and in such cases an objective approach may be best. We've also encountered some photographers who are color-blind and who don't have the luxury of having someone close by to comment on the colors within their images. Sometimes they feel safest using an objective method to correct color casts.

To objectively remove a color cast, use the three eyedroppers in a Levels adjustment layer. However, first identify and set the white and black points and then have Photoshop define them as neutral.

As you already know, you can hold down the Alt/Option key while pulling the endpoint sliders within Levels to identify the lightest and darkest pixels within your image. However, you don't want to have to rely on your memories as to exactly where they're located. Instead, we'll show you how to mark them to be sure you're accurately targeting the darkest and lightest pixels within your image.

To objectively remove a color cast, take the following steps:

1. Begin by choosing the Color Sampler tool. It's located on the Tool palette with the Eyedropper tool (see Figure 6.9). Make certain to set the Sample Size option on the Options bar to 3×3 Average rather than to its default value, which is a one-point sample. The 3×3 option causes Photoshop to read an average of nine pixels, which prevents you from accidentally selecting a pixel that is different from its neighboring pixels.

Figure 6.9 (left) The Color Sampler tool allows you to mark particular pixels within the image. (right) It's best to set the Color Sampler tool to use a 3×3 sample to avoid accidentally sampling an aberrant pixel.

2. Create a Threshold adjustment layer via the same icon and drop-down menu that you've been using to access the other adjustment layers, as shown in Figure 6.10.

Figure 6.10
Open a Threshold adjustment layer to identify the darkest and lightest pixels within the image.

3. You see a histogram with only one slider, and your image is in black and white, with no tones in between (see Figure 6.11). Move the slider all the way to the right until the image preview becomes totally black.

Figure 6.11
Your image will appear in black and white, with no in-between tonalities.

4. Slowly move the slider to the left and stop when you see the first pixels begin to turn white. These are the lightest pixels in your image.

5. Zoom in by pressing Ctrl/⌘++ to clearly identify the lightest pixels. Accuracy is vital here. Click OK.

6. Now, with the Color Sampler tool still selected, place your cursor over the lightest pixels in your image and click. The tool leaves a small circle with the number 1 on your image.

7. Zoom out to see your entire image by pressing Ctrl/⌘+0.

8. Double-click the Threshold layer icon to reopen it. This time move the slider all the way to the left so that the preview becomes entirely white. Gradually move it to the right and note where the first black pixels appear. These are the darkest pixels in the image.

9. Again, zoom in as necessary to clearly see these pixels and then click OK.

10. Place your cursor over one of the darkest pixels and click. This time, the Color Sampler tool leaves a small circle with the number 2.

11. Zoom out again by pressing Ctrl/⌘+0 to see your whole image.

12. Since you no longer need the Threshold adjustment layer, drag it to the trash can to remove it. The selected pixels remain marked, and you have an objective indicator of the darkest and lightest pixels within your image, as shown in Figure 6.12.

Figure 6.12
The darkest pixel (bottom edge) and lightest pixel (corner of the mouth) in your image are marked with a numbered circle so you can easily identify them.

13. Now create a Levels adjustment layer as usual. Be sure to rename it to indicate you're using this one to remove a color cast.

14. Next, you're going to set the values for the black and white points that you want Photoshop to use. If you have previously saved default values for black and white, you can skip this step:

   a. Double-click the black eyedropper to open the Color Picker dialog box. Type in values of R = 12, G = 12, and B = 12 for the black point and click OK. (If you have established a different set of black values for your printer, use them here.)

   b. Double-click the white eyedropper, and the Color Picker dialog box reappears. Type in values of R = 244, G = 244, B = 244, as shown in Figure 6.13, for the white point and click OK.

   c. Click OK in the main Levels dialog. Because you've changed one or more eyedropper values, Photoshop asks if you want to set these as your default values. Click OK.

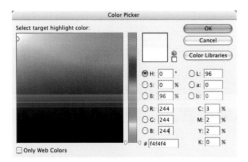

Figure 6.13

By typing values into the Color Picker, you can set the black and white points within your image and then save them as the default values for Photoshop to use in the future.

> **Note:** Because our printers can't print in ways that allow us to differentiate shades of black all the way to 0,0,0 or whites all the way to 255,255,255, we have to use slightly different values. Once those are set, we can save them as default values. The actual ideal values for your printer may vary and can be determined by printing out test strips of blacks and whites at various values—(8,8,8), (12,12,12), (15,15,15), etc.—to determine where you can begin to see differences in the dark tones. You can do a similar test strip for the whites. The values suggested in step 14 work for many people.

15. Now click the white eyedropper and then move your cursor onto your image. Align the cursor with the point the Color Sampler tool marked with the number 1. When you have precisely aligned the cursor and the sampled point, click OK. This remaps that point to an RGB value of 244,244,244, or neutral white. Verify this by looking at the Info palette, which shows you the before and after values of the targeted points.

16. Repeat the same process with the black eyedropper. In most cases, the color cast within the image is neutralized (see Figure 6.14). In some images, however, you also need to use the gray (middle) eyedropper and click somewhere in the image that should be neutral.

Figure 6.14

Compare this neutral version of the heron with the original in Figure 6.12. (Photo by Ellen Anon.)

17. To remove the little circles with the numbers by them, reselect the Color Sampler tool and hold down the Alt/Option key. As you approach a circle, your cursor changes to a scissors. When you click, the circle is removed. Alternately, simply hide them by choosing View > Extras from the menu. This toggles the visibility of the Color Samples. Simply hiding them can be a time-saver if there is any possibility that you might want to modify your color-cast adjustments.

Try It! Open the image on the CD named Colorcast3 or one of your own images and try removing the color cast using the objective method. You can compare the results with what you obtain using your favorite subjective method.

This approach may seem quite long, but actually it's pretty straightforward and a good way to set your black and white points as well as to remove a color cast objectively. You could also use the eyedroppers in a Curves adjustment layer to achieve similar results. You would follow the exact same procedure described in this section from within a Curves dialog.

Award-winning nature photographer John Shaw agreed to share his version of the color-cast correction process with us.

Neutralizing a Color Cast

by John Shaw

Some images—particularly scans from certain film stocks—may show a distinct color cast. The neutral colors are just not neutral. Of course, at times that's exactly what you want since you photograph at sunset just to get that golden, warm glow on your subjects. But if you have images in

© John Shaw

which you would like to neutralize the colors, here's an easy way to do it if there are areas of the image that should be black or white.

Let's open a scan of a film image taken during a Colorado blizzard. There is a definite blue bias to the image, and while snow in overcast conditions often really does show a blue component, this is rather extreme.

Let's use a Levels adjustment layer (adjustment layers are always the best way to do non-destructive editing) and Threshold to find the lightest and darkest areas of the image. To do this, choose Layer > New Adjustment Layer (actually I always use the shortcut icon at the bottom of the Layers palette, as shortcuts are a great help in Photoshop), and click Threshold for the type of layer you want to create. Your image turns into black and white, and a dialog appears with one slider.

As you mouse over your image, notice that you get an eyedropper tool. Right-click or Control+click to get a context menu and set the eyedropper to a 3×3 sample. Move the slider to the left and watch your image for the last place there is a solid black. When you find this location, position the eyedropper over it and Shift+click to set a color sampler point. Now pull the slider to the right, watch for the last solid white area of the image, and Shift+click again with the eyedropper to set another color sampler point. You might have to enlarge your screen image while setting these points.

Click Cancel in the Threshold dialog; you used it only to set those two color sampler locations, nothing else.

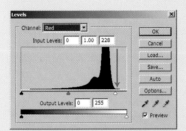

Make sure your Info palette is visible and open a Levels adjustment layer. You'll see three eyedroppers in the dialog box. Click the white eyedropper (the right one) and then click the white color sampler point you set in the image. Look at the Info palette for this point, and you'll see two sets of RGB values displayed for that point. The first set is the original "before" values, the second ones are "after" you clicked the sampler point. Note the highest numerical "before" value. Now in Levels, open each channel and move the white input slider until the "after" numbers in the Info palette all match that highest "before" value.

Repeat this process for the black color sampler point you set. Select the black Levels eyedropper, click the black point, and move the Levels black output slider until all those numbers match in numerical value also.

You have now neutralized any color cast. Of course, if you don't want a perfectly neutral result, you can change the numbers just partially, leaving one channel more prominent.

© John Shaw, www.johnshawphoto.com

© John Shaw

Adding a Color Cast

The reality is that nature photographers get up ridiculously early in the morning and stay out photographing until the sunset is completely over because we *like* our pictures to have the warm special light of early and late day. We tend to prefer the color casts imparted by this light because our photos have a different feeling in them and often create more impact on the viewer than more neutral versions of the same subject. It's possible to create color casts to simulate that light using the same subjective techniques we used before to remove color casts.

For example, if you're using the middle (gray) eyedropper from within Levels or Curves and you click an area that should not be neutral, Photoshop will still be obliging and redefine the values of that point to be neutral anyway and the rest of the image then has a color cast. This can be a good thing! You can introduce a slight warmth to your images this way by clicking a point that actually should be slightly bluish or cyanish, as shown in Figure 6.15. Conversely, you can make them appear cooler by clicking a pixel that should actually be slightly yellowish or reddish. Remember that Ctrl/⌘+Z undoes your last step, so you can use a trial-and-error approach in finding the right spot to use. Obviously, this is a subjective way to determine the color balance within your picture that relies on Photoshop to do most of the work for you.

Figure 6.15 By clicking the middle eyedropper on a point that should be slightly bluish, you can impart a warmer color cast to an image. (Photo by Ellen Anon.)

If you prefer to use a Color Balance adjustment layer, simply adjust the sliders to achieve the desired effect. No one but you has to know that the picture wasn't taken in the earliest morning light!

Photoshop also offers a Photofilter adjustment layer option. Choosing this adjustment layer allows you to select from a drop-down menu containing a variety of color tints, including some with familiar names like 81A (see Figure 6.16). You can adjust a Density slider to control the strength of the effect. Although this is a quick and easy way to add a color cast to your image, the disadvantage is having to settle for tints predetermined by the folks at Adobe who wrote Photoshop rather than choosing the exact color cast that suits your image.

Figure 6.16
The Photofilter adjustment layer contains a number of familiar sounding filters.

Modifying Colors to Match Nature or Add Impact

After you've adjusted the overall color cast of your image—whether to neutralize it or to add a color cast—you often want to work with the colors a little more to help convey the mood and impact you have in mind. Colors elicit emotional reactions from those who view your pictures. For example, pastels can be calming, while bold primary colors can be energizing as seen in Figure 6.17. A blue cast in a snow scene can add to the sense of coldness and perhaps isolation. Warm yellow light rays drifting through trees or lighting flowers may give a sense of peacefulness and well-being or spirituality.

Figure 6.17
Colors elicit emotional reactions from the viewer so it makes sense to adjust the colors accordingly. (Photo by Ellen Anon.)

It's well worth the effort to spend the time to make certain the colors in your pictures elicit the reactions you have in mind. The two primary tools you'll use for this are Hue/Saturation adjustment layers and Selective Color adjustment layers.

Adjusting Hue and Saturation

Most photographers who use Photoshop are comfortable opening the Hue/Saturation dialog (which of course we recommend you do as an adjustment layer) and adjusting the saturation of their image. This is one of the more intuitive adjustments within Photoshop, and it can make your images come to life. However, be careful not to go to excess with Saturation, not only because the colors will look fake, but also because you risk losing detail as you increase the saturation. This is the result of more and more pixels being shifted towards the purest colors, resulting in a loss of detail in those areas. With most images, you'll find a saturation increase in the composite channel of between 6 and 12 is usually effective. Of course, this varies among files from different cameras as well as individual preferences.

Although you can modify the saturation of all the colors within your image by using the composite or "Master" channel, which is the default when you open the Hue/Saturation adjustment layer, one extremely useful feature is the ability to target a particular color range from the drop-down menu (see Figure 6.18). This way you can modify colors individually by selecting the desired color. Now you can change the saturation—or hue—of a single color within your image.

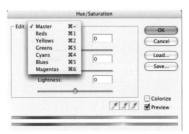

Figure 6.18
The Hue/Saturation dialog box enables you to target not only the composite channel, but individual colors as well.

In addition to choosing a particular color, you can target a specific range of colors to modify within the Hue/Saturation dialog box. However, you can't do this from the composite channel; you have to begin within a specific color channel from the drop-down menu. Select the range of colors to modify by first clicking the eyedropper in the Hue/Saturation dialog box and then clicking the color you want to adjust.

Don't worry if you're not sure which color to choose from the drop-down menu. It doesn't matter which one you begin with, because once you click with the first eyedropper, Photoshop automatically changes to the correct color channel. You can increase the range of colors to be modified by clicking with the plus eyedropper or decrease it by clicking with the minus eyedropper.

Alternately, you can refine the range of colors to modify by adjusting the Color Range bars that appear between the two color gradients when you have specified a particular color channel (see Figure 6.19). This process is a bit more advanced than the other adjustments you've been making.

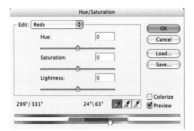

Figure 6.19
You can set the range of colors to be adjusted by moving the Color Range Bars that appear between the two color gradients at the bottom of the Hue/Saturation dialog box.

To refine the range of colors to modify, follow these steps:

1. We recommend initially dragging the Saturation slider all the way to the left so that the selected range of colors is shifted to gray. This helps you to see what areas of the image you're modifying.

2. Click the bars and drag them to increase or decrease the targeted range of colors. This limits or expands the colors that will be affected by the adjustments you make to the sliders.

3. Click the two triangles outside the bars to define the extent of feathering of the color adjustments. These triangles control how gradual the transition is between the modified and original colors so that the adjustment is less obvious.

4. Having selected the target range of colors, move the hue, saturation, and lightness sliders to achieve the desired effect.

Try It! Open the file HueSat from the accompanying CD or one of your own images, and select a single color and then a range of colors to adjust. Try changing not only the saturation but the hue as well.

There are times when your original image may contain very little color information. For example, one of our students had a lovely image of a gray covered bridge set amidst trees. He wanted to make the bridge red so he used the following procedure.

To add color to neutral areas such as the gray bridge:

1. Select the area to be colorized using any of the selection tools discussed in Chapter 3, "Basic Tools."

2. Check the Colorize box in the Hue/Saturation dialog box.

3. Notice that the Hue and Saturation sliders have moved substantially. Adjust all the sliders to colorize the targeted portion of your image as desired.

Another use of the Colorize option is to create a tint such as a sepia tint with a black-and-white image. We'll cover how to do this, as well as how to convert images to black and white, in Chapter 8, "Creative Effects."

Fine-Tuning with Selective Color

There are times when a color may still not look right despite your best efforts at adjusting the color cast and making Hue/Saturation adjustments. The Selective Color adjustment layer, accessible from the same place as the other adjustment layers, enables you to modify the hue of specific colors, as well as whites, neutrals, and blacks (see Figure 6.20). This tool enables far greater control over the exact hue of any specific color than is possible within Hue/Saturation, as well as the ability to adjust color casts in whites, neutrals, and blacks.

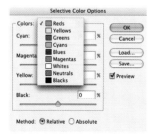

Figure 6.20

The Selective Color dialog box allows you to modify the color components of specific colors as well as the whites, midtones, and blacks within your image.

First, select the color you wish to modify by clicking the appropriate color. For example, if you've adjusted an image but the blue of the sky seems off, you can alter the shade of blue, as shown in Figure 6.21. Notice that the sliders are labeled Cyan, Magenta, Yellow, and Black this time, because Selective Color was originally designed for use with CMYK output. But it works equally well with RGB! If you increase cyan, you are decreasing red, and if you decrease cyan, then obviously red increases. Similarly, increasing or decreasing magenta alters the percentage of green used in the color, and changing the amount of yellow will alter the amount of blue. By changing the percentage of each component of a color, you have fine control over the specific hues.

Figure 6.21 Selective Color was used to improve the shade of blue in the sky by making it slightly warmer. (Photo by Ellen Anon.)

So in the case of your blue sky, you might want to increase the cyan and blue components to make a better shade of sky blue (which is composed of both blue and cyan tones). If you increase the black within the Blues menu, the blue will get darker. In a sky, it's likely you'll need to work with the drop-down menus for Blue and Cyan and adjust the components within them.

Extremely precise adjustments are possible within each of the colors in the Selective Color dialog. Those photographers who are latent artists may particularly enjoy this ability to fine-tune colors.

You will find that as you make a color more pure, there may be less need to increase overall saturation as much. This can lead to a more natural and pleasing final result in your image.

To add a little extra "pop" to your pictures, select Black as your target color and then increase the percentage of Black by a small amount such as 2. The actual amount varies by image. This gives many images the illusion of being slightly sharper. Some images benefit from having the blacks within the Neutrals increased slightly as well.

Selective Color can also be used to remove some stubborn color casts by choosing Neutrals in the Colors list and adjusting the sliders as needed. One of our students came to a workshop with a shot, taken under unusual lighting in a mausoleum, that had a strong cyan cast. The only method that was successful in removing the color cast was to virtually eliminate cyan from the Neutrals and Whites within Selective Color.

Note: For more in-depth coverage of controlling color within your image, see *Color Confidence* (Sybex, 2004).

Layer Masks and Color Adjustments

So far we've described a variety of approaches for modifying the color within your entire image, all of which use adjustment layers and all of which adjust the color across the entire area of your photo. But there will be times when you want to target a specific part of your image to change, a part that will be determined by the subject matter rather than by a particular color range. For example, you may wish to increase the saturation of your subject more than the background to help draw attention to your subject. Of course you'll be using layer masks to do that. Given the importance of gaining a solid understanding of layer masks, rather than force you to flip back to Chapter 5 to refresh your memory, we'll review the process here.

Creating Layer Masks via Selections

One way to affect only a portion of your image is to select that area, using any of the selection methods covered in Chapter 3, before you make the adjustment layer. This technique works well if you have a well-defined area you wish to adjust, and it's Tim's preferred method. By making a selection prior to opening an adjustment layer, whatever adjustment you choose will impact only the selected area. If you then look at the layer mask that Photoshop automatically includes with every adjustment layer, you'll see that the area you selected appears white and the rest of the mask is black. As discussed in Chapter 5, any place in your image that corresponds to where the layer mask is white is affected by the adjustment in that layer, while any part of your image corresponding to where the layer mask is black is not affected. White shows the changes, black hides the changes.

You might want to draw attention to your subject's eyes, for example in the portrait of a crane in Figure 6.22.

Figure 6.22

If you have selected only the eyes of your subject, most of the layer mask will be black while the area representing the eyes will be white. (Photo by Ellen Anon.)

To draw attention to the eyes, take these steps:

1. To begin, select the eyes using the Lasso or Magnetic Lasso tool.

2. Create a Hue/Saturation adjustment layer (using the icon at the bottom of the Layers palette). Notice that the layer mask is almost entirely black. The only parts that will be white are two small shapes that correspond to the eyes you selected, as shown in Figure 6.22.

3. Increase the saturation of the eyes as desired to make them more prominent and also slightly increase the lightness by a value of 1 or 2. This subtly draws attention to the creature's eyes.

Just as when making tonal adjustments using selections, we don't recommend that you feather the original selection, because there's no way to tell how many pixels you should use. You could use a trial-and-error approach, but what we prefer is to apply a Gaussian blur to the adjustment layer after you've made your adjustment. The blur actually affects the layer mask and enables you to create a feather or blending between the areas that were changed and those that were not. The benefit to this method is that you can control exactly how much feathering is needed.

Continuing on with our example…

4. Choose Filter > Blur > Gaussian Blur from the menu.

5. Make certain the Preview box is checked and then move the Radius slider to change the blur on the transition edges (see Figure 6.23). The result is a feathering amount specific to the needs of the individual image and a pleasing transition between the areas that were and were not modified. Usually you will need a very small radius, often less than 1.0, but of course this varies by image.

Figure 6.23
Using a Gaussian blur on your layer mask feathers the transition between the areas that were changed and those that weren't.

Try It! Open the image called Eyes from the accompanying CD and try not only increasing the saturation of just the eyes, but also changing the hue using a Hue/Saturation adjustment layer. Using the same selection, try also adjusting the hue using a Selective Color adjustment layer.

Creating Layer Masks Without Prior Selections

Many people (including Ellen) prefer not to have to make selections whenever possible. We find that it is often easier to simply paint on the layer mask to define the areas we want to be affected, as outlined in the following steps:

1. First, use an adjustment layer to make the desired changes. Train yourself to focus only on the parts of the image you want to change and ignore what happens to the other parts since they will masked out later.

2. Make certain your colors are set to foreground black and background white. To do this press D, or click the small black and white boxes at the bottom-left of the color swatches in the Tool palette .

3. Now, making certain that the adjustment layer is still selected in the Layers palette, select a moderately soft-edged paint brush, place your cursor on your image and begin to paint over the areas you do not want to be affected. Zoom in as needed so you can paint accurately.

4. Continue editing your mask, as described in Chapter 5:

   - To undo your painting (for example, if you accidentally paint over some areas you do wish to be affected), toggle your foreground color to white and paint over those areas.

   - To have an adjustment only partially affect an area of your image, reduce the opacity of your brush.

   - To see a preview of the mask, Alt/Option+click the layer mask icon. You can paint directly on the mask preview if desired.

   - When you've finished, if necessary, Alt/Option+click the layer mask icon again to return to your image preview.

Note: Although learning to use a pen tablet, such as the Wacom Intuos 3, takes time, using the tablet can ultimately help you easily make far more effective layer masks.

Using a Mask for Color Adjustment without a Selection

Let's apply the no-selection mask technique to an image of a burrowing owl with a green background. (This image is called BurrowingOwl on the accompanying CD.) To increase the saturation of the colors within the owl but not affect the background in order to help draw attention to the bird, take these steps:

1. Create a Hue/Saturation adjustment layer by clicking the Create A New Adjustment Layer icon at the bottom of the Layers palette.

2. Increase the saturation to make the owl look good. Ignore what's happening to the background.

3. You could continue to follow the steps exactly as outlined above, but in this case, it would be easier to have the mask be entirely black—hiding the effect of the layer—and then paint with white over the bird to reveal the effect on the bird. To quickly fill the layer mask with black, choose Edit > Fill from the menu and choose Black for the Contents.

Note: A shortcut for filling a layer mask with black is Ctrl+Backspace/⌘+Delete.

4. Now use your Brush tool to paint on your image preview using white as your foreground color. As long as your adjustment layer is still selected, you are actually painting on the layer mask and not the image itself. Paint with white over the bird to reveal the increased saturation only on the bird, as shown in Figure 6.24.

Figure 6.24 Filling with black allows you to quickly create a black layer mask, upon which you'll paint with white to reveal the changes you made in that layer. (Photo by Ellen Anon.)

5. Next, modify the hue of the background using Selective Color. Create a new Selective Color adjustment layer (via the icon in the Layers palette) and label it Background Hue.

6. Modify the colors until they are pleasing and click OK.

7. To save the time of re-creating a mask to affect only the background, click the Hue/Saturation adjustment layer to make it active.

8. Hold down the Alt/Option key, click directly on the layer mask icon, and then drag it on top of the Selective Color adjustment layer. A dialog box appears asking if you wish to replace the mask. Click Yes.

9. Unfortunately, this mask is the opposite of what you need, because you want to change the background on this layer. To invert the mask, choose Image > Adjustments > Invert from the main menu. Then you can modify the background without affecting the bird. Copying layer masks from layer to layer and inverting them as needed can be a time-saver.

Note: If you've created a layer mask on one layer and want to further modify the same areas using another adjustment layer, Ctrl/⌘+click the layer mask icon in the first adjustment layer *before* creating the new adjustment layer. Photoshop creates an active selection based on that mask. Then when you open a new adjustment layer, the same mask appears.

Using layer masks is easy and gives you incredible ability to fine-tune the color within specific areas of your image. Regardless of which approach you prefer for creating your layer masks, being able to enhance parts of your image—such as the eyes of your subject—is invaluable. In fact, Arthur Morris, one of the world's foremost bird photographers, contributed the following section describing several tricks he uses to enhance the eyes of the birds in some of his outstanding photos.

Digital Eye Doctor

by Arthur Morris

In *The Art of Bird Photography,* I wrote, "When viewing wildlife, or wildlife art, we tend to make immediate eye contact. Consequently, if a bird's eye is in sharp focus, it gives the photograph an impression of overall sharpness." While optimizing my bird photographs in Photoshop, I often have the chance to improve the look of a bird's eyes, and I have developed a useful bag of tricks for doing just that. Doing so can add greatly to the drama and impact of an image.

In many cases, simply sharpening the eyes can substantially improve an image. To do so, first zoom in so the eye fills the window. Next, select the eye using either the Lasso or Magnetic Lasso tool. (Sometimes I will select both the eye and a patch of sharply defined feathers surrounding the eye.) Feather the selection one pixel before sharpening to avoid the cookie-cutter look. Then choose Filter > Sharpen > Unsharp Mask. I generally sharpen (to taste) with an Amount from 300 percent to 500 percent, a Radius from 0.2 to (rarely) as much as 0.5 pixels, and Threshold at 0. On average, I work with these settings: 375, 0.25, and 0.

The same technique can be used to lighten or darken the eye and possibly the feathers of the face that surround the eye or eyes. Many birds have dark or black eye masks, and some have black hoods. With these, it is often necessary to lighten the eye so that it becomes visible. At times you may wish to lighten the eye and the surrounding feathers. When optimizing images of birds with light or pastel lores (the area between the eye and the base of the bill) or patches of light-colored feathers around the eye, it is often helpful to darken these areas to intensify the color. To lighten or darken an area, simply use the Lasso tool to select the area and then feather the selection; I use one pixel of feathering for an eye, two pixels when working with tracts of feathers. Then create a Levels adjustment layer (Layer > New Adjustment Layer > Levels) and lighten or darken the selection by moving the middle slider.

When using flash to photograph birds, the eyes are often rendered quite funky. Red-eye and steel-eye (an odd-looking silvery crescent on the eye) were common when using flash with film, but with digital (which is more sensitive to flash than film), the effects are both wider ranging and even more detrimental to the image. When examining a flashed bird's eye at high magnification, unnatural highlights and lightened and artificially colored pupils are often revealed. Most folks simply ignore these problems, but the fix takes only minutes. I always examine the eye closely by magnifying it greatly, using a box drawn around the eye with the Zoom tool to do so.

Continued on next page

Digital Eye Doctor *(Continued)*

I often use the Clone Stamp tool to repair red-eye, purple-eye, steel-eye, and other unnatural highlights that may affect small or significant areas of the pupil. After making such repairs, however, the pupil, which should be black, often appears far too light. Simply select the pupil with the Lasso tool, feather the selection one pixel, create a Hue/Saturation adjustment layer (Layer > New Adjustment Layer > Hue/Saturation), and then reduce the Saturation as much as 100 percent. Next, choose Select > Reselect (Shift+Ctrl+D/Shift+⌘+D) and feather the selection again. Then create a Selective Color layer (Layer > New Adjustment Layer > Selective Color) and add blacks to either the Neutrals or the Blacks until the pupil is rendered a pleasing black. It often helps to compare the eye of a flashed bird with the unflashed eye of the same bird or species.

Original

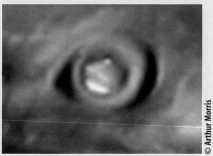

Before correction

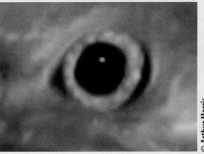

After correction

After correction

After correction

After my recent trip to Homer, Alaska, to photograph eagles in the dead of winter (−5 degrees Fahrenheit!), I found often that I needed to either lighten or darken the yellow iris and to intensify the yellow as well. To select the iris only, first circle it with the Lasso tool. In the Options bar, click the Subtract From Selection button, and then use the Lasso tool to circle the pupil. This *removes* the pupil from your previous selection, which included the iris *and* the pupil. The end result is that you now have only the iris selected. After feathering the selection one pixel, lighten or darken the iris as needed. If you wish to boost the color, reselect and refeather and then either work the Yellow channel only in Hue/Saturation or add Yellow (and possibly a point or two of black) to the Yellows in Selective Color. (Similarly, click the Add To Selection button when you want to work on both pupils or on both eyes.)

By carefully examining the eye or eyes of their subjects, repairing and improving the damaged areas, and then lightening or darkening them as needed, nature photographers can quickly and easily improve the impact and the quality of their images. With wildlife, the "eyes" have it!

If you've followed our workflow so far, you've cropped and rotated your image if necessary, removed any dust or scratches, made any necessary exposure adjustments, and modified the colors so that your image has the desired impact. Be sure to save your image at this point with your layers intact as your master file. The next two chapters provide additional ideas of ways to create and present your images.

Composites

Many nature photographers are initially loathe to consider making composites, believing that this is somehow "cheating" or "dishonest." There is a clear need for photographers using Photoshop to be ethical and reveal when they have made changes so that their images no longer reflect the reality of what they saw and what existed. Few photographers want to create pictures of cows jumping over the moon, but sometimes combining elements from several pictures can be more expressive and even representative of an experience. Ironically, compositing techniques can actually enable photographers to more accurately and realistically depict what they see in certain circumstances.

7

Chapter Contents
Creating Panoramas
Expanding Dynamic Range
Extending Depth of Field
Combining Elements from Multiple Pictures

Creating Panoramas

The advent of the digital darkroom freed photographers from being tied to the constraints of any one particular camera format, whether it is 35mm, 2×2, or some other format. By using Photoshop, you can stitch together a series of images to create a photograph of a particular shape that better suits the subject. An added benefit of stitching together several frames is that the larger file you create enables you to make prints that are substantially larger than you could if you simply used a wider lens and cropped a single frame.

In-Camera Considerations

When photographing images to be combined into panoramas, following certain techniques while shooting enables you to stitch the images together with a minimum of headaches. If you choose to ignore some of the following procedures (and we admit that at times we do), you may still be able to stitch the segments together, but it's likely it will take longer and the results may not be quite what you had hoped:

- Use a tripod.

- Not only do you need to use a tripod, but you need to level it! If your tripod does not have a level built into it, place a small bubble level on a top flat surface to help get it level. This is important because you want the camera to rotate on a level axis. If you enjoy shooting panoramics, consider buying a tripod leveler such as the panning clamp with level from Really Right Stuff (www.reallyright-stuff.com).

- Level your camera as well by adding a double bubble level to the flash shoe of your camera (see Figure 7.1). Taking the time to level both the tripod and the camera means there will be a minimum of "stair-stepping" as you combine the images. Otherwise, you'll lose part of the image because you'll have to crop to get rid of the stair-stepping.

Figure 7.1
Using a bubble level on top of your camera as well as leveling your tripod will make your panoramics stitch together much more easily. (Photo by Ellen Anon.)

- You can shoot a panorama without a tripod, but you will lose part of the image near the top and bottom with a horizontal panorama, and near the sides on a vertical panorama. When the segments are combined, you're likely to discover that you accidentally changed the relative height and angle of the camera slightly between shots. If you must shoot without a tripod, allow extra room in your framing.

- Plan out your shots, allowing for an overlap of about 20–30 percent in most cases, as shown in Figure 7.2. It's helpful to identify key objects/points within each frame that you will use as anchors to help line up each segment. In the first image, this should be within the right 20–30 percent of the frame for a horizontal panorama; for a vertical panorama it would be in the bottom 20–30 percent. As you rotate the camera to take the next shot, place that same anchor point in the left (or top for a vertical panorama) 20–30 percent of the frame and identify a new object on the right (or bottom). Repeat this process for as many frames as necessary.

Figure 7.2 Plan your shots ahead of time, allowing for an overlap of 20 to 30 percent between frames and an identifiable anchor point. (Photo by Ellen Anon.)

- Although it may seem counterintuitive, it can be quite helpful to shoot a horizontal panorama using the camera in vertical format since it reduces distortion.

- Meter the scene and *manually set your exposure* to a compromise between the readings for the various segments. While some exposures for some of the frames that you shoot will be slightly off this way, you avoid having huge exposure variations that may result if you use one of the autoexposure techniques such as aperture priority. The autoexposure modes may set an entirely different exposure for each frame, making the final panoramic image a series of mismatched exposures.

- If you are using a digital camera, *set your white balance manually.* Auto white balance can lead to a slightly different temperature being used in each frame.

- Avoid using a polarizer because the intensity of the polarizing effect varies as your shots vary their angle in relation to the sun, causing parts of the sky to be darker in some frames than in others.

- To minimize having to correct for distortion, use a focal length longer than approximately 35mm.

- Always start by taking the farthest left (or top) image first. This helps avoid confusion later when you combine the sections.

- When shooting a panoramic series digitally, it's beneficial to shoot a frame at the beginning and at the end of the sequence that will clue you in when you're editing that these images are part of a panoramic series. Otherwise, it's all too easy to delete images, wondering why you composed them so poorly. One trick we use is to take a shot of our hand at the beginning and end of each series.

- Compositionally, you need a logical beginning and end to the panorama, just as you would have if you were shooting a single-frame image.

Note: Photographers who shoot panoramas frequently are aware of the benefits of eliminating, as much as possible, the distortion effects of parallax. This is achieved by pivoting the lens around what is commonly termed the nodal point. Technically, this requires moving the camera and lens back slightly from the tripod pivoting point. Companies such as Really Right Stuff (www.reallyrightstuff.com) produce accessories, including the Omni-Pivot Package, to help with this.

Manually Creating a Panorama in Photoshop

Although we are also going to explain how to use the automated Photomerge feature in Photoshop, it's important to know how to put together a panorama manually. That way, you will be equipped to intervene when the automatic methods fail, which they do all too often.

To manually create a panorama in Photoshop, take the following steps:

1. Open the images to be joined and make sure they are all the same resolution. We recommend setting them to a resolution of 300 ppi for printing by choosing Image > Image Size. Make certain the Resample Image box is not checked. If you're starting with images that are still in a raw format, select them all in Bridge and open CR. Then in CR, synchronize the settings—i.e., use the same settings for all of the images—to quickly convert the series, as discussed in Chapter 4, "First Steps."

2. Place a black stroke about two pixels wide around each picture. To do this, you first need to "unlock" the background layer. Double-click the background layer and click OK in the dialog box that appears. The background layer is now labeled "Layer 0." Go to Edit > Stroke and fill in the dialog box, making sure to choose Location > Inside. The stroke helps you later to identify the edges of each image (see Figure 7.3).

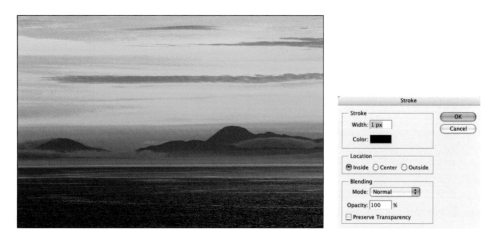

Figure 7.3 Placing a stroke around each image helps you later to easily identify the edges. (Photo by Ellen Anon.)

3. You must determine how large a canvas you need to serve as a background for the panorama. To do this, first note the size and resolution of the images. If you're creating a horizontal panorama consisting of three images, each 4 inches wide by 6 inches high at a resolution of 300 ppi, you must create a new canvas slightly less than 12 inches wide at a resolution of 300 dpi: 4 inches (width) × 3 (number of pictures in panorama) = 12 inches. However, the actual finished width will be smaller due to overlap of images. The new canvas needs to be slightly larger than 6 inches tall in case some images do not line up perfectly.

> **Note:** Don't resize your images at this point. For now just note the size in inches and resolution so you can create a background layer to hold the segments of the panorama. Later you can resize the panorama as desired.

4. Choose File > New and create a new file of the appropriate size for your panorama with a white or transparent background and a resolution of 300 ppi (the same resolution as the individual images).

5. Click each image and using the Move tool, drag them, one at a time, into the new file you just created. Begin with the image that goes farthest to the left (in a horizontal panoramic) or at the top (for a vertical panoramic). Place them in the approximately correct position, as shown in Figure 7.4.

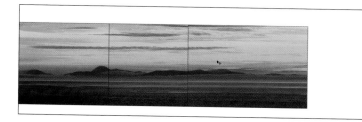

Figure 7.4
Drag your images into the new file you created and place them in roughly the correct position.

6. Turn off the visibility for all but the first two layers above the Background by clicking the "eyeball" icons next to each layer. This helps avoid confusion as you are lining up the images.

7. Select Layer 2 and reduce its visibility to 50–70 percent (see Figure 7.5). This makes it easier to precisely line it up with Layer 1.

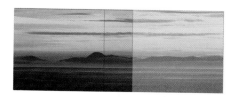

Figure 7.5
Reducing the visibility of the layer you are moving to about 50 to 70 percent, as well as turning off the visibility of the other layers, makes it easier to place each layer.

8. Zoom in and use the Move tool to move Layer 2 so that it precisely aligns with Layer 1. Chances are that not all points will line up perfectly, so target one point to align, as shown in Figure 7.6. When you get close, use the arrow keys to nudge the layer one pixel at a time into the exact position needed. When the layer is in position, click the Lock Position icon ⊕ to lock it so you don't accidentally move it out of alignment.

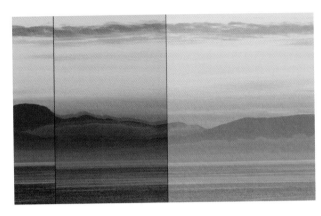

Figure 7.6
Zoom in and select one target point to align, since the chances are that not all points will perfectly align.

9. Return the Opacity of Layer 2 to 100 percent. Click the Create Layer Mask icon ▣ to create a layer mask on Layer 2.

10. Make sure the foreground and background colors are set to black and white by pressing D.

11. Choose a soft-edged brush of a reasonable size and paint with black in the layer mask to erase the edge of Layer 2 and blend it seamlessly with Layer 1. You may need to zoom in and check to ensure that some objects such as an animal or a wave come entirely from one layer or the other, rather than partially masking it in Layer 2 (see Figure 7.7). Occasionally, you may need to use a harder edged brush to ensure an object is clearly from one layer or the other. It can be helpful to turn off the visibility of Layer 1 while doing this.

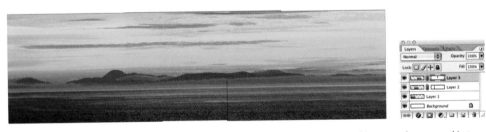

Figure 7.7 Use a soft brush and paint on the layer mask to seamlessly blend the two layers, making sure to have some objects come entirely from one layer or the other.

12. Turn on the visibility of Layer 3. Click it to make it the active layer. Reduce its opacity, move it into position as you did with Layer 2, and finish by blending the edges with a layer mask, as you did with Layer 2. Repeat this sequence as many times as necessary to blend all the individual images of the panorama into one picture.

13. Zoom in and check carefully to make sure no edges are visible. Turning the visibility eyeball icons off and on may help with this process.

14. Crop the excess canvas, as illustrated in Figure 7.8.

15. Save this layered file as a master file of the panorama stitching and then duplicate and flatten it (Layer > Flatten Image). Use the new flattened image as the beginning of your normal workflow.

Figure 7.8 Crop the excess canvas from your panorama and save this as a master file of the panorama itself.

Try It! Open the series of images Pano 1a, Pano 1b, and Pano 1c on the accompanying CD and practice stitching them together. If you prefer, use a series of your own images. We recommend starting with a panorama of no more than three or four sections.

Matching the Exposures of Each Segment of the Panorama

There are times when the exposure of the different segments of the panorama vary, as shown in Figure 7.9. This may happen if you inadvertently used aperture priority or auto white balance, or if a cloud suddenly obscured the sun in the midst of a series of manual exposures for a panorama that were calculated when the sun was shining.

Figure 7.9
Unless you manually set the white balance and exposure for your panoramas, you're likely to get some variation in colors and tonalities between the files.

If you discover that the exposures of the various segments of the panorama do not match, continue on from step 14 in the preceding section and following these steps. (Do not flatten your image yet.)

1. Click Layer 2 (the second segment of the panorama) to make it active.
2. Zoom in to magnify the area where Layers 1 and 2 overlap and where the differences in exposure are evident.
3. Click the Channels palette.
4. Select the Red channel by clicking the word "Red." When viewed in grayscale, the differences between the two layers are usually easy to see, as shown in Figure 7.10.

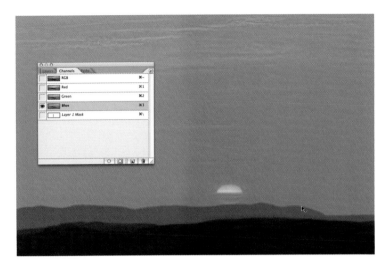

5. Choose Image > Adjustments > Levels on the menu bar. Note that this is one of the few times we'll have you working directly on the pixels. Unfortunately, when you're working within channels, there's no way to use adjustment layers.

6. Click the midpoint slider and drag it to match up the gray tones in Layer 2 with those in Layer 1. When they appear the same, as in Figure 7.11, click OK.

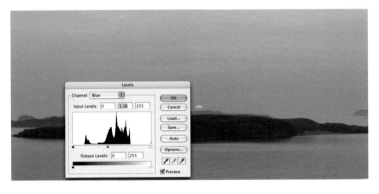

Figure 7.11
Adjusting the midpoint slider in Levels within each channel enables you to easily match exposures.

7. Repeat the same process for the Green and Blue channels, one at a time.

8. Repeat these steps for each frame you need to match to another until your final image matches in color and tonalities (see Figure 7.12).

Figure 7.12
The final image has consistent color across the various segments.

Occasionally, a simple linear correction (which Levels applies) can't resolve the changes in exposure between the segments, in which case you need to use Curves rather than Levels in each channel to accurately match up the different segments. This happens more often when the quality or quantity of the lighting is changing dramatically. Follow the same procedure as described in this section, but use Curves instead of Levels.

Try It! Open PanoMatch1 on the accompanying CD and practice adjusting the exposures to get them to match. If you're looking for a challenge, open PanoMatch2 and match those exposures! (Hint: You'll need to use Curves rather than Levels to get them to match.)

Photomerge

Photomerge automatically arranges and combines multiple images to create a panorama. This can be a tremendous time-saver when it works. Although Photomerge has some surprisingly powerful and flexible features, unfortunately, it often does not blend the images as seamlessly as you can manually. Further, it only works with 8-bit images. Nonetheless, it can provide a quick start to creating a panorama that you finish manually when necessary.

1. There are two ways to get started with Photomerge:
   - The easiest way to begin is to highlight the images you wish to use in Bridge—by holding the Ctrl/⌘ key and clicking the images—and then choosing Automate > Photomerge from Bridge's menu. Photoshop then attempts to align the images for you. If these images are raw files, Photoshop automatically converts them using whatever default you have set within CR. If you have not made any changes to the default, Photoshop uses the Auto Adjust settings. It does, however, convert them to 8-bit images rather than 16-bit images. Photomerge does not work with 16-bit images.
   - If you prefer, select the images to use within Photoshop by going to File > Automate > Photomerge. You need to set the Source to use either images you have previously opened, files you specify, or a folder. Check the box to have Photoshop attempt to automatically arrange the source images (see Figure 7.13).

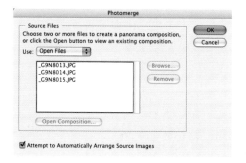

Figure 7.13

Instruct Photoshop which images to select to merge by specifying open files or folders, and check the box to have Photoshop automatically arrange the images.

2. Sometimes Photomerge does a good job, but frequently it fails. If Photoshop knows it failed, you get a message that it could not arrange all the images and that some must be dragged in manually. Click OK and then place the images close to where they belong by clicking them and dragging them. If you have the Snap To Image option checked, Photoshop snaps the images into place when you get close.

3. Zoom in to ensure that Photomerge has done a good job of aligning each segment.

4. Once the pictures are arranged, you can still fine-tune the placement using the tools along the left side of the Photomerge screen (see Figure 7.14).

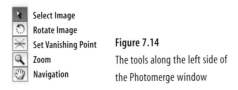

Figure 7.14

The tools along the left side of the Photomerge window

Note: The Set Vanishing Point tool only works when you have applied the Perspective Correction tool. You can use the Zoom tool or the Navigation window to zoom in, but you cannot zoom in as far as you can when aligning the segments manually.

5. Use the options at the right of the Photomerge window to control the perspective and exposure blending of your panorama:

   • If you choose to have Photoshop apply Perspective Correction, it generates a preview that you can keep or you can revert to the normal view. With Perspective Correction you can also choose to have Photoshop apply Cylindrical Mapping to reduce the "bow-tie" effect sometimes caused by the Perspective Correction. You can also set the vanishing point using the Vanishing Point tool. We rarely use these options with nature photographs, but you may wish to experiment with them to preview the effects. If you like the results, go ahead and use them.

   • You can also choose to have Photoshop apply Advanced Blending to combine the layers, although this cannot be done if you have selected the Keep As Layers option (which we recommend). Keeping the layers allows you to fine-tune both the placement and the color/exposure of the various segments of your panorama. However, the Advanced Blending option tries to make transition areas as smooth as possible by blending across a wider area where there is less detail, and across a smaller area where there is more detail (see Figure 7.15).

Figure 7.15

You can preview the results of the Advanced Blending option to see how effective it was.

6. You can preview the results by clicking the Preview button after selecting one of these options. Then click Exit Preview to return to the main window.

7. When you're satisifed, click OK. Photoshop generates a panorama for you (layered, if you have checked the Keep As Layers option).

Note: Even when it appears that Photomerge has done a good job of aligning the images, it's worth keeping the layers. Then, recheck the alignment more closely in the main part of Photoshop where you can zoom in farther and check for accuracy.

If you have the layers, you can proceed as you did when putting a manual panorama together to match the exposures or fine-tune the panorama as necessary.

Composites

by Joe McDonald

Shooting digitally, my photography now has far fewer limitations. Think about it. The basic laws of optics normally restrict our vision, but for virtually my entire career I've been further limited not by what I could see but what my camera could capture. Limitations imposed by the depth of field or the angle of view or the exposure latitude all conspired to force me to make images not as I saw them but as I knew my medium could render them. We all lived with this and probably didn't even think about it, for it was the reality of photography at the time.

Digital has changed all of that for me: I now make images with the "reality" of the scene in mind. This can take any number of forms. Sometimes I simply have too much lens, but by shooting a panorama, I still get the image size and detail I wanted, while encompassing more of the habitat as well. On other occasions I'll shoot focus composites, focusing on the foreground if it bears interest and on the main subject so that the finished image lacks the unnatural dimension typical of long lens shots. If necessary, I'll add some Gaussian blur to a background to draw more attention to the subject.

Restrictions created by a broad exposure latitude have been significantly reduced. Often I'll "shoot for the middle," knowing that I can convert a raw image twice, once biasing for the underexposure, and once for the over. Usually I'll cover myself for those shots by shooting two exposures, metering for each value. That way, if the exposure latitude was indeed too broad for a single image, I'll have a good chance of recording the scene if I use two separate images.

This has simply made my photography more fun because I'm not frustrated or stymied by past limitations. I'm free to try things, probably way more than I'll ever have time to work with in the digital darkroom, but that's secondary. The fun part is the shooting, and with digital, I feel I have the potential of capturing what I truly see.

© Joe McDonald, www.hoothollow.com

Expanding Dynamic Range

Until recently, the dynamic range or exposure latitude that we could capture in a single image was limited by camera and film technology. Often, especially during the midday hours, there was too much contrast to be able to capture in a single shot. We had to choose to give up detail in the highlights, the shadows, or both. Photoshop enables us to combine several images of the same subject, taken using different exposures, to retain detail in the highlights and shadows while simultaneously having the midtones properly exposed. It's almost magical how we can create an image that reflects what we actually saw, no longer limited by the latitude of film.

There are three techniques we'll describe to extend the exposure latitude in an image:

- Manually
- The "cookbook" approach, where Photoshop does most of the work for you
- Merge To HDR, new in CS2

Expanding Latitude Manually

When you encounter a situation in which there is too much contrast to capture detail in the entire scene in a single shot, take several shots at different exposure levels and combine them using these steps:

1. Use a tripod and take your first shot, exposing for the shadow areas. Check your in-camera histogram to ensure that the shadow areas do *not* spike against the left side of the histogram. If they do, take another shot, adding more light to the exposure.

2. Without moving the camera, take another shot, this time exposing for the highlights. This time when you check the histogram, make certain that there are no spikes against the right side of the histogram. If there are, reduce the amount of light in the exposure (see Figure 7.16).

Figure 7.16 Check the histograms to make certain that the dark exposure has captured detail in the highlight areas and similarly that the light exposure has captured all the shadow detail. (Photo by Ellen Anon.)

3. In some cases, you may want a third shot exposing for the midtones.

> **Note:** It's not enough to simply expose for the midtones and bracket the shot by half a stop in both directions. Bracketing that way is usually insufficient to allow ample differences in the exposures to re-create as much detail as your eyes saw. Instead, make sure to check the histogram with each shot to ensure that the portion of the image you are exposing for falls within the bounds of the histogram, as discussed in Chapter 1, "Thinking Digitally in the Field."

4. Open each image in Photoshop.

5. Choose the Move tool and while holding the Shift key, click one image and drag it on top of another. By holding the Shift key, they should line up in perfect registry.

6. To check to see if they are lined up perfectly, reduce the opacity of the top layer to 50 percent. If perchance they are not perfectly aligned, use the arrow keys to nudge the top layer until it does line up. (If you are using files from a film scan, you'll almost certainly need to fine-tune their alignment.)

7. Return the opacity of that layer to 100 percent.

8. Click the Add Layer Mask icon to create a layer mask on the top layer.

9. Choose a brush tool that is soft to medium hardness and set the Brush Opacity to 100 percent initially.

10. Make sure the foreground color is set to black and the background color is set to white by hitting the D key.

11. Paint with black in the layer mask to reveal parts of the underlying image layer, leaving the well-exposed parts from each layer visible, as shown in Figure 7.17.

Figure 7.17
Create a layer mask on the top layer to reveal parts of the image below that are better exposed.

12. Zoom in and work carefully.

13. If you make a mistake, simply switch to white (by pressing X) and paint with white in the layer mask.

14. You may want to reduce the brush opacity to partially reveal the underlying layer in areas.

15. If you have a third exposure, follow the same procedure and drag it on top of the other two while holding down the Shift key.

16. Add a layer mask to this layer and paint with black to reveal the underlying layers in the appropriate places.

17. There are two ways to proceed with the rest of your workflow:

- Flatten the image when the desired tonal range is achieved and proceed to modify it using your normal workflow as you would a single image.

    or…

- Make a Stamp Visible layer (see Figure 7.18)—a single layer containing your desired final exposure. To do this, first create a new layer on top of the others. In CS2 it is not necessary to create the new layer first—Photoshop will do it for you automatically. Then, while holding down the Alt/Option key, click the triangle at the top of the Layers palette to open the palette menu. Continue holding the Alt/Option key and click Merge Visible. Do not release the Alt/Option key until you see a new thumbnail icon appear in the layer you created.

Figure 7.18
A Stamp Visible layer contains all the information of the layers beneath it in a single layer that serves as the initial layer in your normal workflow.

The "Cookbook" Approach to Expanding Latitude

Sometimes combining two exposures is fairly straightforward, as it was in the example we used for the manual method of combining exposures. But sometimes the highlight and shadow areas are scattered throughout the image, making the manual method quite time-consuming. Fortunately, there's an easy way to have Photoshop do most of the tedious work for you in combining two images (see Figure 7.19).

Figure 7.19
You can have Photoshop use the lighter image to create a mask to use while combining two different exposures. (Images courtesy Rick Holt.)

Take these steps to combine the two images:

1. Drag the *dark* image on top of the light image by using the Move tool while holding the Shift key. It's important that the darker image goes on top.

> **Note:** For this approach to be successful, the images must align perfectly. After dragging the darker image on top of the lighter one, reduce the opacity of the dark one and nudge it into place using the Move tool and the arrow keys on the keyboard, as you did when arranging the sections of a panorama.

2. Add a layer mask to the dark image layer.

3. Make the background image active by clicking the background image layer and press Ctrl/⌘+A to select the entire background image.

4. Press Ctrl/⌘+C to copy the image to the clipboard.

5. Highlight the dark image layer; hold down the Alt/Option key and click the layer mask icon to make the mask appear where you usually see your image. It will be completely white at first.

6. Press Ctrl/⌘+V to paste the contents of the clipboard onto the white mask. Your layer mask should now appear to be a black-and-white version of the Background, as shown in Figure 7.20.

Figure 7.20
Hold down the Alt/Option key, click the Layer Mask icon and then press Ctrl/⌘+V to make the mask appear in place of the image preview.

7. Apply a Gaussian blur (Filter > Blur > Gaussian Blur) with a radius between 0.5 and 2.0.

8. Click the image icon on the darker layer and press Ctrl/⌘+D to deselect. Your image should now reflect the best of both exposures (see Figure 7.21).

Figure 7.21
By using the lighter image to create a mask for the darker image, Photoshop does most of the work to create a composite using the best of both exposures.

9. You may want to fine-tune the tonality of the image using a Curves adjustment layer if necessary or by further modifying the layer mask.

10. Create a Stamp Visible layer, as you did in the final step of the completely manual method and continue with the regular workflow.

Try It! Open the images on the accompanying CD called CanyonDark and CanyonLight and try combining them using the "cookbook" approach.

Expanding Latitude via Merge To HDR

Photoshop CS2 offers an option to use Merge To HDR both from Bridge and from within Photoshop itself. This tool combines multiple exposures (ideally three to seven exposures of the identical subject) into one 32-bit image!

Using 32-bit enables the image to have a greatly expanded dynamic range so that the final image can contain detail in shadow areas and in highlights that normally cannot be present in a single image. In fact, 32-bit offers more latitude than what you can even see on your monitor. However, the 32-bit image can then be converted back to 16-bit or 8-bit. Merge To HDR creates an image containing the maximum amount of detail and color information possible, with very little work on your part. It ensures that the transitions among the exposures are gradual, with no harsh obvious edges. It sounds too good to be true, doesn't it?

Unfortunately, nature photographers are likely to experience several difficulties using this tool. If anything changes between exposures—a tree branch blowing slightly in the wind, a leaf, anything moving—Merge To HDR probably won't give a good final image. Similarly, if there is any camera movement, it also won't work. There is no option in this version of the tool to allow you to manually align the images. Although it would seem the answer would be to take a single raw file and convert it at numerous settings, this won't work, because the algorithms used in Merge To HDR require different *linear* data.

All this means that there are only limited situations for nature photographers that can benefit from Merge To HDR. Situations with high contrast and static subjects are best. For example, the sun rising or setting behind a mountain offers an ideal opportunity. Normally, some of the detail in the mountain would be lost while trying to capture the colors of the sunset.

If a scene lends itself to using Merge To HDR, then in the field, take the following steps:

1. It's essential to use a tripod and not move your camera between exposures. Use a cable release if possible.

2. Take a series of shots, varying the exposure by changing the shutter speed, not the aperture (which would change the depth of field). If you use aperture priority, then you simply need to dial in different exposure compensation amounts for each shot.

3. Vary the exposures by one to two f/stops each. Don't try to bracket by small increments such as 1/3 to 1/2 stops, as you might if you were trying to capture a single well-exposed frame.

4. Check the histogram to make sure that your darkest picture includes detail in the brightest part of the image, i.e., there are no spikes on the right of the histogram and no flashing highlight warnings. Similarly, check to make sure that your lightest image (which has flashing highlights) has no spikes on the left side of the histogram. You want to make certain to capture detail in all the shadows.

5. Don't vary the lighting by using flash in one picture and not the next.

After you have downloaded your images to your computer, access Merge To HDR through Bridge directly or through Photoshop using these steps:

1. To select the files to use in Photoshop, choose File > Automate > Merge To HDR. The Merge To HDR dialog box (see Figure 7.22) appears. Click Browse to select the desired images and then click Open, or if you have already opened the images, simply select Use Open Files.

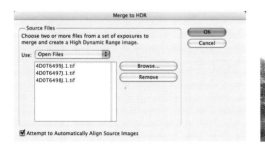

Figure 7.22 Select your desired images in the Merge To HDR dialog box. (Images courtesy Josh Anon.)

2. Check the Attempt To Automatically Align Source Images check box.

3. To select the images to use directly from Bridge, simply highlight the desired images and choose Tools > Photoshop > Merge To HDR.

4. Click OK.

5. This leads to a Merge To HDR dialog box, shown in Figure 7.23. You can zoom in to see the results more closely if desired, or uncheck one of the source images displayed along the left side to exclude it from being part of the final image. The image preview automatically updates to reflect this change.

Figure 7.23
The Merge to HDR window allows you to preview the results of the merge as well as specify the white point and bit depth for the composite.

6. Choose a bit depth for the merged image from the Bit Depth menu. To store the entire dynamic range, you must choose 32-bit.

7. Move the slider below the histogram to set the white point for previewing the merged image. This affects the preview only in a 32-bit image, since there is more information than what can be displayed on a monitor (or print). You are not discarding any information yet. If you choose to save the merged image as an 8- or 16-bit-per-channel file at this point, then moving this slider is applying exposure edits to your final image, and you are discarding some information. The same conversion dialog box shown in Figure 7.24 will appear. There you can specify the exact conversion settings.

8. Click OK, and Photoshop creates the merged image.

   Currently, there are only a few tools and adjustments that can be used with 32-bit images, so you have to convert your image back to a 16-bit-per-channel file. To do this, continue with these steps:

9. Choose Image > Mode > 16 Bits/Channel.

10. In the HDR Conversion dialog box (see Figure 7.24), choose from among several options in the Method drop-down list:

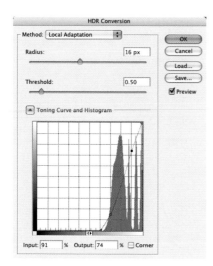

Figure 7.24
You can choose from several different approaches to convert your image back to 16-bit (or 8-bit).

- Choose Exposure and Gamma to manually adjust the brightness and contrast.

- Choose Highlight Compression to compresses the dynamic values in the HDR image to fall within the bounds of a 16-bit image. Photoshop automatically converts the image for you.

- Choose Equalize Compression to compress the dynamic range of the image while trying to preserve some contrast. This is also an automatic method.

- Choose Local Adaptation (see Figure 7.25) to adjust the tonality by calculating the amount of correction necessary for specific brightness regions throughout the image. If you choose this option, you can adjust the tone curve in a manner similar to adjusting curves, as discussed in Chapter 5, "Exposure Adjustments." This is often the most useful choice.

Figure 7.25
Using Local Adaptation and modifying the tone curve allowed us to convert this HDR image to 16-bit, while retaining a great deal more info in the shadows and highlights.

Merge To HDR is a new tool that holds considerable promise for nature photographers. In its current initial form, its applications are limited, but as Adobe continues to develop and refine this tool, it will offer considerable possibilities for us.

 Try It! Open the images from the accompanying CD called HDR1, HDR2, and HDR3 and experiment with creating a 32-bit file and then converting it back to a 16-bit file.

Extending the Depth of Field

Nature photographers sometimes encounter situations where we want to maximize our depth of field (the range of apparently sharp focus within an image) but we encounter technical limitations. Perhaps the range we want to be in focus is too great for the lens, or the wind is blowing so we have to use a relatively fast shutter speed to freeze the motion. Using the faster shutter speed may mean we can't use as small an aperture as we'd like for a correct exposure, without resorting to higher ISOs, which can lead to problems with noise.

Using a compositing technique similar to that for manually increasing the exposure latitude, you can combine two or more photographs in which you varied your focus to increase the depth of field. This can be a huge advantage at times, since you can shoot at whatever shutter speed you need to freeze the action. It can also allow you greater depth of field than would be possible in certain situations, such as macro photography.

 Note: When using zoom lenses, changing the focus changes the focal length slightly, so this technique tends to work best with fixed focal length lenses.

Here are the steps you can take to extend the depth of field by combining two or more images:

1. Take two or more shots, varying the focus for each. For example, focus on the foreground in one shot and on the mid ground for the next shot while the camera is on a tripod as shown in Figure 7.26.

Figure 7.26 Take two or more shots, varying the focal point. (Photo by Ellen Anon.)

2. Do not change the exposure, only change the focus.

3. Use your depth-of-field preview button to see what areas will be in focus and allow for overlap between the shots.

4. Open all the shots in Photoshop. If they are raw files, synchronize the settings for all the files, as discussed in Chapter 4.

5. Drag one image on top of another with the Move tool while holding down the Shift key to align the images in perfect registry.

6. Check to see that they are aligned perfectly by reducing the opacity of the top layer. Use the arrow keys if necessary to slightly move the top image and then return the layer to 100 percent opacity.

Note: Sometimes you may not be able to perfectly align the images, in which case later you'll have to zoom in and carefully create the layer mask.

7. With the top layer highlighted, click the Add A Layer Mask icon at the bottom of the Layers palette.

8. Press D to make sure the foreground and background colors are set to black and white. Press X to toggle between white and black as the foreground color.

9. Choose a medium hardness brush of the appropriate size with 100 percent opacity. You need to zoom in and work carefully, adjusting the size and hardness of your brush as necessary.

10. Paint with black on the layer mask to reveal parts of the underlying image (see Figure 7.27).

Figure 7.27
Use the layer mask to reveal the sharp areas of both images, which creates the appearance of increased depth of field.

11. Repeat this process if you have more than two shots you are combining.

12. Make a Stamp Visible layer that will be a single layer containing a flattened version of your composite image. To do this, first create a new layer on top of the others by clicking the Create A New Layer icon at the bottom of the Layers palette. (It's not necessary to create the new layer first if you are using CS2.) Then, while holding down the Alt/Option key, click the right-facing triangle on the Layers Palette. Continue holding the Alt/Option key and click Merge Visible. Do not release the Alt/Option key until you see a new thumbnail icon appear in the layer you created.

13. Continue with your normal workflow.

Try It! Open the images called DOF1 and DOF2 on the accompanying CD and practice combining them.

Combining Elements from Multiple Pictures

When you start combining elements from various pictures, you begin to be more creative with your images. Ethically, it's important to acknowledge that what you're presenting is not a documentary photograph but rather a photo illustration or photo art. That doesn't make it inherently more or less valuable than a straight photograph—just different. Often, a photo illustration can convey the essence or spirit of a place better than a single straight photograph. But creating something that didn't exist and claiming it is not a manipulated photograph creates trouble for all photographers. The owl image in Figure 7.28 has impact, but it's a composite and needs to be presented as such.

Figure 7.28
Images like this can often be confused with "lucky" shots and ethically must be presented as composites. (Photo by Ellen Anon.)

Advanced Selection Methods

Chapter 3, "Basic Tools," explained some of the basic selection tools, but when you make composites, sometimes you need more sophisticated means of making selections. Different techniques work most effectively with different images, so it pays to understand several different approaches.

If you know ahead of time that you're likely to want to use one part of a picture as a composite, it's a good idea to try to photograph it so that it contrasts as much as possible from the background. That makes it easier to select, no matter which technique you choose!

Color Range

The Color Range tool is similar to the Magic Wand, but it's more powerful. It's particularly useful in selecting skies when there are trees in the foreground. To access it, choose

Select > Color Range. This tool allows you to select multiple areas of different colors at one time. You can even specifically select the highlights, midtones, or shadows with this tool. In addition, you can preview the effects of some of your settings.

Let's use Color Range to select the sky in an image by taking the following steps:

1. Make certain the Select box is set to Sampled Colors and use the left eyedropper to click an area in your image to specify as the target color. (You can also use the pull-down menu from the Select box and choose a specific color, such as red, or highlights, midtones, or shadows.)

2. Your selection is white in the preview box. (Selected areas are white, unselected areas are black, and gray areas are blurred selection edges.)

3. Drag the Fuzziness slider to adjust the tolerance. Higher tolerances select more colors; lower values select fewer colors. The preview box shows how the Fuzziness value is affecting the selection (see Figure 7.29).

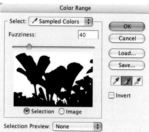

Figure 7.29 With just a couple clicks of the eyedroppers and adjusting the Fuzziness slider, you can easily select a sky from this image. (Photo by Ellen Anon.)

4. It's likely you'll need to use the Add To eyedropper (the one with the + by it) and click additional areas of the background until you have successfully identified the entire sky area. Similarly, you may need to use the Subtract From eyedropper to remove areas from the selection. As you do so, you'll need to readjust the Fuzziness slider.

5. Click OK, and Photoshop turns the white area into a selection.

6. If Color Range has identified other areas that you do not want to be selected and you cannot eliminate them using the Subtract From eyedropper and the Fuzziness slider, use any of the other selection tools (such as the Lasso or Magic Wand) to remove them from the selection, as discussed in Chapter 3.

Note: You can use more than one color as the basis for your selection by selecting the middle eyedropper tool and clicking an additional color in your image. Similarly, you can use the farthest right eyedropper to click a color range to remove from your selection.

The Color Range tool tends to create selections with blurry edges, whereas the Magic Wand creates more definite selections with anti-aliased edges. Color Range is often an extremely effective way to select a sky. Later in this chapter we'll explain how to actually replace a sky that you select this way.

Creating a Selection from Within a Channel

This sounds a lot more difficult than it is, but don't let let the sound of it intimidate you. Recall that your images have pixel information in three channels: a red channel, a blue channel, and a green channel. You access these channels by clicking the Channels palette, as shown in Figure 7.30. By default, Channels shares a palette window with Layers.

Figure 7.30
To access the individual channels, click the Channels palette.

Sometimes it's easier to make a selection using one of the three color channels rather than the RGB image itself. This is the case when there is good contrast within a particular channel. For example, making a selection of a sky based on a channel is quite useful when the sky meets trees and vegetation with many fine branches.

Use this approach to select the sky in the poppy image you just used with the Color Range tool:

1. Choose Channels and then click each of the three channels, one at a time, to determine which has the best contrast in the area of interest. With your poppy picture, clearly the blue channel offers the best contrast to separate the sky and the flower, as you can see in Figure 7.31.

Red channel   Green channel   Blue channel

Figure 7.31 Looking at the red, green, and blue channels, it's clear that the blue channel offers the most contrast between the sky and the flower.

2. Make a copy of the channel offering the most contrast—in this case, the blue channel—by dragging that channel layer to the New Channel icon at the bottom of the Channels palette.

3. Maximize the contrast between the area you want to select and the rest of the image by choosing Image > Adjustments > Levels. This is one of the few times you make changes directly on the pixels, because there is no way to create an adjustment layer for a channel. Drag in the Black Point and White Point sliders to turn the preview nearly black and white, as illustrated in Figure 7.32. A small transition area of gray is actually beneficial.

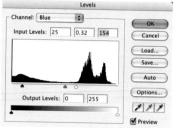

Figure 7.32

Use the sliders in the Levels dialog to turn this channel into black and white.

4. To fine-tune the selection, you'll most likely need to use the Brush tool and paint some areas with black and some areas with white.

5. Once you have a black-and-white preview created (which is actually a mask), click the Load Channel As Selection icon ⬚ at the bottom of the Channels palette. This creates a selection based on the mask you just created. The white areas are selected.

6. You can invert the selection (by choosing Select > Inverse on the main menu) if you find that you have selected the opposite part of the image.

7. After going through all this to make a selection, it's a good idea to save the selection by choosing Select > Save and naming it (see Figure 7.33). That way, you can refer back to it in the future.

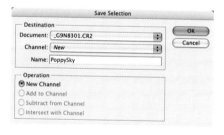

Figure 7.33

After making a time-consuming selection, it's a good idea to save the selection.

Extracting an Object from Its Background

Photoshop provides the Extract dialog box to select an object and remove the background. You might want to do this if you have a subject that you're preparing to import into another image. For example, if you have been on an African safari and have a great picture of a lion you'd like to put in another setting, use the Extract tool to select the lion.

Most people find it takes some practice to use this tool successfully. The trick is to use it carefully to retain edge detail in the portion you're preserving. Fuzzy-edged objects, such as furry or feathered critters, are often challenging. Nonetheless, this tool can work well at times and is worth a try if other selection methods don't seem to work easily.

Note: The Extraction filter only works on 8-bit files.

Take the following steps to extract an object from its background using the Extract tool:

1. Open an image with an object you want to separate from the rest of the image.

2. Choose Filter > Extract.

3. In the Extract dialog box, choose the Edge Highlighter tool 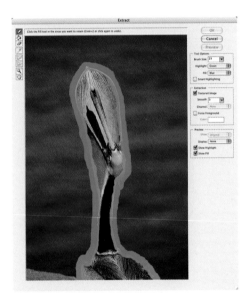 and use it to trace along the edges of the object you wish to preserve.

4. Try to have about two-thirds of the border outside the object and one-third inside it. You can change the brush size as you work. Use a smaller brush when outlining well-defined areas and a large brush for less well-defined areas such as fur or feathers (see Figure 7.34).

Figure 7.34
Outline the object to be extracted, trying to keep two-thirds of the border outside the object. Use a larger brush on less well-defined areas such as feathers. (Photo by Ellen Anon.)

5. Make sure your outline completely surrounds the object to be extracted. You can use the edge of the image as part of the outline.

6. Click the Fill tool 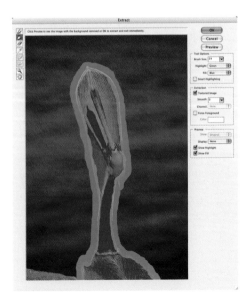 and click once inside the outlined object. This fills the inside of your highlighted outline with a colored tint and tells Photoshop that this is the part you want to keep (see Figure 7.35).

Figure 7.35
Filling an area tells Photoshop that this is the area you want to keep.

7. Click the Preview button to see how your extraction will look, as in Figure 7.36.

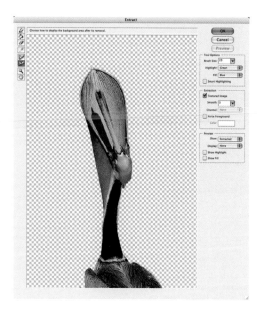

Figure 7.36
Click the Preview button to
see the extraction results.

8. You may have to go back and work on your highlighting along some of the edges if the extraction isn't as accurate as you hoped; zooming in may be helpful. Use the Eraser and Edge cleanup tools while in the Preview to perfect the edges.

9. Click OK to perform the extraction.

10. After performing the extraction, use the History Brush (as described in Chapter 3) to help perfect the extraction if areas were removed by mistake. To do this:

   a. Choose the History Brush .

   b. Click the original image in the History palette to set it as the source, and then paint back in any missing areas in your selection. If the original image was 16-bit you'll need to place the History Brush by a pre-extraction layer in which the image is 8-bit.

   c. Use the Eraser tool to remove any pixels that should not be there.

> **Note:** For more information on making selections, see *Photoshop Masking and Compositing* by Katrin Eismann (New Riders, 2004).

Combining Elements from Various Images

Perhaps you have several images, each containing elements that you would like to combine into a single image. Often, the relative sizes of the various elements need to be modified—you can take care of that during the process of compositing the elements. In the next example, we'll create a composite of some birds, a background, and a moon:

1. Open your destination photo the photo that you are going to use as the main photo—and set its resolution to 300 ppi by choosing Image > Image Size and *uncheck* the Resample Image option. You don't want to interpolate the file now, just set it to the same resolution. See Figure 7.37 for our destination photo.

Figure 7.37
This is the destination photo that we'll use as the foundation for our composite. (Photo by Ellen Anon.)

2.   Open a file containing an element you're going to use and also set it to a resolution of 300 ppi. In our example, we'll use an image with a group of cranes flying (see Figure 7.38).

Figure 7.38
We're going to select these flying cranes to use in our composite. (Photo by Ellen Anon.)

3.   Use your preferred selection tool to isolate the element. In this case, it's easy to use the Color Range tool to select the cranes.

4.   Choose Select > Save Selection and type in a name for the selection. This enables you to return to this selection at any time by choosing Select > Load Selection.

5.   Use the Move tool and drag the selection you just made to the destination image.

6.   Use the Edit > Free Transform tools to size, rotate, and place these elements (see Figure 7.39).

Figure 7.39
Size, rotate, and place the new elements using the Free Transform tool.

7. Note that the elements you just dragged in are on their own layer. It's quite possible they may need some tonal or color adjustments to match the destination image. To make an adjustment layer that only affects a specific layer, hold down the Alt/Option key while clicking the icon to make a new adjustment layer. Check the box that says Use Previous Layer To Create Clipping Mask, as shown in Figure 7.40.

Figure 7.40

By holding down the Alt/Option key while creating a new adjustment layer, you can check the option to have only the previous layer affected by the adjustments you make.

8. Repeat this process if there are other elements from other pictures you wish to include. In this case, add a moon as well (see Figure 7.41).

Figure 7.41

The final image also contains a moon that was added.

9. You may wish to save the composite with the layers intact as a master file so you can further modify it in the future. It's quite possible that you may want to slightly adjust the position of one of the composited items or its size.

10. Proceed with your normal workflow.

Lighting Angles Matter

It's important to pay attention to lighting angles. Many Photoshop novices create composites that would require the earth to have several suns. This detracts from the impact of the final image. Paying attention to subtle details can make the difference between an impressive image and one that evokes comments of "Oh, that was Photoshopped." While you will be ethical and indicate when an image is a composite, you still want to elicit reactions of "Wow!"

Replacing a Sky or Other Background

Now that you've learned a variety of methods for selecting a sky, you're going to put them to use. Nature photographers often find they have a great subject with a boring sky (or other background). It's wonderful when things naturally come together and the subject, lighting, and background are all perfect. But realistically, all too often the sky or background may be great when there are no subjects, and the subjects may be great when the sky is not. This happens on African safaris, it happens while photographing birds anywhere, you name the situation, and you can bet there will be times when the sky/background just doesn't cooperate. Photoshop makes it easy to replace the dull background with one that enhances your subject matter

To replace a sky (You can follow along using the images ReplaceSky1 and 2 on the accompanying CD):

1. Open an image that needs a new sky (destination image) and set it to a resolution of 300 ppi.

2. Open an image of a preferred sky (or other background) and set it to a resolution of 300 ppi as well. Make sure that your new sky is at least as large as the destination image. Making it slightly larger can be helpful too, as you can see in Figure 7.42. The sky image should be a picture of just a sky, not including other subject elements.

Figure 7.42 Open an image with a sky that needs to be replaced and open an image with a better sky. (Photos by Ellen Anon.)

Note: Sometimes the better sky may simply be a more dramatic cloudy sky. You don't want to combine a bright blue sky with billowy clouds and a foreground taken on a very cloudy day unless you're prepared to make some sophisticated color changes to your foreground. Paying attention to the subtleties of color will make your composites more believable.

3. Click the destination image and make a selection of the dull sky using your preferred selection method. The Color Range tool is often the most efficient choice for selecting the sky.

4. Choose Select > Modify > Expand and enter 1 pixel. Click OK. This expands the entire selection by one pixel to help ensure that there are no sky pixels left.

5. Click your good sky image and use the Move tool to drag the new sky image on top of the destination image.

6. Rename the sky image layer "New Sky."

7. Create a layer mask on the New Sky layer by clicking the Add Layer Mask icon at the bottom of the Layers palette. Magic! Your new sky replaces the old one, since the layer mask reflects the selection you just made, as shown in Figure 7.43.

Figure 7.43 When you create a layer mask on the New Sky layer, it reflects the selection of the old sky you already made, and magically the new sky appears.

8. To soften the edge of the selection, select the layer mask by clicking it. Make certain the layer mask is highlighted, not the image thumbnail. Choose Filter > Blur > Gaussian Blur and enter a value of 0.5 to 1.5 pixels. You can see the results on your image and gauge how much blur to add by what looks good. Click OK.

9. With the layer mask still active, you can further control exactly where the mask begins by choosing Image > Adjustments > Levels and moving the sliders. You are modifying the tonalities in the mask, which in turn modify the edges of each image layer.

10. You can choose the area of the new sky (the background) you want to show by *unlinking* the layer mask on the New Sky layer. To do this, click the link icon between the New Sky image thumbnail and the New Sky layer mask, as shown in Figure 7.44. Now click the image thumbnail and choose the Move tool. You can move the New Sky without affecting the mask, so you get to choose which part of the sky to show. Very cool!

Figure 7.44 By unlinking the image thumbnail and the layer mask, you can move the new sky to reveal whatever part of it best complements your picture.

Once you grasp the basics of compositing, you're free to create images that more accurately reflect the realities of some situations as well as images that reflect your imagination and subjective experiences. Experiment and have fun!

Creative Effects

For some nature photographers, the goal is simply to take the best shot they can to document what they see, and then to optimize it in Photoshop. That's fine. Other photographers are latent artists at heart, but may believe (rightly or wrongly) that they have no inherent ability to create art from a blank canvas. But given a camera as the starting point, and a digital darkroom, they can make magic.

Of course, creativity is an artistic form; not every technique appeals to every photographer, and some images are more suited for one approach than another. As you read through this chapter, consider each technique as a jumping-off point for your own ideas rather than a cookbook approach to creative imagery.

Chapter Contents
Black-and-White
Filters
Digital Montages
Digital Multiple Exposures
The Evolution of an Image

Black-and-White

Some images lend themselves to black-and-white, to say nothing of the fact that right now black-and-white images are very popular. In fact, there is a timeless quality to many black-and-white prints.

Converting to Black-and-White

Digital cameras capture images in color, but there are a variety of ways that you can easily convert them into black-and-white. While some folks may opt to simply desaturate their images by creating a Hue/Saturation adjustment layer and sliding the saturation slider all the way to the left, or by choosing Image > Mode > Grayscale, we don't recommend those approaches because the results are often very flat and bland (see Figure 8.1). Instead, we recommend using a Channel Mixer adjustment layer.

Figure 8.1 Simply desaturating, or just changing the mode to grayscale, often converts an image to a rather bland black-and-white version. (Photo by Ellen Anon.)

Recall from Chapter 7, "Composites," that when you wanted to make a selection of part of an image, you could look at the red, green, and blue channels and see what information was in each. You can use this same information to help convert to black-and-white. The channel mixer allows you to specify how much information you want each channel to contribute to the final image. It's a good idea to begin by opening the Channels palette and clicking each channel individually to see what detail is present in each (see Figure 8.2). That will give you an idea of where to begin in the Channel Mixer.

Red channel   Blue channel   Green channel

Figure 8.2 Check each channel to see what information it is contributing to the final image. (Photo by Ellen Anon.)

It's likely that by experimenting with the sliders, you'll find a combination of values that creates a strong image. To convert an image to black-and-white, take the following steps:

1. Return to the Layers palette and create a Channel Mixer adjustment layer (Figure 8.3) by clicking the same adjustment layer icon at the bottom of the palette and choosing Channel Mixer from the drop-down menu.

Figure 8.3

Create a Channel Mixer adjustment layer to use for converting the image to black-and-white.

2. Check the Monochrome box.

3. Modify the percentages from each channel to create a more dramatic black-and-white version of your file. You can choose settings from –200 percent to +200 percent for each channel. As you adjust one, you're likely to need to tweak the other settings. Usually it's best to have the percentages from the three channels total close to 100 percent. Sometimes we go a little beyond 100 percent for a more contrasty image with a lot of punch, but you have to make sure you're not sacrificing image detail for increased contrast (see Figure 8.4).

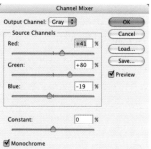

Figure 8.4 Experiment with the settings for each channel to create a black-and-white image with considerable impact. (Photo by Ellen Anon.)

4. Usually we leave the Constant option at its default of 0, but moving it to the left darkens the image and moving it to the right lightens it. After a little experimenting with the settings for each channel, you'll have a more dramatic black-and-white image.

When you first open a Channel Mixer adjustment layer, the default values are red = 100, green = 0, and blue = 0. Often, the red channel provides the most contrast, but it's likely you may find some information in the green or blue channels that you want to emphasize, so you may increase those channels somewhat. If you do, you may need to decrease the red channel. Alternatively, you may even choose to increase the red channel and use a negative value for the green or blue channel. Make this decision based on your taste and the characteristics of the individual image. Often, noise is more prominent in the blue channel, so if noise is a problem in your image, you may opt to use a negative value there. There really are no typical values that apply to most images.

If you're not certain that the values you have selected are the best possible combination, click the Snapshot button in the History palette to take a snapshot of the image this way. Then, reopen the Channel Mixer adjustment layer (by double-clicking its icon in the Layers palette) and try a new combination of values. You can repeat this process as many times as you desire. To go back to an earlier snapshot, return to the top of the History palette and click the desired snapshot, as shown in Figure 8.5. Note that snapshots disappear when you close the image.

Figure 8.5
By taking snapshots of previous combinations of settings in the Channel Mixer, you can try a variety of settings and choose which one you prefer.

Note: Because you used an adjustment layer to convert the image to black-and-white, as long as you save the image with the layers intact, you can go back and modify the settings.

Colorizing Black-and-White Images

You may be quite content with the black-and-white rendition of your image, or you may want to experiment with adding color back into your image, depending on the effect you're after.

For example, you may decide that you'd like to emphasize one particular aspect of the picture by having it in the original color while the rest of the picture remains black-and-white. This look—popular in greeting cards—is incredibly easy. All you need to do is select the Brush tool, set it to black, make sure the Channel Mixer layer is active (highlighted) and paint over the areas you want to be in color (see Figure 8.6). It's that simple!

Figure 8.6
By painting with black on the layer mask in the Channel Mixer layer, you can return color to selected portions of the picture. (Photo by Ellen Anon.)

Hopefully by now you recognize that you're using the layer mask that came with the Channel Mixer layer to mask out the monochromatic effects. If you'd prefer the color to be more subdued, reduce the opacity of the brush by going to the Options bar and setting it accordingly

If you wish to have a *different* color in that one area than what was originally there, create a Hue/Saturation layer on top of the Channel Mixer layer and adjust the Hue slider (as well as the Saturation and Lightness sliders if desired) until the target item is the shade you prefer.

Some people prefer a more hand-tinted look. An easy way to create such a look is to take the following steps:

1. Create your black-and-white file using the Channel Mixer, as described in the preceding section.

2. Reduce the opacity of the adjustment layer to achieve the desired look, using the Opacity slider in the Layers palette (see Figure 8.7). The final opacity is a matter of individual preference.

Figure 8.7 By reducing the opacity of the Channel Mixer adjustment layer, you can create a hand-tinted look. (Photo by Ellen Anon)

3. If you wish to change the hue of the colors, add a Hue/Saturation adjustment layer and adjust the Hue slider to taste. The Hue/Saturation adjustment layer changes the color of the entire image, albeit with reduced saturation due to the Channel Mixer layer.

4. If you wish to change the color of only part of your image and leave the remainder with the look created in step 3, add another Hue/Saturation layer and create a layer mask so that only the areas of the mask corresponding to the areas you wish to change are white and the rest of the mask is black. Adjust the Hue slider to taste.

An alternate approach to adding color to a black and white image is to create a Stamp Visible layer after using the Channel Mixer. Set the Brush tool to Color mode in the Tool Options Bar and select the desired color in the Color Picker. Reduce the opacity of the brush to subdue the colors. Paint each area as appropriate.

Sepia-toned images have an aged look that is also quite popular and is easy to create. It's another approach to colorizing a monochromatic image. To create a sepia-toned image, take these steps:

1. After you have converted your image to black-and-white, open a new Hue/Saturation adjustment layer.

2. Check the Colorize box. Notice that the Hue and Saturation sliders change their default positions, and when you adjust the Hue slider, you're adding an overall tint to your image.

3. For a sepia tone, we use a Hue setting of 30–40, along with a Saturation setting of 17–25. These numbers are guidelines; you'll choose the precise numbers that work best for your taste (see Figure 8.8).

Figure 8.8 Checking the Colorize box in the Hue/Saturation adjustment layer makes it easy to create a sepia tone. (Photo by Ellen Anon.)

Try It! Open the image called BlackAndWhite on the accompanying CD, or one of your own color images. Try converting it to black-and-white using the Color channel. Experiment with restoring color in part of it or giving it a hand-tinted look.

Filters

Photoshop includes a huge array of filters that make it easy to distort your picture in all sorts of ways. It's beyond the scope of this book to cover them all, but we'll describe a few that we find useful. However, the best way to get familiar with filters is to open an image and begin experimenting.

Before you apply any filter, it's a good idea to make a copy of the layer you wish to affect. That way you can reduce the effect later by adjusting the opacity of the layer, or you can add a layer mask to apply the filter to specific parts of the layer only.

Not all filters work on 16-bit images; some require 8-bit mode. If necessary, you may have to convert to 8-bit mode by choosing Image > Mode > 8 Bit. The blur and sharpen filters work on 32-bit images as well as on 16- and 8-bit files.

Many of the filters take considerable time to process. If you are going to experiment with different effects, a useful trick is to duplicate your image by choosing Image > Duplicate and significantly reduce the size of the duplicate file. Then experiment with the filters on the smaller file. When you have established a combination of filters and settings that you are satisfied with, apply the same combination to your original file.

Blurs

There is an impressively long list of blurs in Photoshop CS2, but we'll cover only a few of them that are particularly applicable to nature photographs. We find that Gaussian Blurs, Smart Blurs, and occasionally Lens Blurs are the main ones we use. You may wish to explore Motion and Zoom Blurs as well.

Gaussian Blurs

Gaussian blurs produce a hazy effect and blur the image by an adjustable amount. They're quite useful when you want to blur a section of your image. However it's important to remember that if you make a selection of the area you wish to blur, a Gaussian blur considers that selection a general guideline, but not an absolute mandate, for the boundaries of the blur. This transition area between blurred and not blurred sections is more apparent the more blur you apply. At times it can create a glow around your subject, as it does in the photo in Figure 8.9.

To apply a Gaussian Blur, take the following steps

1. Make a copy of your Background layer.

2. You may choose to first select the area to apply the blur to using any of the selection tools, or you may prefer to rely completely on a layer mask.

3. Apply the blur to the copy layer, if you have made a selection first, by choosing Filter > Blur > Gaussian Blur. If you prefer to rely on a layer mask, it will be easier to apply the blur to the Background layer and then add a layer mask to the background copy layer that will be the sharp layer. You will be using the layer mask to reveal blur wherever desired.

4. Using the preview as a guide, set the radius to determine how much blur you want.

5. Add a layer mask, if desired, by clicking the Add Layer Mask icon at the bottom of the Layers palette to further hide or reveal the blur effect.

Lens Blur

The Lens Blur filter mimics the appearance of a reduced depth of field so that your subject remains in focus while the background fades away. With this filter, you specify part of the image as your subject that you want to remain in sharp focus and then set it to progressively blur other areas. You can also control the creation and appearance of specular highlights.

Note: Although the Lens Blur filter can be helpful at times, it's still more efficient to use the correct aperture setting in the field.

1. Duplicate the Background layer by dragging it to the Create A New Layer icon in the Layers palette.

The key to the Lens Blur filter is creating a *depth map*. Don't let the name scare you. This is where you define what parts of the image you want sharp and what parts to blur, as well as how much blur you want to add. The depth map is essentially a layer mask.

There are two ways to create a depth map; one way is to use an alpha channel and the other is to use a selection. The easiest way, and one that works well with scenics, is to create it from an alpha channel. Figure 8.10 shows an image in which the Lens Blur filter is being used to blur the trees in the background. An alpha channel with a gradient was created to tell the filter which parts of the image to keep sharp and which parts to blur.

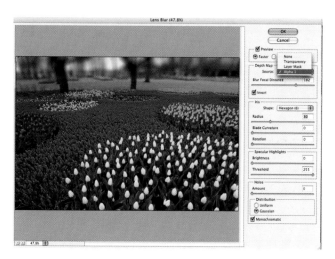

Figure 8.10

The Lens Blur filter was used to blur the trees in the background. The depth map was based on a gradient on an alpha channel. (Photo by Ellen Anon.)

2. To create a depth map based on a selection, skip to step 3. To create a depth map using an alpha channel, follow these steps:

   a. Open the Channels palette and create a new alpha channel by clicking the Create New Channel icon ▣ . Your preview becomes entirely black.

   b. Select the Gradient tool ▣ from the Tools palette. The gradient is used to define a gradual transition from black to white so that the blur tapers off gradually.

   c. On the Options bar, open the Gradient Picker (click the arrow next to the first field) and then click the third option in the drop-down panel (see Figure 8.11). This produces a gradient from the black to white. Set the gradient type to Linear by clicking the first icon to the right of the Gradient Picker in the Options bar.

Figure 8.11

Choose the black-to-white gradient to use as the basis of your depth map.

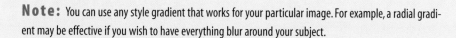

Note: You can use any style gradient that works for your particular image. For example, a radial gradient may be effective if you wish to have everything blur around your subject.

d. After you apply the blur, *wherever the gradient is black, the image will be sharp; where the gradient is white, the image will be blurred.* So if you begin near the bottom of your image and drag the gradient towards the top; the blur affects the top of your image but not the bottom. Note that you can create this gradient anywhere in your image or invert it if desired. Later—in the Lens Blur Filter dialog—you can also refine where it begins.

e. Your alpha channel is now ready, containing the gradient that determines where the blur is strongest and weakest. Click the RGB channel and then return to the Background copy layer in the Layers palette. *Continue on with step 4.*

3. An alternate approach to creating the depth map is to create a selection first and use this selection as the basis for the depth map. This approach is frequently useful with a discrete subject such as an animal or bird rather than a scenic one:

a. Create a selection using any of the selection methods to define the area you want to blur.

b. Save the selection by choosing Select > Save Selection. Do *not* feather the selection.

c. In the Save Selection dialog (shown in Figure 8.12), do the following:

- Leave the channel set to New.

- Enter a name that will allow you to easily recognize your selection. In this example we used "whitepeacock."

- Under Operation leave New Channel selected

- Once you've done this, click OK.

Figure 8.12
Save your selection with an easily recognizable name as a new channel.

d. Deselect the selection by choosing Select > Deselect.

e. To feather the selection, go to the Channels palette and click the channel you saved, to make it visible. It appears as a black-and-white version of your image.

f. Choose Blur > Gaussian Blur and, using your mask as a preview, determine how soft the edge of the mask should be.

g. Click the RGB channel and return to your Background copy. Proceed as follows.

4. Now, regardless of how you created your blur depth map, choose Filter > Blur > Lens Blur.

5. At the right of the Lens Blur dialog, under Depth Map, set the Source for the depth map to Alpha Channel 1 (shown in Figure 8.13) or to the selection, depending on which method you have followed.

Figure 8.13

Choose the alpha channel to use as the basis for your depth map (if you created a depth map using a gradient on an alpha channel) or the name of the selection (if you made a selection to serve as the basis of the map).

6. Set the preview to Faster initially to generate previews to help you select your settings. Then change it to More Accurate when you have made your final choices to preview the effect.

7. The Blur Focal Distance slider allows you to fine-tune where the blur begins. (It's similar to setting your camera at a certain focal distance.) To use it, click the part of the image you want to remain sharp. Photoshop sets the Blur Focal Distance automatically for you.

8. Drag the Radius slider to define how much blur to add, checking the preview (see Figure 8.14).

Figure 8.14

Preview the amount and placement of the blur. Note that this image uses a saved selection in the alpha channel as the basis of the depth map. (Photo by Ellen Anon.)

9. Once you've set your Source and Blur Focal Distance, adjust the other options to get the look you want, using the preview to see how the settings interact:

- The Iris settings allow you to specify the shape and size of specular highlights. Some readers will appreciate the fine control this offers, while others may prefer to use the default settings. If your image doesn't have any specular highlights, then don't worry about setting the Iris values.

- The Specular Highlights settings enable you to determine which values should be used as specular highlights The Brightness setting allows you to specify how bright to make the specular highlights, while the Threshold setting specifies which values are to be used as specular highlights. (You can choose from 0 to 255.) True specular highlights should have a value of 255, but you may want to create specular highlights by using a slightly lower setting. Many images have no specular highlights.

- Some people choose to add some noise to simulate the appearance of film grain. If you choose to add noise, check the box to make it monochromatic. (Adding color noise will look like digital noise…which we try to eliminate!) Usually the Gaussian distribution appears more natural than uniform.

10. When you are satisfied with your settings, click OK to perform the blur.

11. If you find that you blurred areas you didn't intend to, you can modify them by adding a layer mask to your blurred image layer. Make sure to use as soft a brush as possible on the layer mask.

Smart Blur

The Smart Blur filter (Filter > Blur > Smart Blur) blurs pixels throughout the entire image based on how similar or dissimilar they are and the settings you specify. Of course, you can use a Smart Blur filter in conjunction with a layer mask to apply the blur only to specific portions of your image. Smart Blur offers several options, as shown in Figure 8.15:

Figure 8.15
The Smart Blur filters offer several controls, including radius, threshold, and mode, which determine not only the strength of the blur but also the appearance.

- The Radius setting refers to how large an area Photoshop checks for dissimilar pixels. The larger the area, the more chance of finding dissimilar pixels and so the more likely blur will be applied.

- The Threshold value refers to how different two pixels must be before Photoshop recognizes them as different enough to blur. The lower the value, the more blur that will be applied.

- Quality refers to the quality of the preview. Initially, to save time you may prefer to use the Low setting and change it to High when you are close to your desired values.

  Smart Blur also offers three modes, which are illustrated in Figure 8.16:

- In Normal mode the blur is applied to the entire selection and works as anticipated. In some images it can create a painterly effect, while in Edge Only or

Overlay Edge, you can get some very creative outlined effects.

- Edge Only applies black and white edges and may convert your entire image to a maze of black and white lines and shapes. This can be useful if you want to create an outlined version of your image.

- Overlay Edge retains the general colors of your image but applies white lines and shapes to edges where significant contrast occurs.

Normal mode

Overlay Edge mode with Filter reduced to about 25%

Edge Only mode with Filter faded to 45%

Figure 8.16

Depending on the mode and settings used in Smart Blur, you can create a gentle blur or some unusual painterly effects. (Photo by Ellen Anon.)

The effects generated using the three mode settings are quite different and fun to explore. We find it helpful to use them in conjunction with reduced opacity of the Background copy layer to obtain unique versions of our images.

> **Note:** To reduce the effect of any filter immediately after applying it, choose Edit > Fade and reduce the effect by adjusting the slider. This option only exists immediately after applying the filter.

The Liquify Filter

The Liquify filter can be a lot of fun. It's a lot like finger painting with the pixels but with a lot more control and much cleaner hands! You can stretch, push, pull, pucker, or bloat any area to create subtle or dramatic distortions. This is one of Ellen's favorite filters to use to create artistic effects with flowers (see Figure 8.17).

Liquify can be used with 16-bit or 8-bit images, but be aware that unless you have a fast computer with a lot of memory, processing the Liquify effects may be slow. For that reason, you may wish to convert a copy of your image to 8-bit and use the filter on that version. Once you have established effective settings for your image, you can save them and then apply them to a 16-bit version if you prefer. Don't forget to work on a copy of your Background layer, both for safety and so you can apply a layer mask or reduce the opacity of the layer.

Perhaps more than any other filter in Photoshop, this is one you have to play with to use effectively. Let's look at the Liquify dialog box, which you open by choosing Filter > Liquify. There are a variety of tools in the toolbox column on the left, shown in Figure 8.18. Some of these tools apply the distortions, while others, such as the Freeze tool, enable you to apply a quick mask to certain areas to "freeze" the effects. The Hand and Zoom tools work as usual. The primary tool we tend to use is the Warp tool, although it's worth experimenting with the others.

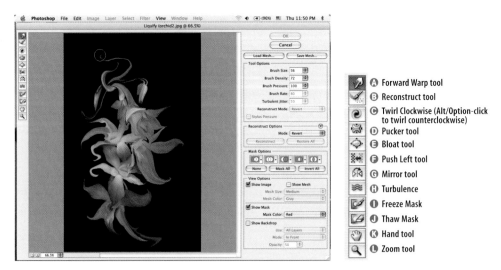

Figure 8.18 The Liquify dialog box offers several tools. (Photo by Ellen Anon.)

On the right side of the Liquify dialog box (shown in Figure 8.19) are options for using the tools:

Figure 8.19

On the right side of the Liquify dialog box are the controls for the various tools.

- Brush Size is as expected: it refers to the size of the brush and can be controlled by the bracket keys on your keyboard or via the setting in the dialog box.

- Brush Density controls how the brush is feathered at the edges. The effect is strongest in the center of the brush and lighter at the edges.

- Brush Pressure controls how quickly the distortions are applied when you drag a tool across your preview image. Using too large a pressure may make it difficult to stop exactly where you want.

- Brush Rate controls how quickly distortions are applied when you use a tool that can be held stationary, such as bloat or twirl.

- Turbulence Jitter sets how tightly the Turbulence tool scrambles the pixels.

- Reconstruction Options allow you, with the Reconstruct tool selected, to specify a mode for the reconstruction, which can either create further distortions or revert to the original image.

When you have achieved the desired effect, if you're working on a full-resolution image, you can simply click OK to apply your work to the picture. If you are using a small file version of your image as we suggested at the start of this section, click Save Mesh. Another dialog box appears in which you can name the effect and specify where to save it (see Figure 8.20).

Figure 8.20

After you are satisfied with the effect, save the mesh to apply to your full-sized file.

Once the mesh is saved, open your full-sized file, choose Filter > Liquify and click Load Mesh. Choose the mesh you just saved and click OK to perform the distortion. If you are feeling adventurous, apply a saved mesh to an unrelated image—sometimes serendipity comes into play and you create something unexpected but wonderful!

Try It! Open the image called Liquify on the accompanying CD, or one of your own images, and see what you can create with it. Be sure to vary the settings and tools to get different effects.

Using the Filter Gallery

Recent versions of Photoshop (CS and newer) contain a filter gallery (Filter > Filter Gallery) rather than just a simple list of individual filters. This gallery enables you to preview the effects of a variety of filters, as well as to preview the effects of combining them and reordering them. This saves a lot of time as you experiment with different effects, but unfortunately, it only works on 8-bit images.

We often find that when using filters, one thing leads to another and pretty soon you may have created something you love but perhaps couldn't have imagined ahead of time. The more you experiment with these filters, the more predictable they will become for you.

The Filter Gallery contains thumbnails that give you an idea of each effect. As shown in Figure 8.21, this dialog box also previews the various effects and settings on your image. You can vary the settings, combine filters, vary the order (which can substantially change their effect), and even repeat filters. The filters are applied in the order you select them, but you can drag the filter name to a different position to reorder them. To select an effect, click the corresponding thumbnail. If you wish to add an additional effect, Alt/Option click each additional filter. Clicking the eyeball icon toggles the visibility of the effect.

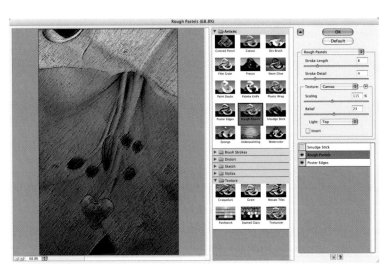

Figure 8.21
The Filter Gallery allows you to preview various combinations of filters and settings.

Before beginning with the Filter Gallery, you should take several preparatory steps:

1. Usually when we experiment with filters, we're using files that have already been optimized. To avoid accidentally mucking up an image you've already put effort into, work on a copy of the master file by choosing Image > Duplicate.

2. Close the original file. This ensures you won't accidentally save changes to your master file such as flattening it.

3. Flatten the image by choosing Layer > Flatten Image.

4. Duplicate the Background layer by dragging it to the Create A New Layer icon at the bottom of the Layers palette. Now you'll be adding your creative effects on a layer so that not only are you not damaging your pixels, you can also later reduce the opacity of the layer or add a layer mask to it to control where the effects are applied.

Some of the filters we frequently try are Poster Edges and Rough Pastels (which are in the Artistic group) and Water Paper (which is in the Sketch group). You will find your own favorites the more you experiment with the filters. However, don't forget to use the filters that are not part of the Filter Gallery as well. They are available from the Filter menu on the main menu bar.

Sometimes the distortion filters can lead to some exciting results, as shown in Figure 8.22. This poppy was distorted using polar remapping, then copied, liquefied, and a bit of the original image returned to complete the effect. Pretty wild, but that's what happens when you let your imagination go along with the filters in Photoshop!

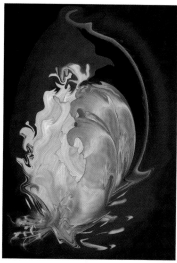

Figure 8.22
This rather boring picture of a poppy was transformed into a fantasy image using a variety of the filters found in Photoshop, along with a little imagination. (Photo by Ellen Anon.)

Additional Filter Effects

There are quite a few software companies that have produced filter effect plug-ins for Photoshop. Many of these can lead to interesting effects as well. Often, you can download a free sample to see if it's something you might want to use.

Michael Sommer, winner of a recent Sybex photo contest, used the ChromaSolarize plug-in from Flaming Pear (www.flamingpear .com, in their Goodies & Freebies section) to develop this dramatic image he calls "Fiery Rose." Initially, he worked with Curves to add contrast to his image and selectively lighten and darken portions of it. He applied the filter and then followed up by burning, dodging, and selectively sharpening the image to create the desired effect.

Try It! Open the image called FilterGallery on the accompanying CD, or one of your own images, and experiment with a variety of filters. Try different combinations and orders of filters while varying the settings.

Digital Montages

Combining shots, or creating "slide sandwiches," has been a popular film technique for years. Traditionally, one slide had to be overexposed by about two stops and the other by a single stop to yield an acceptable exposure. At best, it's an approach that requires a lot of trial and error and bracketing.

André Gallant's slide sandwiches are among the most impressive and inspiring. He creates several types of montages, including surreal, mirror, and cross montages, which he describes in his book *Dreamscapes*.

It's not only possible to emulate these same effects in Photoshop, it's actually easier to do so! One reason is that we have the flexibility to alter exposures as needed. Another reason is that if you didn't think of using a particular image as part of a montage while you were in the field, it doesn't matter. You can make several versions of the same file in Photoshop. And in Photoshop, you can go further and combine numerous images in a variety of ways.

Before you begin to make your montages, remove any dust in your images. After all, double the dust means double the cleanup required later! Final exposure and color changes are usually best made after creating the montage.

Mirror Montages in Photoshop
by André Gallant

Photo courtesy André Gallant

Whether working with transparency film or using Photoshop, I'm fascinated by photo montages. *Dreamscapes*, a book I wrote and illustrated on the subject, is a result of my obsession. Although mirror montages are not for everyone, I particularly like their symmetry and the intricate designs they create. Your imagination is your only boundary.

The mirror montages illustrated here were created in Photoshop using one of the two identical slides that render a similar result on film. Here is how I achieve this:

1. First, I choose File > New and produce a file the same size as the final mirror montage (for example, a width of 12" and height of 8" for a full-frame 35mm horizontal image). This is where I'll be inputting the two images that will create the mirror montage.

2. I scan my slide (or negative) and then crop the image to 8"×12".

3. I then sharpen, adjust the levels, and brighten the image if it's dark in tone.

Photo courtesy André Gallant

4. I drag the image to the new file.

5. I then go back to the original scan (still on my desktop) and choose Image > Rotate Canvas > Flip Canvas Horizontal ().

6. I drag the reversed image over the original one in the new file.

7. In the Layers palette blending mode list, I choose Multiply. This merges the images and creates the mirror montage.

8. The final photograph often needs to be brightened. You can do so by brightening the images individually, or you can choose Layer > Flatten Image, and then brighten your final creation.

There are other combinations to mirror montages. You can also invert one image over the other (rotate canvas 180 degrees), or you can reverse and invert an image over the other (flip canvas vertically). There is a substantial difference in the possible combinations.

© André Gallant, www.andregallant.com

Blending Modes

Before proceeding with ways to combine images, you need to have some understanding of blending modes.

Way back in Chapter 4, "First Steps," you learned about layers. Recall that in many ways, pixel layers in Normal blending mode—which is what we've been using—act like prints. Whatever is on top is what you see. If you "cut a hole" in the top layer by using a layer mask to partially hide that layer, you see what's underneath. If you reduce the opacity of the top pixel layer, you see some of the top layer and some of the layer beneath it. In Normal mode, the layers blend together in an intuitive way.

However, Photoshop at its core is a series of mathematical algorithms, and there can be (and are) other instructions (algorithms) for how to blend two layers. These are called *blending modes*. Photoshop CS and CS2 have 23 blending modes. Don't panic! The good news is that you don't have to memorize what each one does. Instead, you can simply scroll through the drop-down list in the Layers palette (see Figure 8.23). You'll soon realize that the most useful blending modes for photographers are

- Normal
- Multiply
- Screen
- Overlay
- Soft Light
- Difference
- Luminosity

But sometimes, one of the other modes will create magic for you, so don't hesitate to try them all.

Figure 8.23

Photoshop CS and CS2 offer 23 different blending modes to combine layers.

Each blending mode is a different set of instructions for how to combine two layers. For those of you who are more intuitive, don't worry about fully grasping each algorithm. Feel free to skip ahead and experiment with actually using the blending modes. For those of you who are more analytical, we're providing this explanation.

The different blending modes are grouped together in the drop-down list according to those with somewhat similar functions:

Normal   Every pixel in the top active layer is displayed normally, regardless of the colors of the underlying layer.

Dissolve   If the active top layer is 100 percent opaque with hard edges, this mode has no effect. It affects feathered edges only and layers using reduced opacity. Instead of giving a translucent appearance with reduced opacity settings, it simply turns some pixels on and others off.

Darken   This mode uses pixels from the top layer only if they are darker than those in the layer below. However, it compares the pixels on a channel-by-channel basis and may use channels from both layers for any particular pixel.

Multiply   This provides an effect similar to holding two slides together and looking through them.

Color Burn and Linear Burn   Both of these blending modes use colors in the active layer to reduce brightness, often resulting in extreme color changes with darkened edges.

Lighten   This is the opposite of Darken. Photoshop uses the pixels in the active layer only if they are lighter than those in the layer below. Again, lightness is determined on a channel-by-channel basis in each layer.

Screen   This is the opposite of Multiply, and lightens the image as if you had overexposed it.

Color Dodge and Linear Dodge   Both of these use colors to increase brightness. Light colors have the greatest effect and can simulate intensely bright effects.

Overlay, Soft Light, and Hard Light   These are three of the blending modes that darken the dark colors and lighten the light colors. Note that Overlay and Soft Light can be used for nondestructive dodge and burn techniques.

> **Overlay**   Multiplies or screens the colors depending on the background color. The base color is mixed with the blend color to reflect the lightness or darkness of the original color.

> **Soft Light**   Works similarly but gives an effect similar to shining a diffused spotlight on the image.

> **Hard Light**   Also multiplies or screens the colors depending on the base color, but the effect is more similar to shining a harsh spotlight on the image.

Vivid Light and Linear Light   These are useful for increasing contrast. Vivid Light is akin to combining Color Dodge and Color Burn; Linear Light gives an effect similar to combining Linear Dodge and Linear Burn.

Pin Light   This is an extreme effect that keeps only the darkest blacks and lightest whites, and makes everything else invisible.

Hard Mix   Hard mix produces a posterized image consisting of up to eight colors, including red, green, blue, cyan, magenta, yellow, black, and white. The blend color is a product of the base color and the luminosity of the blend layer. It can be used to sharpen by blending a blurred layer using Hard Mix and then decreasing the Fill to about 10 percent or less.

Difference and Exclusion   These modes either subtract the colors of the top active layer from the underlying layer or vice versa, according to which layer has the greatest brightness value. Blending with whites inverts the base colors, while black produces no change. Exclusion is slightly lower in contrast than the Difference mode. These modes can lead to striking creative effects when combining two images.

Hue   This mode creates a blend color with the luminance and saturation of the base color and the hue of the blend color.

Saturation   Saturation retains the values from the active layer and mixes them with the hue and luminosity values of the underlying layer.

Color   This mode creates a color with the hue and saturation values from the active layer combined with the luminosity values of the underlying layer. This is useful if you want to replace the color in part of your image and have it maintain the expected variations in tonal value.

Luminosity   This final blending mode retains the lightness values from the active layer and mixes them with the hue and saturation values from the underlying layer. This can be useful when applying Curves or Unsharp Mask to avoid unexpected color shifts.

Figure 8.24 shows the results when a Background layer of an image is copied and flipped horizontally upon itself in six different blending modes. Note that for this image, Exclusion and Hue provided interesting results, so they were included in this illustration.

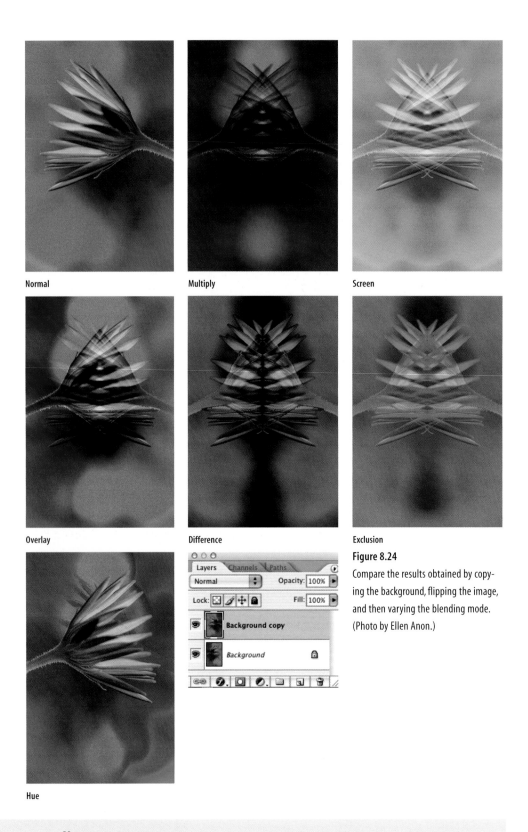

Normal

Multiply

Screen

Overlay

Difference

Exclusion

Hue

Figure 8.24

Compare the results obtained by copying the background, flipping the image, and then varying the blending mode. (Photo by Ellen Anon.)

Note: To preview the effects of the various blending modes, scroll through them by highlighting the top pixel layer and clicking Shift++ (plus) or Shift+- (minus).

Surreal Montages

A very common effect photographers seek is a dreamy blur. You've seen it in many artistic photos: a kind of glow or soft focus around the subject that I call a *surreal montage* (see an example in Figure 8.25). Even the most mundane subjects can become evocative when done in this way.

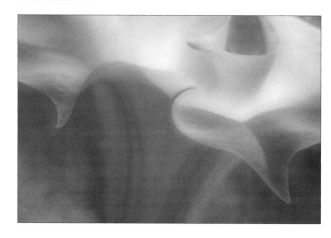

Figure 8.25
Surreal montages seem to have an ethereal glow around them that makes them quite evocative. (Photo by Ellen Anon.)

Note: The surreal montage in Figure 8.25 would not be possible using film because of the amount of white and nearly white in the image.

The traditional way to capture a surreal dream montage is to take two shots with your camera on a tripod, not moving it between shots. Take one image two stops overexposed at f22 or comparable, and sharply focused, and the other one stop overexposed with a wide open aperture and blurred. You want to defocus in the direction that makes the blur get larger than the subject rather than smaller, because the blurred version is going to provide the glow around your subject. The first image is going to provide the detail.

When done with a film camera, you couldn't use a wide angle lens because the blur would be insufficient. You were also limited to subjects that were close to middle toned. If you wanted to do a surreal montage of a light subject, it was often impossible because you would lose all detail in the overexposed versions.

Photoshop enables you to go beyond these restrictions and create surreal montages using any lens, since you can use a Gaussian blur to blur the image as much as needed. Also, you can capture light images while retaining detail and adjust the exposure after the fact as necessary.

If you know you want to make a surreal montage, go ahead and capture two versions of the image as described in the preceding paragraphs. However, if it wasn't until editing your pictures that you realized an image would be great as a surreal montage, convert the same image twice, making one considerably lighter than the other. You can try plus two and plus one exposures in the raw converter, but we usually try to avoid clipping any data, so adjust the exposures accordingly. You can always lighten the exposure of the composite using Levels or Curves.

To create the surreal montage, take the following steps:

1. Open your two images, as shown in Figure 8.26.

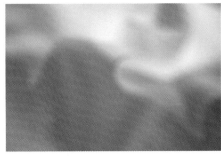

Figure 8.26 Open a light, but detailed, image as well as a slightly darker, but blurred, version of the same image. (Photo by Ellen Anon.)

2. Select the Move tool, and while holding down the Shift key, drag the darker, blurred image on top of the lighter one.

3. If the blurred one is not as blurred as you would like, select that layer and then choose Filter > Blur > Gaussian Blur. The blur should be sufficient to allow you to retain the general shape of the main objects but remove all detail. If you are working from an in-focus original, you may need a blur ranging from 15 to 40, depending on the amount of detail in the original image.

4. Change the blending mode of this layer (in the Layers palette) to Multiply.

5. Adjust the overall exposure as needed with a Curves or Levels adjustment layer.

Cross and Flip Montages

Another approach to combining images is to take the same image and combine it with a second identical shot that is rotated 90 degrees or flipped 180 degrees; André Gallant calls these *mirror montages*. This can yield some amazing abstract designs. One of the keys is to experiment with the different blending modes. Often, Multiply, Overlay, Difference, Exclusion, Luminosity, or Color yield some interesting results.

Usually, you begin with well-exposed images, and lighten the montage as needed after you combine the layers. Depending on the choice of blending mode, you may or may not need to adjust the exposure.

To create mirror or flip montages, take these steps:

1. Open an image and duplicate the Background layer by dragging it to the Create A New Layer icon.

2. Ctrl/⌘+click the icon for the Background Copy layer to select it.

3. Choose Edit > Transform > Rotate and select either 90 degrees in either direction, or flip horizontal or vertical. The choice depends upon the particular image and what you think might look good.

4. Scroll through the different blending modes to see what looks good. Sometimes nothing works, and sometimes you hit a winner, as you can see in Figure 8.27.

Figure 8.27 Flipping this image horizontally and selecting the Difference blending mode resulted in a dramatic abstract design. (Photo by Ellen Anon.)

5. If you have elected to rotate your image 90 degrees, the chances are you will want to crop and use the center square formed by the overlap of the two images.

6. Sometimes you can repeat the process and copy the montage, rotate, or flip it and blend it to create a virtual kaleidoscope, as shown in Figure 8.28.

Figure 8.28
Duplicating the montage, flipping it, and blending it upon itself resulted in a kaleidoscope. (Photo by Ellen Anon.)

Try It! Open the image called Flip on the accompanying CD, or one of your own. Duplicate it and then rotate or flip it to create various effects. Be sure to scroll through the blending modes to see how they affect the montage.

Mirror Images

Mirror images are very similar to flip montages, except that the two images are side by side rather than on top of each other. This creates an obvious dramatic symmetry that can be quite compelling. Natural phenomena that have strong design components, such as sand dunes, rock formations, waves, and even trees, lend themselves to this approach. Remember that the center of your image is formed by what is on the edges of your file, so your subject may need to be placed toward the edges of the original rather than your typical composition.

To create a mirror montage, take the following steps:

1. Open your file (see Figure 8.29) and duplicate it by choosing Image > Duplicate. This is easier for this technique than simply copying the Background layer, as you did earlier.

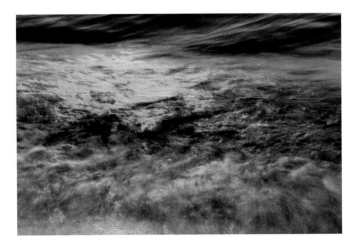

Figure 8.29
Open a file you think will work as a mirror. (Photo by Ellen Anon.)

2. Select your original file and choose Image > Canvas Size to determine the size of your image.

3. If you are going to create a horizontal montage, double the width of the canvas but leave the height alone (see Figure 8.30). Anchor the original to the right or left as desired by clicking the anchor arrow. (If you are creating a vertical montage, then double the height and leave the width alone. Anchor the image at the top or bottom as desired.) Click OK.

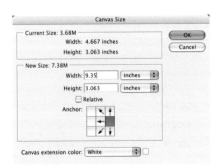

Figure 8.30
Double the canvas size in width if you are creating a horizontal mirror or double it in height if you are creating a vertical mirror.

4. Select the copy of the image and drag it onto the original using the Move tool.

5. Ctrl/⌘+click the thumbnail icon for the Background copy layer, and choose Edit > Transform > Flip Horizontal (or Vertical).

6. Use the Move tool to align the flipped layer next to the original.

7. When you get close, it's easier to use the arrow keys on your keyboard to nudge the layer into place.

Using this technique creates symmetry that sometimes creates what appears to be odd creatures or faces (see Figure 8.31). These often add to the intrigue of images created this way.

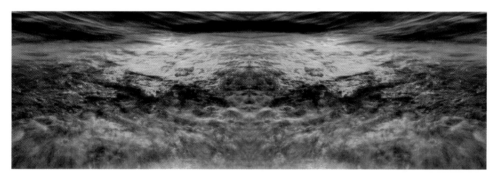

Figure 8.31 The symmetry of mirror montages often creates what appears to be creatures in unexpected places. (Photo by Ellen Anon.)

Multiple Subject Montages

So far, we've been describing a variety of ways to combine two versions of the same image, but it's also possible to combine two different images. One approach to combining two different images to have one image provide texture and to have the other provide the subject matter. You can stack one on top of the other, rotate, or flip one as desired. And of course, the effect is going to vary dramatically depending on the way you combine the two images. You could simply reduce the opacity of the top image and leave it in Normal blending mode, or you could choose any of the other blending modes.

Note: Shots of wood, tree bark, textured glass, frost, rocks, snow, rain, and lots more can be used as texture shots.

Figure 8.32 shows a flower image and a shot of the rain on the greenhouse wall. The greenhouse wall file was dragged on top of the flower using the Move tool. Scrolling through the blending modes, the image jumped to life in the Difference mode. However, the flower was a little too unrecognizable, so we added a layer mask to the second layer and used it to reveal the center of the original flower in the layer below.

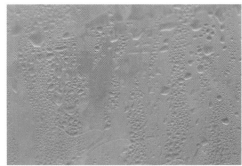

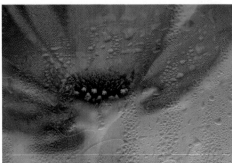

Figure 8.32
Combining two very different shots in the Difference mode led to this striking image. (Photo by Ellen Anon.)

There are no simple rules and absolutes to follow when creating montages. You are the artist, and you have to decide what works and what doesn't. It's your chance to apply all the knowledge you've gained in the previous chapters!

For example, you could add texture to a surreal montage created from the steps in an earlier section:

1. Open two versions of an image that you want to use to create a surreal montage and follow the steps described earlier. We'll use the surreal montage shown in Figure 8.33.

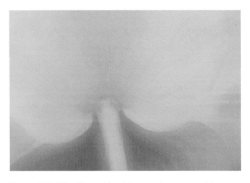

Figure 8.33 We will combine this surreal montage with a texture shot of wood siding. (Photo by Ellen Anon.)

2. Open a shot that you want to use as texture.

3. Drag the texture shot on top of the other layers using the Move tool.

4. Reduce the opacity of this layer in the Layers palette so that it provides a subtle, but not overpowering, texture. Often, you may be in the range of 10 percent to 20 percent opacity, but of course, this varies depending upon the particular images you're using.

The final result (see Figure 8.34) should be subtly different than a straight shot, and it is this unexpected texture that captures your viewer's attention.

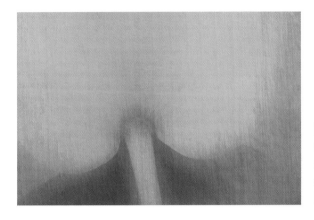

Figure 8.34
Combining a texture with a surreal montage can give a subtle soft feel to the image. (Photo by Ellen Anon.)

On occasion, we have combined all of the techniques discussed so far into one image. Figure 8.35 is the result of two totally different images of sand dunes montaged together, then mirrored horizontally. Note that unlike in the previous examples, two different images were combined equally as the foundation for the montage. That entire montage was then duplicated and mirrored vertically, and the image was cropped.

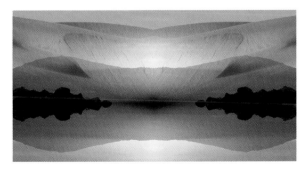

Figure 8.35
Almost all the techniques described so far in this section were combined to create this dramatic image. (Photo by Ellen Anon.)

The ways to combine images in Photoshop is infinite. The only limit is your imagination!

Digital Multiple Exposures

Ever since Ellen was exposed to some of Freeman Patterson's creative multiple exposures, she decided there *had* to be a way to create the same effect digitally. Although some methods were available on the Internet, none worked reliably and well. It took some time and experimentation, but at last she figured out how to create multiple exposures of as many images as desired in Photoshop.

For those not familiar with Freeman's techniques, he uses film and takes multiple images (9, 16, or 25) slightly moving his camera between shots. Sometimes he moves the camera in a vertical or horizontal direction, depending on what would be a natural movement for the subject. Sometimes he zooms the camera between shots, and at other times he combines zooming the camera with rotating it slightly between shots. The results are artistic, soft-abstract renditions of familiar subjects (see Figure 8.36).

Figure 8.36
Multiple exposures can render familiar subjects in pleasing artistic abstract ways. (Photo by Ellen Anon.)

Note: To learn more about the in-camera and artistic techniques for taking multiple exposures, see *Photo Impressionism* by Freeman Patterson and André Gallant (Key Porter Books Limited, 2002).

To use a digital camera to create multiple exposures, you have to decide whether to capture the images in RAW or JPEG. Ellen usually takes advantage of the Canon 1DsMKII's ability to capture both simultaneously. Although it is tempting to use RAW, particularly since CS2 enables you to select all the images that will be used in the composite at once and synchronize the settings in the raw converter (described in Chapter 4), there is a potential problem. The issue is memory. For example, with a 1DsMKII camera, each 16-bit converted file is roughly 95 megabytes. If you have 9 or 10 images to combine, your multiple exposure file is going to be close to one gigabyte in size before you do anything else to it. You're going to need a lot of RAM and hard drive space to deal with files that large. If you don't have enough memory, you can either use the JPEG versions of the files, or convert the raw files to JPEGs.

The key to combining multiple images within Photoshop is as follows:

1. Open the first image. If you are combining two images, the first should be at 100 percent opacity.

2. Open the second image.

3. Shift+drag the second image on top of the first (hold the Shift key while clicking the second image and drag it on top of the first image, still holding the Shift key). Using the Shift key automatically centers the new image on top of the original.

4. Reduce the opacity of the second image to 50 percent.

5. If you have a third image to add, drag it on top of the others, but reduce its opacity to 34 percent.

6. For a fourth layer, reduce the opacity to 25 percent; a fifth layer is 20 percent, a sixth layer is 17 percent, a seventh layer is 15 percent, an eighth layer is 13 percent, and a ninth or tenth layer is 10 percent (see Figure 8.37).

Figure 8.37
Reduce the opacity of each layer according to how many layers you are combining to create abstract expressive images.

7. Leave the blending mode for these layers set to Normal except for the final layer, which you may want to set at Overlay or Soft Light to add a little punch to the image.

8. You can adjust the exposure using a Levels or Curves adjustment layer, and you can adjust the color using any of the color adjustment layers.

The ability to create digital multiple exposures opens up entire worlds of creativity. The only downside is the need for a lot of memory, both Compact Flash card space as well as computer memory. Often it's a good idea when shooting a multiple exposure to do it more than once; subtle differences in the amount you moved the camera can make a huge difference in the success of the image.

The Evolution of an Image

To give you an idea of the mental process as well as the specific technique that can be followed when attempting to become more expressive with an image, here are the various steps that I (Ellen speaking here) took with this rather unimpressive photo (Figure 8.38). Note that I could have decided to stop with any of the versions of this photo.

Figure 8.38
This is the original image, which at best was documentary. (Photo by Ellen Anon.)

1. I made a copy of the Background layer by dragging it to the Create A New Layer icon. That way, when I applied a filter, I could later modify the strength of the filter effect by changing the opacity of the layer. I could also use a layer mask if I wished to limit the areas affected by the filter.

2. I chose Filter > Stylize > Find Edges. Often this effect leads to a rather pale, subtly colored, outlined version of the image that needs to be boosted by a Levels, Curves, or Hue/Saturation adjustment layer. In this case, I reduced the opacity of the filtered layer to 72 percent to slightly decrease the effect and increase the color. This led to the colored-pencil look of Figure 8.39.

Figure 8.39
Applying the Find Edges filter, followed by exposure and color boosts, led to this version of the picture. (Photo by Ellen Anon.)

3. Next, I duplicated the Background copy (the filtered version) and dragged that layer to the top of the stack. I increased the opacity of the layer to nearly 100 percent (it was at 72 percent since that was the opacity of the layer that was copied). Then, I scrolled through the various blending modes and settled on Difference mode. This dramatically changed the picture, as you can see in Figure 8.40.

Figure 8.40
Duplicating the filtered layer and changing the blending mode to Difference made a dramatic change in the image. (Photo by Ellen Anon.)

4. Although I liked the effect I had achieved, I wanted another version of it that might seem a little more natural. This time I made a Stamp Visible layer (a layer that contains all the information in all the visible layers below it). To do this, I held the Alt/Option key, while clicking Layer > Merge Visible.

 Note: When making a Stamp Visible layer, be sure to continue holding the Alt/Option key until you see the thumbnail icon for the new layer appear with all the information in it.

5. Again I experimented with the various blending modes and chose the Hue mode. This resulted in more natural colors that some may prefer (Figure 8.41).

Figure 8.41
By creating a Stamp Visible layer and changing its blending mode to Hue, the image was transformed to more natural-looking colors. (Photo by Ellen Anon.)

6. I created a Hue/Saturation adjustment layer and wondered what would happen if I checked the Colorize box. Adjusting the Hue slider slightly resulted in a golden image reminding me of a tapestry. I used the layer mask to return the color to just one of the flowers and liked the result (see Figure 8.42).

 Note: The key to any creative endeavor is to wonder "what if" and then find out.

Figure 8.42
Experimenting with checking the Colorize box in a Hue/Saturation adjustment layer turned the image golden, and using the layer mask to reveal the color in one flower completed the image. (Photo by Ellen Anon.)

This chapter has only touched the tip of the iceberg in terms of what you can do with your images. Hopefully, you'll use these ideas as a starting point to create imaginative versions of some of your own photographs.

Output

Photographers are often inspired by the desire to share their view of nature's beauty, whatever their motivation may be. While we all love to create beautiful photographic images, more often than not, what we really want to do is produce beautiful output so we can share the images with others. In this chapter, we'll take a look at how to produce the best prints possible, and how to create a web gallery to share your images with an even broader audience.

9

Chapter Contents
Output Workflow
Printing Your Images
Creating a Web Gallery

Output Workflow

The output workflow actually starts very early in the process of optimizing your photographic images in Photoshop. Of course, we could go so far as to say that every optimization step is part of the output workflow, since you're generally trying to make the image look its best in order to produce the best output. However, what we're referring to here is saving the image. Although we tend to talk about saving the image near the end of the workflow, in actual practice you should be saving from early in the workflow. As a general rule, every time you perform any significant optimization step on your image, you should resave so you won't lose any changes should something go wrong.

The idea is to save a master image (as well as archiving your original capture) that contains all of the image and adjustment layers in a single file, which becomes your master image to be used as the basis for all future output (see Figure 9.1). After you've saved the final result safely, you're ready to move on to actually preparing that image for output.

Figure 9.1
Your master image file should contain all of the image and adjustment layers used to create the optimal output. (Photo by Tim Grey.)

Try It! To get a feel for the best output workflow, open the image PrintWorkflow.psd on the accompanying CD and follow the steps in the next few sections to prepare that image for an 8"×10" print.

Duplicating the Image

By this time, you can well imagine how important your master image is. As you'll see in the next few sections, the process of preparing your image for output results in changes to the number of pixels in your image as well as to the actual color and tonal values for those images. Therefore, we recommend using a working copy of your image while preparing it for output. This ensures that the original master image remains safely saved without risking a permanent loss of pixels.

As a result, the first step in the output workflow is to create a duplicate copy of the image by choosing Image > Duplicate. The Duplicate Image dialog box (shown in Figure 9.2) appears, allowing you to enter a name for the new image document. The name in the text box is simply the name of the document you are duplicating with the word "copy" appended to it. You can enter a different name if you like, which becomes the filename if you save this duplicate image later.

Figure 9.2

The Duplicate Image dialog box allows you to specify a name for the image, as well as to specify whether you want to flatten the image through the Duplicate Merged Layers Only checkbox.

The Duplicate Image dialog box also contains a check box labeled Duplicate Merged Layers Only. This check box is only enabled if the image you're duplicating contains multiple layers. If you check it, the duplicate image is a flattened version of the original image you started from. We recommend checking this box for two main reasons. For one thing, it flattens the image into a single layer, reducing the amount of memory required by the image. (Remember, the master image with all layers intact has already been saved and you're working on a duplicate copy.) This can speed up the process of preparing the image for output and sending the data to the printer. The other reason is that sharpening can only be applied to a single layer, so if you have multiple image layers in the image, this streamlines the sharpening process.

When you have established the desired settings, click OK to actually create the working copy of your image file, and then you can close the original master image.

Resizing

Chances are the native size of your image doesn't match the final output size you're targeting, so you need to resize it. This involves both setting the resolution for the final output and the actual output size. To change the size of the image, choose Image > Image Size, which bring ups the Image Size dialog box (shown in Figure 9.3).

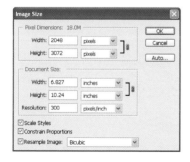

Figure 9.3

The Image Size dialog box allows you to resize your image for the final output.

Although you would normally start at the top of a dialog box and work your way down, in the case of the Image Size dialog box, it makes more sense to start at the bottom and work your way up. At the bottom, be sure the Resample Image check box is checked, which enables Photoshop to resize the image using interpolation, changing the number of pixels within the image. The drop-down list to the right of the Resample Image check box provides options for the algorithm to use for interpolating the data in your image, as shown in Figure 9.4.

Figure 9.4

There are five options to choose from for the interpolation algorithm in the Image Size dialog box, but you generally only use Bicubic or Bicubic Smoother.

Bicubic is an all-purpose option. If you're creating a particularly large enlargement from your original, the Bicubic Smoother option is a good choice, and it can be used any time you're enlarging. Bicubic Sharper is designed to maintain sharpness when reducing the size of an image, but we prefer to control the sharpening ourselves and therefore don't usually use this option.

Note: The other two options—Nearest Neighbor and Bilinear—are not appropriate for producing high-quality photographic output and should not be used.

The Constrain Proportions check box ensures that you maintain the aspect ratio for the image. If you clear this check box, it's possible to stretch the image in one direction or the other. While this isn't a problem when done to a very small degree, it can produce a distorted result if taken too far, and we recommend eliminating the possibility altogether by keeping this check box checked.

The Scale Styles check box determines whether layer styles are scaled when you resize the image or whether layer styles are kept at their same size. This isn't an issue at this point since you have already flattened the image. However, you generally want to scale any layer styles, so if you are resizing an unflattened image, keep this check box checked.

The Resolution box in the Document Size section of the Image Size dialog box determines how the pixels are distributed when the image is output, and plays a role in determining how many pixels are required in the final image. For digital display (monitor and digital projector, for example), this number is actually irrelevant. However, because some applications where you may import your images do indeed look at this number, we recommend setting it to about 96 dpi for those situations. For printing, the best resolution depends on the output method being used, but 300 dpi is a good standard value.

Note: If you're working with film scans, it's particularly important to keep an eye on the Resolution setting. If you've scanned at 4000 dpi, you don't want to resize to a 20"×30" print without changing the resolution to a more appropriate value, or you'll produce an absolutely huge file that takes forever to resize and likely crashes your computer.

The next step is to set the actual output size. For printed images, this should be done in the Document Size section, setting either the Width or the Height. You can change the unit of measure with the drop-down list to the right, and if you have the Constrain Proportions check box checked (as we recommend), then setting the Width or the Height causes the other to be adjusted automatically.

For images that will be displayed digitally on a monitor or digital projector, the size should be adjusted using the Width or Height text boxes in the Pixel Dimensions section. This allows you to set the specific pixel sizing for your intended purpose. For a digital slideshow, for example, you might set these dimensions to fit within the resolution of your digital projector. For a website, you might set them to a standard output size you deem appropriate for your specific site design.

Once you've established the sizing parameters in the Image Size dialog box, click OK, and the image is resized accordingly.

Reducing Noise

Although you could certainly insert steps to reduce noise earlier in your workflow, it often becomes more apparent as you are preparing your image for output. We recommend applying any noise reduction before sharpening to make sure the process of sharpening won't exaggerate the noise, so this is a good time to apply such a correction, if you haven't done so already.

It is best to apply this correction to a separate layer, so start by creating a copy of your background image layer by dragging it to the New Layer button at the bottom of the Layers palette. This ensures that you are preserving the original image data, as well as providing you with the opportunity to mask out any areas of this layer if the noise reduction isn't needed or introduces color problems.

Photoshop CS2 has added a new noise reduction filter called Reduce Noise (found under the Filter > Noise submenu). If noise exists in your image, it's most likely found in the dark shadow areas, both because it contrasts better there and because that is where the digital camera or film scanner has the most difficulty reading accurate values. Zoom in on the dark shadow areas looking for pixels with random colors that don't match their surroundings, as shown in Figure 9.5. If you find noise that is problematic in the image, try using Reduce Noise to minimize it.

Figure 9.5 Noise is most often found in the dark shadow areas of an image when high ISO settings or long exposures are used with a digital camera. (Photo by Tim Grey.)

To use the Reduce Noise filter, choose Filter > Noise > Reduce Noise from the menu. This brings up the Reduce Noise dialog box (see Figure 9.6), which includes a number of settings that allow you to adjust its behavior.

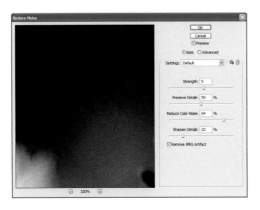

Figure 9.6

The Reduce Noise dialog box allows you to control the behavior of this filter to reduce the effect of noise in your photographic images. (Photo by Tim Grey.)

Make sure to zoom in on the preview image in the Reduce Noise dialog box so you can see detail in the image clearly. The zoom percentage for the preview can be adjusted using the plus and minus buttons below the preview image. You can click the preview image to see the "before" version without the effect of the Reduce Noise filter, releasing the mouse to see the "after" version again.

Note: It's a good idea to set all of the settings in Reduce Noise to 0 before starting, so you'll be able to see the effect of each individually as you work to find the best settings.

The Strength setting controls the amount of noise reduction you'd like to have applied to luminosity noise in the image—that is, noise exhibited by tonal rather than color variations. This is noise that is exhibited by tonal variations at the pixel level, and generally, this isn't a significant issue in digital images, and increasing the Strength setting too much effectively blurs the detail out of your image. However, we still recommend adjusting this setting for images that have significant noise to see if it provides a benefit.

The Preserve Details slider controls the amount of edge detail you want to maintain. Adjusting this too high reduces the effect of luminosity noise reduction controlled by the Strength setting (and in fact, this setting is only available if the Strength is set higher than 0). However, generally you want to use a relatively high setting here, such as 50 percent to 60 percent, to ensure you are maximizing the amount of detail in the image (see Figure 9.7).

The most important setting in the Reduce Noise dialog box is the Reduce Color Noise slider. This setting determines how aggressively color noise, exhibited by random color variations (as opposed to luminance noise exhibited by tonal variations), should be reduced in the image (see Figure 9.8). The potential risk is that you'll reduce the overall color in the image by using a setting that is too high, because it causes an averaging of pixel values within the image. To help ensure you're getting the best results with a minimum of unintended effects, we recommend starting with a very low setting and then gradually increasing the value until you have effectively minimized the noise.

Figure 9.7 You can use the Preserve Details slider to ensure that maximum detail is maintained in the image despite the changes being applied by Reduce Noise. (Photo by Tim Grey.)

Figure 9.8 The Reduce Color Noise slider, as the name implies, allows you to reduce the effect of noise exhibited by color variations in your images. (Photo by Tim Grey.)

After you've reduced the noise in your image, you may want to enhance detail slightly to compensate for the slight loss caused by the noise reduction process. The Sharpen Details setting allows you to enhance edges within the image (see Figure 9.9). We recommend starting with a low setting and gradually increasing the value until you have achieved the desired level of edge enhancement, without creating any quality problems within the image.

Figure 9.9 Use the Sharpen Details setting to enhance edges in your image after applying noise reduction, starting with a low value and gradually increasing it until you have achieved the desired result. (Photo by Tim Grey.)

While we recommend capturing in RAW whenever possible, we do recognize that many nature photographers are still going to utilize JPEG capture at times. The Reduce Noise filter includes an option that helps reduce the appearance of JPEG artifacts in the image, which are a by-product of how the JPEG file format compresses the image data. To help compensate for visible JPEG artifacts, select the Remove JPEG Artifact checkbox (shown in Figure 9.10).

Figure 9.10 The Remove JPEG Artifact checkbox in Reduce Noise allows you to minimize the effect of JPEG compression in your images. In this image, you can see the artifacts above the thorn in the center of the image. (Photo by Tim Grey.)

Advanced Settings

If you select the Advanced radio button, the area with the settings controls is divided into tabs, as shown in Figure 9.11. The settings discussed in the previous section appear on the Overall tab, while new settings become available on the Per Channel tab.

Figure 9.11
When you select the Advanced option in the Reduce Noise dialog box, the settings will be divided into tabs.

The Per Channel tab allows to you adjust the noise reduction individually for each color channel in your image. When you select one of the color channels from the drop-down list below the smaller preview on the Per Channel tab, that preview is updated to reflect that channel, and you can adjust the Strength and Preserve Details settings individually for the channel, as shown in Figure 9.12.

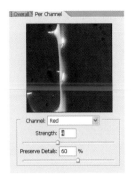

Figure 9.12
The Per Channel tab allows you to adjust the Strength and Preserve Details adjustments individually for each channel in your image. (Photo by Tim Grey.)

While this allows you to fine-tune noise reduction for each individual channel, which can be helpful for some images, to us the greatest benefit of these advanced settings is the ability to target additional noise reduction to the blue channel, which is typically where the most noise exists within digital images. If you have an image with strong noise, it's helpful to examine each of the channels and set individual settings for each to minimize the amount of noise each channel contributes to the overall image.

Once you have applied appropriate noise reduction to your image (if necessary), click OK in the Reduce Noise dialog box to apply the settings to your image.

Sharpening

Sharpening is an important aspect of preparing your image for output, and is of particular importance for nature photographers who tend to be focused on maintaining maximum detail in their images. Because sharpening enhances edge contrast, it helps to improve the overall perceived detail in your images.

Though it's important to evaluate the effect of your sharpening settings based on a view of the actual pixels in your image, we don't work with the image set to 100 percent scale while applying sharpening. Doing so only allows you to view a portion of your image (in most cases). Instead, we prefer to set the image to fit the screen (View > Fit On Screen) and use the 100 percent preview in the dialog box for the sharpening filter being used to make judgments about the settings. This allows you to then click any area of your actual image to set the preview to show that area.

> **Note:** Although most images benefit from sharpening, it's important to keep in mind that images without significant detail—such as a photo of the sky at sunset with no foreground detail—may not need to be sharpened.

At this point, we're sharpening a flattened version of our master image file. The flattening is important so we can apply sharpening—which only affects one layer at a time—to the entire image in the event that we have additional layers for things like the Clone Stamp. Since sharpening is so important to the final appearance, you may wonder why it comes so late in the process. One reason is that the sharpening settings you use vary based on the output size, and should be optimized for the output size and printing process you're using. Another is that sharpening, while beneficial to the image, is a destructive process in that it alters pixel values, so we want to apply it as part of our output workflow rather than to the master image. Although it's possible to sharpen on a separate layer in our master image, that works against the desire to sharpen based on final output size.

 Note: If you're looking for even more detail on this topic, Tim recently wrote an e-book titled *Photoshop Sharpening*. It's for sale by download at **www.sybex.com**.

The Unsharp Mask Filter

The most common tool for sharpening images is the Unsharp Mask filter. This filter provides excellent control over the sharpening process, enabling you to improve the overall appearance of the image without introducing quality problems in the process. To use Unsharp Mask, choose Filter > Sharpen > Unsharp Mask from the menu. The Unsharp Mask dialog box appears (see Figure 9.13), which contains three settings you can adjust to modify the sharpening effect: Amount, Radius, and Threshold.

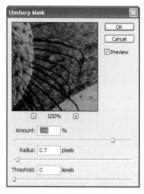

Figure 9.13

The Unsharp Mask dialog box allows you to control the sharpening effect on your image with three individual sliders for Amount, Radius, and Threshold. (Photo by Tim Grey.)

Unsharp Mask operates by enhancing contrast along the edges of objects within your image. In other words, it's enhancing contrast where contrast already exists. Adjusting the controls in the Unsharp Mask dialog box allows you to change how this contrast enhancement is applied.

The Amount setting determines the extent to which contrast is enhanced along edges. Think of this as an intensity control. The higher the setting, the more intense the edge contrast is in your image. As a general rule, we work in a range between about 100 percent and 300 percent for Amount.

The Radius setting allows you to determine the size of the area to be affected by the boost in contrast along the edges. For images with high detail, you generally want to have the impact only affect a small area for each edge, so work in a range between around 0.4 and 1.0 pixels. For images with low detail, a setting of between 2.0 and 3.0 is probably best. When in doubt, work in a range between about 1.0 and 1.5.

The Threshold setting provides something of a "damage control" function. It determines how much contrast must exist between two pixels for them to be considered to define an edge. With a minimum Threshold setting of 0, virtually all pixels are affected by sharpening. As you increase the value, fewer areas are sharpened because they must exhibit a certain amount of contrast before sharpening is applied. This enables you to maintain smooth textures in areas of the image where that is important.

For high-detail images, you should use a very low Threshold setting of between 0 and 4. For images with areas of smooth texture you want to preserve, a setting of between 8 and 12 is probably appropriate (see Table 9.1).

▶ **Table 9.1** Typical Unsharp Mask Settings

	Amount	Radius	Threshold
High-detail image	200% to 300%	0.4 to 1.0	0 to 4
Low-detail image	75% to 125%	2.0 to 3.0	8 to 12
Average image	150% to 175%	1.0 to 1.5	0 to 8

It's important that you evaluate the effect of Unsharp Mask on a 100 percent preview of your image. Do this by changing the zoom percentage for the image to 100 percent by choosing View > Actual Pixels from the menu. This enables you to evaluate the sharpening effect looking at the actual effect in the image you're working on. If you prefer to see the entire image while you're working so you can choose which areas you want to evaluate for best sharpening effect, set the zoom to fit the image on screen by choosing View > Fit On Screen from the menu. Then click anywhere in your image to set that as the preview area in the Unsharp Mask dialog box. It's important to realize, however, that when you work this way you must use the preview within Unsharp Mask to evaluate the results, not the actual image.

Once you've established your settings for Unsharp Mask, click OK, and the effect is applied.

The Smart Sharpen Filter

Photoshop CS2 includes a new filter called Smart Sharpen you can use to apply sharpening to your images. The Smart Sharpen filter includes the ability to mitigate the sharpening in highlights and shadows in your images individually, which can be very helpful. Tim wishes it included a Threshold control to maintain smooth textures throughout the image. Despite this limitation, however, there are still benefits of Smart Sharpen that can be helpful, especially when you have artifacts or noise in shadow areas of the image that you want to avoid having sharpening apply to. And, of course, you could always work around this by working on a copy of the background image layer and masking out areas where you want to retain smooth textures.

To use Smart Sharpen, choose Filter > Sharpen > Smart Sharpen from the menu. The Smart Sharpen dialog box (shown in Figure 9.14) appears, with the large preview area set to the default of 100 percent.

Figure 9.14

The Smart Sharpen dialog box includes a large preview and settings to help you control how sharpening is applied to your images. (Photo by Tim Grey.)

Note: The key setting in the Smart Sharpen dialog box is the Remove drop-down list, where you choose a blur type to work on. Be patient; we'll explain that in just a second.

As with the Unsharp Mask filter, you can click and hold the preview image to see what the image looks like without sharpening applied, and release to see it again with the effect. You can also drag within this preview area to change your view to a different area of the image. Clicking the actual image centers the preview on that position, just like you're able to do with Unsharp Mask. The Preview check box controls whether the effect is visible in the actual image, as opposed to being visible only in the preview within the Smart Sharpen dialog box.

Below the Preview check box are option buttons for Basic and Advanced. With Basic selected (which is the default), only the Sharpen settings are available. When you select Advanced, tabs are added for Shadow and Highlight, as you can see in Figure 9.15. Because these advanced features represent a large part of the reason you are likely to use the Smart Sharpen filter, we recommend that you always select the Advanced option.

Figure 9.15

When you select the Advanced option in Smart Sharpen, tabs are added for Shadow and Highlight. We recommend always working in Advanced mode for this filter.

The Basic settings in Smart Sharpen include the Amount and Radius settings you're familiar with from Unsharp Mask, as described in the Unsharp Mask section previously. The settings function in exactly the same way, with Amount controlling the intensity of the halos created along edges in your image and Radius controlling the size of those halos. As a general starting point, the default values of 100 percent for Amount and 1.0 for Radius are good. Refer to the settings recommended in the previous section for more details on how you might adjust these basic controls.

At the bottom of the basic sharpening section is a More Accurate check box. Although this option requires additional processing time, it also produces better results in the final sharpening. We recommend keeping this check box selected for every image you are sharpening with Smart Sharpen.

The blur removal settings are the key controls in the basic settings for Smart Sharpen, and in fact is what differentiates this section the most from the features available in Unsharp Mask. Instead of applying simple edge contrast with a fixed approach (with the specific application varying based on settings used) as with Unsharp Mask, the Smart Sharpen filter takes an intelligent approach based on the settings you establish. The primary control here is the Remove drop-down list, which controls the algorithm used to process the image when it comes to reducing the appearance of specific types of blur in the image (see Figure 9.16). These options are described in more detail below, but the point is that instead of just applying added contrast to the image as Unsharp Mask does, Smart Sharpen can counter specific causes of blur in your images to help you produce the best results possible.

Figure 9.16

The Remove drop-down list provides various options for reducing the effect of blur in your image to improve the perceived sharpness.

The default setting of Gaussian Blur causes the Smart Sharpen filter to process the image with the same algorithm used by Unsharp Mask. With this setting used, the results achieved with Smart Sharpen are very similar to the results achieved with Unsharp Mask with the same settings. I use the Gaussian Blur setting when I'm trying to achieve an effect similar to Unsharp Mask, with the additional benefit of being able to mitigate the effect in the shadow and highlight areas of the image.

The next option for blur removal is Lens Blur. This option adds another element to the "smart" aspect of the Smart Sharpen filter. It causes the filter to detect edges and texture detail within the image. The sharpening effect is adjusted in those areas to maintain fine detail and reduce the size of halos. This is the setting we recommend using for most images, as it does the most to achieve the typical goals of the photographer applying a sharpening effect to an image.

The final option for blur removal is Motion Blur. This option is designed to compensate for blur caused by motion of either the camera or subject during the capture. Of course, these are generally the type of images you would discard in favor of better ones, but when you have an important image that exhibits such blur, this option in Smart Sharpen helps you compensate for it.

When you select the Motion Blur option from the Remove drop-down list, the additional Angle control becomes active (see Figure 9.17). This is the same Angle control found in the Motion Blur filter used to create rather than remove such an effect. You can click anywhere in the circle to identify a point you'd like the angle control to intersect with, or click and drag to move the line representing the angle to be used around the circle. Type a specific value in the text box, or use the up and down keys on your keyboard to increase or decrease the value by one degree at a time. If you hold the Shift key while using the up and down arrow keys, the value changes by 10 degrees at a time. It can be a bit tricky to find just the right angle for a given image, so we recommend starting with a setting that seems to be in line with the direction of motion within the image and then use the up and down arrow keys on your keyboard to fine-tune the value until you achieve the best effect.

Figure 9.17

When you select Remove Motion Blur, an Angle control becomes available for you to adjust the direction of the visible blur in your image.

When you select the Advanced option in the Smart Sharpen dialog box, two additional tabs appear: Shadow and Highlight. These tabs contain additional settings that allow you to reduce the sharpening effect in these particular areas (see Figure 9.18). Because these settings represent a significant portion of the advantage to using Smart Sharpen, we recommend using the Advanced option every time you use the Smart Sharpen filter.

Figure 9.18

Among the Advanced options are settings that allow you to control the mitigation of sharpening in the shadow and highlight areas of your images.

Note: The settings available to control Shadow and Highlight sharpening effect in Smart Sharpen are very similar to those found in the Shadow/Highlight adjustment control.

Although there are separate tabs for limiting sharpening for both shadow and highlight areas within the image, the controls and behavior of each are identical. Both tabs allow you to adjust how much you want to reduce the sharpening effect in each area, as well as controls for determining how broad a range of shadow and highlight values should be affected. The controls are discussed here collectively. You simply need to apply the settings as needed on the Shadow or Highlight tab (or both of them) to apply the desired adjustment in the particular tonal areas of the image where you need it.

When adjusting the settings on the Shadow tab, we recommend zooming in to the darkest areas of the image, and for the Highlight tab, zooming in on the brightest areas. This allows you to better evaluate the settings as you adjust them on each of the tabs.

Here are the settings available on the Shadow and Highlight tabs:

Fade Amount   The Fade Amount setting controls how much the sharpening effect should be reduced within the shadow or highlight areas of the image. A value of 0 percent means the sharpening effect is not reduced at all, and the maximum value of 100 percent means the sharpening effect should be completely removed from the affected area of the image. Start with a value of 0 percent and gradually increase the value until the sharpening effect is reduced in the target areas to the extent desired.

Tonal Width   The Tonal Width setting allows you to specify how broad a range of tonal values should be affected by the reduction in sharpening effect. Very low values mean sharpening is only removed from the very dark pixels in shadow areas, and a high value causes the effect to be removed from a broader range of tonal values, extending into the midtone values. We usually use a value in a range between about 10 and 50 so the reduction in sharpening only affects the true shadow areas of the image, but evaluates all shadow areas to determine the best value for your particular image. Since noise is often worst in shadow areas, you may want to focus your attention there.

Radius   The Radius setting provides control over how far out from each pixel Photoshop should look when deciding if a particular pixel is contained within a shadow area. Frankly, even large adjustments of this control have a minimal effect on the final results achieved, so we recommend just leaving it at the default value of 1 pixel.

Targeted Sharpening

Save your sharpening for the end of your workflow, doing it on a flattened copy of your image and treating the whole picture at once. While it can be useful to sharpen the whole image at once, there's a place and time for sharpening only portions of your image. Localized sharpening is particularly helpful when there is a specific subject against an out-of-focus background, such as often occurs with bird or flower photography. In such situations, it can be challenging to find a Threshold setting that adequately sharpens the subject and does not affect the background.

Ellen's preferred method in such cases is to sharpen on a separate layer and use a layer mask to precisely control which areas are affected. The mask allows for various gradations of the sharpening within the image as well as eliminating the sharpening effects from areas, such as sky or water, that sometimes show increased noise when sharpened.

The choice here depends greatly on individual preference. For some, the benefits of masking a sharpened layer can generally be achieved on a flattened image by appropriate use of the Threshold setting in Unsharp Mask; this is the process Tim uses. But for many other nature photographers, masking is the usual method of targeting their sharpening.

This approach is extremely precise, quick, and easy. Beginning with a duplicate copy of the master file, take the following steps:

1. Flatten the image by choosing Layer > Flatten Image.

2. Resize the image by choosing Image > Resize and setting the values as described earlier in this chapter.

3. Make a copy of the background layer by dragging it to the New Layer icon at the bottom of the Layers palette.

4. Choose Filter > Sharpen > Unsharp Mask, setting the values as described earlier in this chapter.

5. While holding the Alt/Option key, click the Create Layer Mask icon to add a black layer mask to the background layer. This temporarily hides the effect of the sharpening from the entire image.

6. Select the Brush tool by pressing the B key and select the default colors of black and white by pressing the D key. Make certain that white is the foreground

color, pressing X to swap foreground and background colors if necessary. Use a soft-edged brush at 100 percent opacity to reveal the sharpening in your primary subject. If there are areas that need some sharpening, but not full sharpening, paint those areas with a reduced opacity. By using a soft-edged brush, you don't have to worry about precisely following the edges of your subject. This should be a quick mask to create, not a painstaking one.

7. Change the blending mode of this layer to Luminosity. This eliminates the chance of any color distortions or rainbow halos resulting from the sharpening.

 Note: You can also use this layered method with the Smart Sharpen filter in place of Unsharp Mask.

Prepping a File for Output

By Lewis Kemper

Let's start with some assumptions:

- There are many ways to do anything correctly in Photoshop, and there is no one right way. I'll discuss my methods, and I have never had anyone reject a print for quality reasons—and I have made prints that measure several feet in width by up to seven feet in length.

- You have completed your "master file," where you have already done all your exposure and color correction, plus whatever other Photoshop wizardry you have applied. Create the master file from the largest original digital file you can get without interpolating data. I save all my master files as PSD files, with the layers intact and unsharpened.

- Your monitor is hardware calibrated, and you've applied the correct paper/printer profile in the printer dialog box to assure consistent and reliable results.

SEDIMENT PATTERNS, DEATH VALLEY NATIONAL PARK, CALIFORNIA

Lewis Kemper

Now let's get onto the process of prepping a file for output:

1. The first step I take is to flatten my file. I do this because I am going to sharpen the image based on file size, and if the image has multiple layers, it is easier to sharpen if it is flattened.

2. Once the file is flattened, I size the image for the output use. If I am sending a file to my Epson inkjet printer, I size it to output size at 180 ppi (pixels per inch). I have done numerous tests and have found that 180 ppi works fine for all my needs, and because it is a relatively low resolution, I can get larger prints from smaller files. (When saving for output on other devices, I consult with the operator of these devices to determine the optimum resolution.)

3. So if I have an approximately 50 MB (8-bit) file from my Canon 1Ds MII camera and I want to make a print that will fit on 16×20 paper, I resize the image to approximately 19"×12.5" at 180 ppi, using Bicubic Sharper interpolation. (If I were enlarging a file, I would use the Bicubic Smoother algorithm.)

4. Once the file is sized, then I apply sharpening. The reason I wait until the image is sized is because the amount of sharpening an image needs is based on the image's size: a smaller image needs less sharpening than a large one. I use a 23-step action that I wrote that does three levels of sharpening on the image: one level to sharpen the edges only, one level to sharpen texture, and one level to sharpen contrast.

   If you are using the Sharpening filters found in Photoshop directly, I recommend the new Smart Sharpen or the old standby Unsharp Mask.

5. Since sharpening can accentuate any small dust I may have missed in my original spotting of my master file, I reexamine the image for dust. To do this, I enlarge the image to 100 percent or the Actual Pixels view. Then, using the Ctrl/⌘ key in conjunction with the Page Up and Page Down keys, I go through the entire image, from the upper-left corner to the lower-right corner. If I find any new dust, I remove it using either the Healing Brush or the Clone Stamp tool, depending on the situation.

6. My image is ready to be sent to the printer. When the printer dialog box comes up, I make sure the printer driver is set to No Color Adjustment and that the proper Paper Type, Print Quality, and Ink Type are set. Then, using the color management options in the dialog box, I apply the proper ICC profile for the paper and printer combination I am using for my output.

If you follow these steps and have a calibrated monitor and accurate profiles for your printing devices, you no longer have to waste time and money doing test prints. What you see on your monitor should match (as close as possible) what comes out of your printer.

© Lewis Kemper, www.lewiskemper.com

Printing Your Images

Once you've prepared the image through the output workflow, you're ready to produce a print, which is typically the ultimate goal for nature photographers. When sending the image to the printer, it's important that the appropriate settings be used to ensure accurate color and optimal quality.

Note: Remember that getting an accurate print depends on a calibrated monitor display. If your monitor isn't calibrated, you can't trust the colors displayed to be accurate, and therefore you can't be assured of a matching print.

An additional step that can be helpful before actually sending your image to the printer is soft-proofing, which enables an on-screen preview of what the print will look like. You can configure and enable a soft-proofing display by choosing View > Proof Setup > Custom from the menu and configuring your output print settings. When you click OK, the image simulates the final printed output, and you can make adjustments to the image before printing to compensate.

To get started, choose File > Print with Preview from the File menu. The Print dialog box (shown in Figure 9.19) appears, which allows you to set basic color management settings (as well as output scaling and layout settings, but we generally leave these for the printer Properties dialog box). It's important to make sure you're looking at the complete range of options available. If the dialog box doesn't include the color management options, click the More Options button to expand the dialog to include these controls. (When you do so, that button name changes to Fewer Options.)

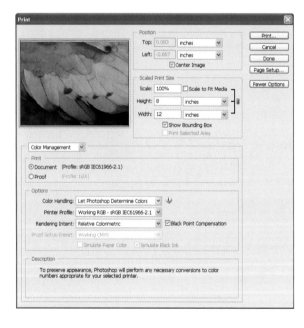

Figure 9.19

The Print dialog box, accessed by choosing the Print with Preview option from the File menu, allows you to control the basic color management settings for output.

Note: The exact same process applies for black-and-white images as for color images. However, some printers are better than others when it comes to producing accurate grayscale output, as discussed in Peter Burian's sidebar later in this chapter.

Make sure the Color Management option is selected from the drop-down list below the image preview on the left side of the dialog box. In the Print section, set the option to Document so the working space or embedded profile is used to determine the color values from your image being sent to the printer.

The Options section contains the key settings related to color management. For the Color Handling drop-down list, select Let Photoshop Determine Colors. The Printer Profile drop-down list is where you need to select the profile appropriate for the printer, ink, and paper you're using to produce the print. Many printers now include "canned" custom profiles, which are designed for the printer, ink, and paper combination their name implies, but were not created specifically for the printer sitting on your desk.

> **Note:** Using the Let Photoshop Determine Colors option assumes you are using a custom profile for your printer, ink, and paper combination. If you're using a generic profile for your printer (which we don't recommend), you need to use the Let Printer Determine Settings option instead.

For Rendering Intent, which deals with how colors that your printer can't produce are changed to colors it is able to print, select Relative Colorimetric, which ensures that colors your printer can produce are rendered accurately, while any color it can't produce is shifted to the closest in-gamut color. To the right of the Rendering Intent drop-down list, select the Black Point Compensation check box so that black in your image is mapped to black in the output.

> **Note:** You may hear the recommendation to use the Perceptual rendering intent rather than Relative Colorimetric, but we don't recommend Perceptual because it compresses the entire color gamut of your image into the printer's gamut, rather than only adjusting the colors that are actually out of gamut.

When you have set the appropriate settings in the Print dialog box, click the Print button to bring up another Print dialog box (shown in Figure 9.20). In this dialog box, select the printer you're sending the image to, and then click the Properties dialog box. The Properties dialog box for the particular printer you are using appears (see the example in Figure 9.21). The settings you use in the printer Properties dialog box depend on your particular printer model, but in general, you need to set the appropriate paper type and size, quality settings, and color management settings. Find the least invasive color management choice—such as a "no color adjustment" or similar option—to ensure that the printer doesn't try to alter the color values in the printing process, leaving Photoshop to handle the color management for the print.

Figure 9.20
The Print dialog box allows you to select the specific printer you want to use for printed output.

Figure 9.21

Clicking the Properties button in the Print dialog box brings up the Properties dialog box for the printer you selected.

With all settings established for the print, click OK in the printer Properties dialog box and then OK in the Print dialog box to send the job to the printer.

The technical editor of this book, Peter K. Burian, is a stock photographer and the author of *Mastering Digital Photography and Imaging* (Sybex, 2004). As a regular contributor to several photo magazines, including *Shutterbug, Here's How, Photo Life,* and *Australian Photography,* he frequently tests digital cameras, lenses, scanners, and printers. We asked him to give us his picks for black-and-white printers.

Ideal Printers for Black-and-White Outputs

by Peter K. Burian

Until recently, most photographers who love black-and-white prints were often disappointed with their inkjet outputs. While it should be possible to make a truly neutral monochrome print with color inks, few machines did a competent job without a frustrating process. That required constant fine-tuning in the printer driver and making test prints until one was very close to neutral.

And there was another problem, especially with printers using pigmented inks, like the very popular Epson Stylus Photo 2200. This problem was metamerism: the tendency for inks to change color under different types of illumination. A print may look quite different under incandescent light, fluorescent light, and sunlight, for example.

Epson and Hewlett-Packard have been working on the problem, introducing improvements slowly in selected models. Recently, both companies introduced new printers employing new inks that should satisfy the most dedicated B&W print makers. HP was first, in early 2005, with the tabloid format Photosmart 8750 that employs a nine-color inkset called Vivera. Although designed to make vividly saturated color outputs, this machine also generates excellent monochrome prints with high-contrast, neutral grays (thanks to two gray inks), rich dark blacks, pure whites, good shadow detail, and a pleasing tonal gradation overall. The on-display print permanence rating is impressive too: 100 years for color prints and 115 years for monochrome prints made on HP Premium papers.

A couple of months later, Epson announced four printers that employ an improved version of the archival UltraChrome inkset: the tabloid-format Stylus Photo R2400 and several wide-format models (Pro 4800, Pro 7800, and Pro 9800). All of these products employ the eight-color UltraChrome K3 pigmented inkset, including three blacks: Light Black, the entirely new Light Light Black, plus either Matte Black or Photo Black, depending on the media type.

Although these machines were not yet available for testing at our press time, the prints exhibited by Epson indicate significantly reduced metamerism. The color prints show an improved range of color and more vibrancy, while the monochrome outputs matched the best silver halide prints that I had seen in the past; the improvement was partly due to a remarkable increase in maximum density. Preliminary testing by Wilhelm Research suggests that the K3 inks are at least as archival as the UltraChrome inks; exact ratings depend on the paper used, but they often exceed 100 years.

The new Epson machines also feature an entirely new driver option—Advanced Black & White printing mode. When selected, only the three black inks are used for prints without any apparent color cast. The new driver provides many of the features that previously required the purchase of a separate RIP (raster image processor), an advanced printer driver that provides maximum control over the entire printing process. With simple adjustments, you can replicate warm or cool tone prints such as sepia or platinum in the Epson software. This additional printing mode expands the range of options available to the monochrome print maker.

At this time, these machines are the most worthy of consideration by those who want to make beautiful black-and-white prints. Before making a final decision as to the one that would best suit all of your needs, read some reviews on all models on the Internet and visit a retailer to evaluate the quality of prints made by each machine in your price range.

© 2005 Peter K. Burian, www.peterkburian.com

Choosing the Best Paper

The choice of paper when producing a print is a very subjective decision. When we're asked by nature photographers what paper should be used, our typical response is that you really need to try various papers for yourself to find what you like best. However, as subjective as this decision is, here are some general guidelines to help you make your decision.

A big part of the decision has to do with the type of effect you want to produce in the print. The first consideration is the surface type. For images where you want to have maximum detail, contrast, and vibrancy of colors, a glossy paper is your best choice. For example, a crisp high-detail image of highly saturated flowers or a strong landscape image with a silhouetted foreground subject generally works well on a glossy paper.

For images that are more muted, such as more delicate flowers with subtle colors or a photo captured under very diffuse lighting on an overcast day, you may want to maintain the subtle mood by printing on a matte paper. This tones down both the colors and contrast to produce a more subtle print.

Of course, many images tend to fall somewhere in between, and those are appropriate for a semi-gloss paper. This is an excellent choice for photographers who don't like the strong reflections you can get from the glossy papers, and who don't like the loss of color and contrast typical of matte papers.

The other consideration for papers is the texture. This decision depends on the content in the image. When in doubt, opt for a smooth paper surface. However, there are many other textures available that add to the aesthetics of an image. Images with deep, rich colors, such as the greens of a rain forest, can produce beautiful results with a canvas surface that lends a painterly look to the image. Images that have smooth and subtle textures can be enhanced by a textured paper that adds a certain random aspect to the surface.

These basic decisions represent only an overview of some of the considerations to think about as you prepare to print your nature photographs. We strongly recommend that you test a wide variety of papers to find the ones you feel work best for your images. Many third-party paper manufacturers offer "sampler" packs that provide an economical way for you to test many papers as you discover your new favorites. Above all, experiment with many different papers so you can find options that enhance the qualities of your images.

Creating a Web Gallery

Prints aren't the only form of output nature photographers want to produce. Displaying images on the Web is becoming more popular, providing a great way to share your images with a large audience easily and affordably. While creating a professional-quality website can require either many hours of learning and creating or a considerable budget, Photoshop makes it easy to create a basic gallery of your images to display on screen through the Web Photo Gallery automation tool.

To get started, choose File > Automate > Web Photo Gallery from the menu. The Web Photo Gallery dialog box (shown in Figure 9.22) appears, where you can establish the various settings that define the appearance of the final gallery.

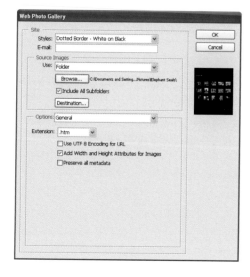

Figure 9.22

The Web Photo Gallery dialog box allows you to establish settings that enable Photoshop to create all the files necessary for a basic gallery for your images on the Web.

Note: If you're reviewing your images in the Bridge application, select the images you want to include in a web gallery and then choose Tools > Photoshop > Web Photo Gallery from the Bridge menu to open the Web Photo Gallery dialog box with the selected images automatically set as the source for the gallery.

At the top of the dialog box is a Styles drop-down list where you can choose the overall appearance of the website. Because the names don't provide a completely clear indication of what the site layout will look like, we recommend that you select the first option from the drop-down list and then use the up and down arrow keys to cycle through the various options. A thumbnail display on the right side of the dialog box gives you an indication (though very small) of what the layout will look like.

In the E-mail box, enter your e-mail address if you'd like it to be displayed in the contact information on the gallery you're creating. This provides a simple link for people to use if they want to contact you with questions about your images or (better yet) information on how to purchase an image.

In the Source Images section, specify both the source of images and the destination for the files to be created as part of your gallery. From the Use drop-down list, select Folder if you would like to specify a particular folder containing image files you want to use in your gallery. If you have selected images in Bridge that you want to include in the gallery, choose the Selected Images From Bridge option.

Note: If you're going to be using a folder as the source of images, you may want to copy those images into a new folder so you can more easily manage the collection of images to be included in the gallery.

If you have set the source to Folder, click the Browse button to open a separate dialog box, where you can identify the folder where the images to be included in the gallery are stored. If there are additional folders within the source folder with images you want to include in the gallery, select the Include All Subfolders check box.

To select the folder where you want all of the files for your gallery to be saved, click the Destination button. As with the Browse button for setting the source, this brings up a dialog box where you can specify a folder or create a new folder.

The Options section of the Web Photo Gallery dialog box contains a large number of settings, broken down into various sections that are accessed by choosing a category from the drop-down list at the top of this section:

General   The General options control some of the basic parameters of the website. You can specify whether you want the file extension for the HTML files that form the website to be .htm or .html, though this isn't a significant concern because all current servers and web browsers support both file extensions. The check box to Use UTF8 Encoding For URL allows you to ensure that URLs containing international characters function properly. The Add Width and Height Attributes for Images check box causes sizing information to be included in the HTML files for images, so the layout of the page remains fixed as the images load. We recommend selecting this option. The Preserve All Metadata check box ensures that all metadata is retained within the image files being created for the web gallery.

Banner   The Banner options allow you to specify the text that appears on the page. Enter values for each field if you want that information displayed on your gallery. Leave any of them blank if you do not want particular text included.

Large Images   The Large Images section provides settings that determine how large the "full-sized" images appear in your gallery. While it's possible to maintain the native size of your image files by clearing the Resize Images check box, we recommend checking this box so the images can be adjusted to a more appropriate size. The Small, Medium, and Large sizes provide basic values for you to use, and we usually recommend the Large setting unless file sizes are a particular concern. You can also select the Custom size and enter a maximum pixel size for your images. The JPEG Quality setting determines the quality setting used for the JPEG images that are saved, which has a direct effect on the size of the image files. We recommend using the High setting for JPEG Quality, although a lower setting could be used if file size is a serious concern for your site, such as if you expect many visitors to be using dial-up Internet connections. At the bottom of this section, set a Border Size in pixels if you want to have a border around your images, and select the desired check boxes below in the Titles Use section if you would like to include additional text as titles for your images.

Thumbnails   The Thumbnails section provides very similar settings to those used for the Large Images section, except that these settings relate to the small thumbnail versions of the images to be displayed in the gallery. We recommend using a Large setting for these so the thumbnails are large enough to be clearly visible and identifiable in the gallery.

Custom Colors   The Custom Colors section allows you to specify the color for text links for those Styles that support this option. We generally recommend leaving these to the defaults so visitors have the Internet-standard experience on your site, such as text links that have not yet been visited appearing in blue and those that have been visited appearing in purple.

Security   The Security section contains various settings to place text over the top of your images. There are many options available that enable you to use specific attributes (such as filename) for this text. You can also choose Custom Text and enter your own text to be placed over your images. Font attributes can also be adjusted as desired.

Once you've established all the settings applicable to your gallery, click OK and Photoshop processes all the files, placing them into the folder you set as the destination. This includes a series of HTML files and resized images, divided into folders (see Figure 9.23). The entire contents of the destination folder can then be uploaded to your website server so the site can be accessed on the Internet.

Figure 9.23
After establishing the desired settings for your gallery in the Web Photo Gallery dialog box, a website is created for you automatically.

Share Your Images

In this chapter we've explained methods for sharing your images after they have been optimized. This is only a starting point for producing great output, and we encourage you to be creative in how you prepare your images for display. In the next chapter, we'll demonstrate some additional techniques for optimizing your workflow and creating other forms of output.

Additional Techniques

Throughout this book we've provided you with the best techniques for optimizing your images at every stage of the digital workflow. In this last chapter, we'd like to present some additional topics to help you improve your efficiency and expand your creativity in the digital darkroom. Think of this as a sampler of various techniques we find fun and helpful, which will hopefully spur your imagination and help you apply the lessons you've learned throughout this book to many other photographic projects.

10

Chapter Contents
Actions and Batch Processing
Borders
Creating a Greeting Card
Creating a Business Card
Slideshows

Actions and Batch Processing

Who decided that being lazy was such a bad thing? You've probably heard the adage that if you want to find the most efficient way to accomplish a given task, ask a lazy person to do it for you. If the person is intelligent as well as lazy, they'll likely come up with a technique that is a marvel of efficiency, allowing them to get back to relaxing in that hammock.

When it comes to getting efficient with repetitive tasks in Photoshop, the key is creating actions and applying those actions to a group of images in batch. Actions allow you to automate just about any series of steps you can perform in Photoshop. You can record a series of steps, and then have those steps applied to an image in exactly the same way. Batch processing allows you to apply the action to a group of images at once, all automatically. The result can be a significant boost to your productivity.

Let's look at an example where your intent is to resize a series of images to prepare them for inclusion in a digital slideshow using third-party software. (We'll show you how to create a basic slideshow automatically in Photoshop later in this chapter).

Creating an Action

The Actions palette is "command central" for creating and managing your actions. So, start by selecting the Actions palette (shown in Figure 10.1). If it isn't visible, choose Window > Actions from the menu.

Figure 10.1
The Actions palette is command central for creating and managing your actions.

On the palette, actions are organized into folders called *sets*. Photoshop includes a Default Actions set with a variety of included actions, but you should divide your actions into sets that define logical groups. For instance, in this example, you might create a new set called "Slideshows" to contain the various actions you might utilize when preparing images for digital slideshows. To create a new set, click the Create New Set button at the bottom of the Actions palette. In the New Set dialog box (shown in Figure 10.2), enter a name and click OK.

Figure 10.2
The New Set dialog box allows you to create a new set that helps you manage the various categories of actions you're creating.

Note: When creating an action, it's a good idea to work with a copy of one of your images. Copy one of your images to the desktop before you start creating the action and use that as the file you adjust in the process of recording the action.

With this set active, the next step is to start recording your new action. Click the Create New Action button at the bottom of the Actions palette. In the New Action dialog box (see Figure 10.3), enter a descriptive name for this action. For this example, let's use "Slideshow Prep." The Set option defaults to the one that was selected when you created the new action, but you can choose a different set from the drop-down list if desired. The Function Key option allows you to set a shortcut key for the new action you're creating, which can be convenient if you're applying this action individually to single images (which probably isn't the case in this example). Finally, the Color setting determines what color the action shows up as if you use Button mode for the Actions palette. This allows you to color-code the individual actions. However, we prefer using the default system of grouping actions into sets, so we leave the Color setting to None.

Figure 10.3

In the New Action dialog box, specify a name for the new action, the folder you want it stored in, and a function key to use as a shortcut key to run the action.

Once you've established the palette characteristics for the new action, click Record and you're actively recording the action. Don't worry though—time isn't an issue. Photoshop doesn't record the time you take between your steps, but instead records the final result of each step you perform so those steps can be repeated as quickly as possible when you apply the action to an image. You can perform any adjustment or command on an image as part of an action. However, keep in mind that any step that depends on specific positioning within the image can be problematic because image dimensions vary from one photo to the next.

For this example, perform the following steps:

1. Open the image being used as the example for the action.

2. Choose Layer > Flatten Image from the menu to merge all layers in your master image into a single layer.

3. Select Image > Image Size from the menu, clear the Resample Image check box, set the Resolution to 96, and click OK. This sets the output resolution to a more appropriate value for those slideshow applications that look to resolution when you insert an image.

4. Select File > Automate > Fit Image from the menu, and the Fit Image dialog box appears (see Figure 10.4). Enter the maximum dimensions of the resolution to be used to display your digital slideshow, which are generally the maximum resolution dimensions of the digital projector you're using. For example, most current digital projectors support a resolution with a Width of 1024 pixels and a Height of 768 pixels. When you have established the appropriate values, click OK.

Figure 10.4

The Fit Image dialog box allows you to specify maximum dimensions in pixels for an image you want to resize.

5. Select Edit > Convert To Profile to bring up the Convert To Profile dialog box, shown in Figure10.5. (In versions of Photoshop prior to CS2, this is Image > Mode > Convert To Profile.) Set the Profile option under Destination Space to sRGB and click OK. This setting ensures that the image is represented with the best color possible by converting it to a color space that closely matches the color gamut of a typical digital projector.

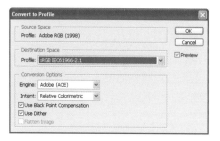

Figure 10.5

In the Convert To Profile dialog box, set the Destination Space to sRGB and click OK.

6. Select File > Save As. In the Save As dialog box, set the Format to JPEG. Select a destination folder and filename that will make it easy to delete this sample file later, because the batch processing explained in the next section override these settings in any event. This may make this step seem unnecessary, but it's important to establish the parameters you want the file saved with. When you click OK, the JPEG Options dialog box appears. Set the Quality setting to 10.

7. Close the image.

With these steps performed, you're ready to stop recording the action. To do so, click the Stop button at the bottom of the Actions palette (shown in Figure 10.6). This completes the process of creating the action, which can then be applied to many images at once using batch processing, which we'll demonstrate later in this chapter.

Figure 10.6

The Stop button at the bottom of the Actions palette allows you to stop recording the action when you're finished.

Actions

By Arthur Morris

At Birds As Art, we often find ourselves in a position to perform the same, time-consuming operations on numerous images day after day. To save time, we have learned to prepare and execute actions. I use a permanent saved action almost every day to prepare images for the Web, and I use another on occasion to prepare images for digital slide programs. In addition, I will often create an action on the spot should I need to process a group of images to a given set of specs for a publisher.

You've just seen how to open the Create New Action dialog and set up such things as a name, keyboard shortcut, or palette color for your action. Once you've done that, you're ready to begin recording the various steps in your action. Let's build an action to be used to prepare an image file for digital projection:

Create a new action named Slide Show JPEGs and assign F5 as its shortcut. We will consider a 16-bit TIFF image with layers as our starting point.

1. Choose Image > Mode > 8-bit.

2. Choose Image > Image Size and change the resolution to 96 pixels per inch. After making sure that that the Resample Image box is unchecked, click OK.

3. Next, choose File > Automate > Fit Image. Enter **1028** in the Width box and **768** in the Height box, because that is the resolution of nearly all digital projectors at present. If you are working with a newer projector with higher resolution, enter the correct numbers for that projector.

4. Then choose Image > Mode > Convert To Profile and select sRGB from the drop-down menu if it does not appear in the Destination Space Profile box. (Note: With some master files, all of these operations may not be needed, but it does no harm to have them included in the action in these cases.)

5. Next, sharpen the image with Unsharp Mask. With digital images to be used for digital projection you'll do three rounds of sharpening. The first round is at 100/0.4/2.0. This is followed by two more rounds at 125/0.2/0. These generic settings usually do a great job with digital images; some scanned film images may require an additional round or two of sharpening after the fact. (If you have lots of scanned film images, you may wish to create a separate action for those images with higher sharpening settings.)

   While it is true that a given image may look somewhat better with a bit more sharpening, the amount of time saved by using an action is considerable; I have never had an image that looked oversharpened using the settings described in this sidebar.

6. Now click File > Save As and select JPEG from the drop-down menu in the Format box. The original filename appears in the File Name box. Make sure that you have clicked through to the correct folder in the Save In window before clicking Save. (We save the images in a folder titled Slide_Show_JPEGs.)

7. In the JPEG Options window that appears select a value of 10 or 11 for a high-quality image file.

8. Click File > Close. A box should open and ask, "Save changes to original file?" Click No, because you do not want to change your master file.

9. Finally, click the square to the left of the red circle on the bottom of the Actions window. This stops the recording of your steps and saves the action. Be sure to remember to end the recording, or you will have to begin the whole process anew! (Been there, done that!)

Now, when you have a finished master file that has been saved, press the F5 key, and the processed file is saved in your Slide_Show_JPEGs folder in a few seconds!

Batch Processing

As you can see, recording an action is relatively straightforward. Just start recording, perform the steps you want included in the action, and then stop recording. Where many photographers run into trouble is in attempting to apply the action in batch to a series of images, which is where you achieve the real benefit of actions. The problem is with the confusing choices that are offered to you in the Batch dialog box.

To get started, select the action you want to apply to a group of images from the Actions palette. Then select File > Automate > Batch from the menu, which brings up the Batch dialog box (shown in Figure 10.7). Because you selected an action first, the Set and Action drop-down lists default to the one you want to apply to your images.

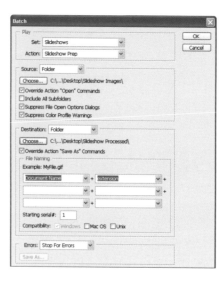

Figure 10.7

The Batch dialog box allows you to specify the action you want to run on a group of images, as well as other settings that determine which images should be processed and how they should be handled.

Note: When you're applying an action to a group of images in batch, we recommend copying the image files to a separate folder to protect the originals.

The Source section provides a number of options related to the images you'll be processing with the action. The Source drop-down list allows you to specify where the source images are located:

- We generally use the Folder option so we can specify a specific location where we've copied the images to be processed.
- The Import option applies to images being imported from a particular source at the time the action is run.
- The Opened Files option applies to all images currently open in Photoshop.
- Bridge applies the action to all images currently selected in the Bridge browser.

If you have included an Open step in the action (as you did in the earlier example), select the Override Action "Open" Commands check box so the source you have set is used within the action rather than having the same image opened repeatedly. In general, you should just keep this check box selected.

If you have used the Folder option for Source and there are more images in sub-folders below that folder, select the Include All Folders check box so those images are also processed.

The Suppress File Open Options Dialogs option causes all images to be opened with default values without bringing up any Options dialog boxes that might be associated with the particular open operation. The most common situation where this would be an issue is for raw files—the Camera Raw dialog box is displayed when a raw file is opened. As a general rule, keep this check box selected, since the point of using batch processing is to allow a group of images to be processed without any user intervention required.

Similarly, select the Suppress Color Profile Warnings check box so the action won't pause for missing profiles or profile mismatches in any of the images you are processing. When this option is selected, the default action specified in the Color Settings dialog box is performed when either of these situations occurs.

The next section of the Batch dialog box is the Destination section, which allows you to specify parameters for the output that is generated by the batch process. From the drop-down list, select the Folder option so that the processed images are saved in a specific folder. The other options are None (which causes nothing to be done other than what is part of the action) and Save and Close (which causes each image to be saved as it is processed, replacing the existing file). If you use the Folder option, click the Choose button to bring up the Browse For Folder dialog box, where you can specify which folder you'd like to save the processed images in (including the ability to create a completely new folder for this purpose).

One of the biggest points of confusion for photographers using the Batch dialog box relates to the Override Action "Save As" Commands check box. This option is important to use when you set the output to a folder, but it only works when you have actually included a Save As option within the action. The Save As step in the action establishes the basic options for saving (such as file type and any special options available for that file type). The options in the Batch dialog box specify the location and filenames for those files. So, if you're saving the results to a folder, be sure to select this check box, but also be sure the action you're using includes a Save As step.

In the File Naming section, you have considerable flexibility in naming the files that are created. You can type specific text into the option boxes, or select a variable from the drop-down list. For example, if you want to save the images with a filename in the structure Slideshow_0001.jpg, enter **Slideshow_** in the first box, select 4 Digit Serial Number from the drop-down list in the second box, and then select the Extension option from the third drop-down list. The default values of Document Name and Extension cause the original filenames to be retained. If you're using a serial number option, specify the starting value in the Starting Serial # box, which defaults to 1.

In the Errors section, choose whether you want to Stop For Errors or simply have Photoshop Log Errors To File without interrupting the batch processing. We prefer to use the Stop For Errors option so we know right away if there is a problem we need to correct.

When you've set all the settings you want to use for the action you are applying to a group of images, click OK, and Photoshop processes all of the images specified in the Source section with the action specified in the Play section, saving the resulting output based on the settings in the Destination section. This processing is done automatically at top speed, making the process very efficient. Whenever you find yourself performing the same task on a group of images, consider making an action to automate that process. The small amount of time spent creating the action pays significant dividends when you apply that action in batch to a large group of images.

Batch Processing

By Arthur Morris

Let's say that you have a folder with 300 family jewels images. Each is a master file ranging in size from 10 to 63 megabytes, and you wish to have them all available for a slide program that you are assembling. Opening and running your Slide Show JPEGs action (the one we built a few pages ago) on each of the images individually would take hours at best. Imagine that you could have Photoshop do all of that automatically.

By learning to set up batches, Photoshop can do just that in about 20 minutes while you are busy working at other tasks.

To have Photoshop perform an action on a group of images, choose File > Automate > Batch. When the Batch window opens, choose the action that you wish to have executed from the drop-down menu in the Action box. In our example, you would choose Slide Show JPEGs F5. Next, select Folder from the drop-down menu in the Source box and then click Choose. When the Browse For Folder window appears, choose the folder that contains the group of images that you wish to process. In our example, you would select Family_Jewels. (If you wish to work only on some of the images in a folder, you need to select them and copy them to a new folder first.) Once you have highlighted the correct folder, click OK.

After making sure that Folder appears in the Destination box, click Choose and when the Browse For Folder window pops up again, choose the Folder to which you want the images to be saved. In this case, it might be Slide_Show_JPEGs/Family_Jewels. Click OK. The next step is extremely important and can be a bit confusing at times: Make sure that the Override Actions "Save As" Command box is checked. This ensures that the images are saved to the folder that you have designated in the Batch commands—not to the folder specified in the Actions. To ensure that the batch runs smoothly and without interruption, check both the Suppress File Open Options Dialogs and the Suppress Color Profile Warnings boxes and choose Log Errors To File in the Errors box. (You will need to type in a filename.)

After you click OK, each image appears briefly on the Photoshop screen, as it opens and then closes after all of the operations that you specified have been performed. When no more images appear, your batch processing has been completed. Do check to make sure that the images in their final form have been saved to the specified folder. It is not difficult to encounter some problems here; at times, I find the images in a folder other than the intended one.

Borders

While your images are no doubt beautiful all by themselves, as you gain more knowledge of optimizing those images with Photoshop, you no doubt want to find ways to add a creative touch to your images. One way to add a creative effect without altering the basic content of the image itself is to add an artistic border around your image.

There are a variety of methods you can use to add such a border to your image. One of these is a plug-in from Extensis (www.extensis.com) called PhotoFrame. This software includes thousands of photo edges you can apply to your images, making the process very easy.

However, you can produce similar effects within Photoshop with no special software. Rather than removing pixels from your image to create the edge effect, we recommend adding a new layer above the image layer to serve as the artistic border around the image. So, start by creating a new layer above your image layer by clicking the New Layer button at the bottom of the Layers palette. Then select Edit > Fill from the menu, choose white from the Use drop-down list, and click OK to fill this layer with white (see Figure 10.8). Of course, you don't really want to cover up the entire image with white, but this provides the foundation for this technique.

Figure 10.8
The first step in creating an artistic border around the edge of your image is to create a new image layer and fill it with white.

To help you better identify the area you want to apply the border effect to, turn off the visibility of the new layer you filled with white by clicking the eye icon to the left of its thumbnail on the Layers palette. Next, choose the Rectangular Marquee selection tool and drag from *near* the top-left corner of the image to *near* the bottom-right corner (as shown in Figure 10.9). This becomes the area along which the edge effect is added, with anything outside the selection hidden and anything inside the selection retained, so be sure to position this selection accordingly. When you're finished, turn the visibility of the white layer you created back on by clicking in the box where the eye icon was.

Figure 10.9
Create a selection with the Rectangular Marquee tool to define the area where the border will be created. (Photo by Tim Grey.)

The next step is to switch into Quick Mask mode, which allows you to modify the selection with a bit more flexibility. To switch to Quick Mask mode, press Q on your keyboard or click the button on the right side directly below the Color Picker on the Tools palette. The selection is now displayed using a mask display, with a color (red by default) showing the area that was not selected and no color (which therefore allows the white layer to appear) in the selected area (see Figure 10.10).

Figure 10.10
Switching to Quick Mask mode causes the selection to be displayed as a color overlay, with the overlay representing areas of the image that are not selected.

To apply a creative shape to this edge, apply a filter to the Quick Mask display. Choose Filter > Filter Gallery from the menu (see Figure 10.11). Start by selecting an initial filter to work with from the sections in the center of the dialog box. We prefer the filters in the Brush Strokes and Distort sections for this purpose, but anything is fair game if you like the final result. As you're adjusting the settings for this filter along the right side, keep in mind when you're looking at the preview that white areas are where the image will be visible and black areas are where the image will be blocked in the final result.

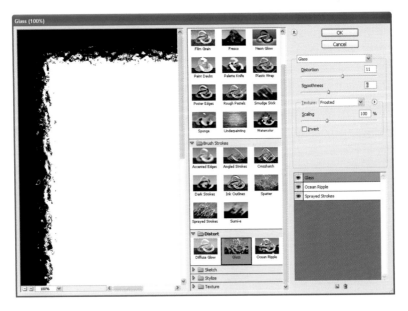

Figure 10.11
Use the Filter Gallery to apply filters that distort the edge of the selection on your image.

After you've established settings for the filter you've selected, you can actually add additional filters to create a more complex pattern. To do so, click the New Effect Layer button at the bottom-right of the dialog box. This initially duplicates the first filter you added, but you can then select a different filter to change it, adjusting the settings as desired.

Once you have a basic shape for the border you want to apply to your image, click OK in the Filter Gallery dialog box. The shape of the Quick Mask display is altered based on your filter selections. Switch back to normal mode for the selection by again pressing Q or by clicking the button on the left below the Color Picker on the Tools palette. The selection reflects the edge shape you created by applying filters in Quick Mask mode.

Note: The selection shape may not perfectly reflect the result of filtering in Quick Mask, because the "marching ants" border of the selection only follows the line along the division between pixels that are at least 50 percent selected and those that are less than 50 percent selected.

Because you want to retain only the outer portion of the white layer that was added to this document, the selection needs to be inverted to include only the outer border area. Choose Select > Inverse from the menu to invert the selection. This selection can then be used as the basis of a layer mask to block out the white layer where it isn't selected. To do so, simply click the Add Layer Mask button at the bottom of the Layers palette. The result is a white border around your image that blocks the outer edge, but with an artistic shape to that edge that can help enhance the textures and mood of the image (see Figure 10.12).

Figure 10.12
When you add a layer mask with an active selection you have modified with the application of one or more filters, the image is masked based on that selection to hide areas outside the selection, resulting in an artistic edge effect. (Photo by Tim Grey.)

Try It! To practice the methods described in this section for applying a border to your image, open the image Border on the accompanying CD and apply this method to the image. Save the result for the next section.

Creating a Greeting Card

With the ability to make your own prints on a wide variety of papers, many photographers have started producing greeting cards featuring their image on the front. Whether these are used to send a message to family or friends, or sold to generate a profit, creating greeting cards featuring your photography can be a fun and rewarding experience.

We've seen many photographers get frustrated trying to create greeting cards, because they're not sure how to create the page layout. Often they'll try to print a single image in the normal way, attempting to change the page layout settings so that image appears in the correct position on the final printed card. Unless you're a master of spatial orientation, this can prove to be very difficult to get right on the first try, much less the tenth try.

Creating the Template

Start by creating a new blank document that matches the dimensions of the sheet of paper you'll actually be printing to. For example, you can print to a standard 8.5"×11" sheet of stock and score the page yourself, or you can purchase pre-scored paper specifically designed for this purpose. We'll use the example of an 8.5"×11" sheet that will be folded in half for this demonstration.

To get started, choose File > New from the menu to bring up the New dialog box (Figure 10.13). Change the unit of measure for the dimensions to inches using the drop-down list to the right of the Width field. (When you change the unit of measure for either Width or Height, the other will also change automatically.) Enter dimensions for Width and Height based on the paper setting, but consider the orientation as you do so. If you want to produce a card with a vertical orientation, you need to create a document with a horizontal orientation, because the page will be folded lengthwise. Similarly, if you want a card with a horizontal orientation, create the new document with a vertical orientation.

Figure 10.13
In the New dialog box, enter the settings for the page you'll use as the template for your greeting card.

Set the Resolution to the value you plan to use for printing, such as 300 dpi. Make sure the Color Mode is set to RGB, the bit depth is appropriate for the images you're using (since you're just preparing a print, using 8-bit is perfectly fine here), and set the Background Contents to White so you're working with a blank page. Then click OK to create the new document you'll use for your greeting card layout.

To help you visualize the actual page layout and where you want to place the image or images to include on the greeting card, place guides on the document you've created. Guides are non-printing lines that you can place at any horizontal or vertical position within a document to provide layout guidance. At the very least, put a guide marking the fold line for the page. You might also want to place guides to identify the margins of the page to keep the images you place within the printable area.

Let's assume a horizontal page that will result in a vertical image layout for our example greeting card. Therefore, the document you've created is 11" wide and 8.5" tall. You want to place a guide halfway along the width to mark the fold location, so select View > New Guide from the menu. This brings up the New Guide dialog box (see Figure 10.14), which allows you to specify a position and orientation for the new guide you're adding. In this example, you set the Orientation to Vertical and the Position to "5.5 in," with the abbreviation "in" representing inches. Click OK, and the guide is added. You can add additional guides in a similar manner, for example, about a half-inch from each edge of the "front" of the card to identify the printable area you want to use for images, as shown in Figure 10.15.

N o t e : Many printers don't actually print content perfectly centered on the page, leading to challenges in creating an effective template. Perform some test prints early in the process to confirm the behavior of your printer—being sure to use the appropriate settings to center the output on the page—and adjust the template layout accordingly.

Figure 10.14

The New Guide dialog box allows you to place a guide at a specific position within your page layout document.

Figure 10.15

Place guides in the template document to help you visualize the page layout for your greeting card, making it easier to properly position images within the layout.

Having the layout of the page clear in your head can be a challenge here. If you're at all unclear on how the page should be structured, take a sheet of paper, fold it in half, and draw a simple sketch on the front of the card. Then unfold the paper and hold it in front of you to match the page layout you're creating in Photoshop. This should help clarify where the front really is on the blank page you're working on. In this section's example, the front of the card is on the right side of the new page.

Adding Images to the Layout

Once you've created your template document and have added guides to help you with the layout, you're ready to start placing images. Start by opening the image you want to add to your layout. You'll probably want to resize the image (for example, down to about a 4"×6" size for our sample card created from an 8.5"×11" sheet). In addition, it's easier to work with if you flatten it, so create a duplicate copy to protect your original. Select Image > Duplicate from the menu, check the Duplicate Merged Layers Only check box, and click OK. Then select Image > Image Size from the menu. Make sure the Resample Image check box is selected and set the Resolution to the same value you used for the new document you created. Then set the size as appropriate for the size of the greeting card document. (You'll be able to fine-tune the sizing later.)

With the image prepared, select the Move tool from the Tools palette (or press the V shortcut key). Point the mouse at the image, click and hold the button, and drag all the way into your new document; make sure the image window isn't maximized, and that you're able to see both documents at the same time. Don't release the mouse until the pointer is over this new document, with a plus sign showing on the pointer to indicate you're creating a copy of the image layer. When you release the mouse, the image is added as a separate layer to the new document.

Fine-tune the position of the image layer by dragging with the mouse or using the arrow keys on your keyboard. Each press of one of the arrow keys moves the image by 1 pixel. You can increase this to 10 pixels by holding the Shift key while pressing the arrow key.

To resize the image on the page, select Edit > Transform > Scale. This places a bounding box around your image layer. Hold the Shift key to constrain the proportions of this image layer and drag one of the corners to resize the image. You can also click and drag on the image itself while you're in the middle of the transform to adjust the position of the image layer. When you have applied the resizing as desired, press Enter/Return or double-click inside the bounding box. Keep any increase in size to a minimum, because repeatedly resizing can degrade image quality.

If you're adding multiple images to the greeting card, follow this same procedure for each of them. If the images will overlap, their order on the Layers palette determines whether individual layers appear above or below the others. The stack in the document is the same as shown on the Layers palette, with an image above another blocking part of any images below if they overlap.

Save and Print

Once you've created your document for your greeting card, save it so it can be printed in the future (see Figure 10.16). We recommend saving the document as a Photoshop PSD file, retaining all layers so you can fine-tune the layout in the future if desired. (You could also use a TIFF image while preserving layers, as discussed in Chapter 9, "Output.")

Figure 10.16
Once you've placed one or more images into your layout document, save the file and you're ready to print. (Photo by Tim Grey.)

To print the greeting card, try not to think of it as a special layout, but rather as a composite image that consumes an entire sheet of paper. Insert the appropriate sized paper in your printer, and then print the image as you normally would (and as described in Chapter 9). In other words, even though your example greeting card will ultimately be a vertical card created from a folded sheet of paper, think of your example as an image in a horizontal format that needs to be printed in Landscape mode to a normal sheet of paper. This helps simplify the process in your mind and makes it easier to get to the final result of a printed card that you can fold, sign, and send to the lucky recipient.

Try It! Open the image you saved in the prior section, when you added a border to the image Border on the accompanying CD, and create a greeting card template, placing the image to the template.

Creating a Business Card

Creating a business card is in many ways similar to creating a greeting card. In some ways it's easier since you don't have the issue of folding the final print and the related layout issues to contend with. However, it is slightly more complicated in some ways because you need to repeat the same design multiple times on a single sheet to be printed. However, if you divide this into two basic tasks—creating the card layout and creating the print layout—you'll find it much more manageable.

Creating the Card Layout

To create the card layout, start by making a new document for this purpose. Select File > New from the menu, and create a document that is 3.5 inches wide and 2 inches tall (the standard dimensions for business cards) at 300 dpi (see Figure 10.17). Be sure the Color Mode is set to RGB, and leave the bit depth at 8-bit. Use White for Background Contents. Click OK, and your new document is created.

Figure 10.17
Create a new document with the dimensions of your individual business card to get started.

Note: If you prefer to make a vertical business card, simply switch the Width and Height settings when creating your new document for the business card layout.

The next step is to add an image to the layout. This is exactly the same as the process used to create a greeting card, except that in this case, the document is much smaller. So, open the image you want to include, create a duplicate copy flattening it in the process, and resize it to fit the dimensions of your business card. Then use the Move tool to drag the image into the business card layout, as shown in Figure 10.18. If you want to rotate the image, select Edit > Transform > Rotate from the menu, move the mouse outside the bounding box, and drag to rotate. When you're happy with the rotation, press Enter/Return or double-click inside the bounding box. You can also resize the image by selecting Edit > Transform > Scale, holding the Shift key as you drag a corner to resize and pressing Enter/Return or double-clicking inside the bounding box to apply. Use the Move tool to fine-tune the position of the image as needed. To include multiple images, simply repeat the process, making sure the correct image layer is selected in the Layers palette when you rotate, resize, or move the image.

Figure 10.18
Use the Move tool to bring your image into the business card layout. (Photo by Tim Grey.)

Adding Text

Of course, while photographers would likely consider a photograph the key component of the perfect business card, you'll need text for it to actual serve the intended purpose. Creating text layers in Photoshop is quite easy, and there is tremendous flexibility you can exercise in the appearance of the text. To add a text layer, select the Text tool from the Tools palette and click on the place in the image where you want the text to appear. A flashing cursor appears, allowing you to start typing immediately. Make sure the text is set to an appropriate size before you start typing so you'll be able to see and manage the text. On the Options bar, there is a drop-down list for text size with two Ts of different sizes to the left of it. We recommend starting with a point size of 12 initially.

As you type your initial text, don't worry about the font attributes, because you'll change those in a moment. Just type the text you want to appear. When you're finished, don't press the text keyboard's Enter/Return key as you may be inclined to do if you want to create multiple lines of text. In terms of adjusting the final layout of your text, it's much easier if each text element or line of text is created as a separate text layer. When you're finished typing that block of text, simply switch to the Move tool or click the Commit button in the Options bar to commit the text (pressing Enter on the numeric keypad does the same thing) and get yourself ready to fine-tune the position of the text.

Note: When you create a text layer, the name of the layer is automatically changed whenever you change the text itself, with the name reflecting that text.

With the Move tool active, drag the text to the desired position, using the arrow keys on your keyboard to get the text into the perfect position. You're then ready to adjust the attributes of the text. To do so, double-click the thumbnail for the text layer on the Layers palette. This selects the text associated with that layer, so that any changes you make to the attributes affect all of the text.

On the Options bar (shown in Figure 10.19), the first setting to consider is the font type. Photoshop CS2 has added a WYSIWYG ("What you see is what you get") sample preview on the Font drop-down list, showing you what the font actually looks like within the drop-down list to the right of the font name. To the right of the Font drop-down list is another drop-down list that allows you to select the style for the text. Your options are Regular, Italic, Bold, or Bold Italic. Keep in mind that some fonts do not support all of these style options directly.

Figure 10.19 The Options bar for the text tool contains a number of settings related to the overall appearance of your text.

To the right of the font and font style drop-down lists is where you choose the font size. This uses the same point size system you may be familiar with from using word processing software, with 12 points being the standard for most documents, but 10 or even 8 points often necessary for the reduced real estate of a business card.

To the right of the font size drop-down list is the anti-aliasing drop-down list. This controls how the lines within the text are refined to avoid a stair-step pattern along curved lines. Choose among the various settings to get a preview of the effect, but we generally find that the Sharp option provides excellent results.

The next set of buttons allows you to control the text alignment, with the standard choices of left, center, and right represented by icons on the buttons. Since you're not going to be creating paragraphs of text, the default setting of left alignment is probably adequate, but at times you may find it helpful to use a different option to help you align text properly.

The colored box to the right of the text alignment buttons is used to define the color of the text. It reflects the current color of the active text layer; click this colored box to bring up the Color Picker and select a new color. Note that the selected text appears inverted, so you don't see the final result until you apply the change to your text (for example, by selecting the Move tool as discussed earlier).

The Warp Text button brings up the Warp Text dialog box (shown in Figure 10.20), where you can adjust the shape of the path upon which the text is written. Normally, the text simply flows across a straight line. However, you can have it move across a curved line or have the text itself warped into a particular shape. The Warp Text dialog box includes a Style drop-down list, where you can specify the particular shape you'd like to use, along with settings to adjust the particular style you've chosen.

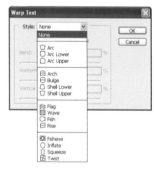

Figure 10.20
The Warp Text dialog box allows you to distort the text so it flows along a path that isn't straight.

Note: For advanced users, the last button on the Options bar for the Text tool brings up the Character palette, which provides more options for fine-tuning the text appearance.

Layer Styles

Once you've created the basic layout for your card, experiment with adding some layer styles to your text or image layers. These allow you to add dimension to the elements that compose your business card design. To add a layer style, first select the desired layer on the Layers palette. Then click the Layer Style button 🍥 at the bottom of the Layers palette. A list of available layer styles pops up (see Figure 10.21). Let's start with a simple drop shadow to add some depth to the current layer. When you select an option from the list, the Layer Style dialog box (shown in Figure 10.22) appears. Along the left side are the available styles, and in the center are the options for the currently selected style. You can add more than one style to the current layer by selecting it from the left. Be sure to click the text rather than the check box, so the option is activated and the options for that style are shown at the same time.

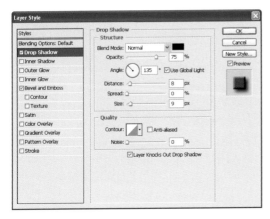

Figure 10.21

When you click the Layer Style button, a pop-up list provides the available options for the effects you can apply to elements within your text or image layers.

Figure 10.22

The Layer Style dialog box allows you to select the various effects to add to the current layer and adjust the settings for those effects.

Adjust the settings in the center section of the dialog box as desired. Remember that a subtle effect is generally best, as it provides the impression of depth without overwhelming the viewer. The best settings are usually those that you feel are a little too subtle. To get you started, add a Drop Shadow layer style and a Bevel and Emboss layer style to your text layers. When you've added the desired settings, click OK to apply them to the current layer.

Chances are you want to apply a consistent style to all of the text elements in your business card layout. When you add a layer style to a layer, an icon that matches the button you clicked initially at the bottom of the Layers palette is added on the right side of that layer in the Layers palette. To copy the styles to a different layer, first right-click that icon and select Copy Layer Style from the context menu. Then select the layer you want to copy the layer styles to, right-click it, and choose Paste Layer Style. You can continue to right-click and paste the styles to as many layers as you need to.

To adjust the Layer Style settings later, simply double-click the icon on the right side of the layer on the Layers palette. The Layer Style dialog box appears, where you can select the style on the left and adjust the settings in the center, clicking OK when you're finished making adjustments.

Saving the Layout

Once you've added image and text layers to the layout, fine-tuned their settings and position, and applied layer styles as desired, you should have a business card that you're proud to hand out. Be sure to save this document as a Photoshop PSD file with all layers intact so you can go back and make revisions as desired at a later date. This master file will be the basis of the print layout we'll create in the next section.

Try It! Open the image BizCard on the accompanying CD and create a business card layout as outlined in this section.

Creating the Print Layout

With the business card layout created, the next step is to create a print layout that includes multiple business cards so you can print sheets of them at a time. While there are pre-scored business card papers available, most of these that we've seen don't provide a material that is adequate for photo-quality printing. Therefore, we recommend using a paper designed specifically for producing photo-quality output on your photo inkjet printer for this purpose. In general, you'll get the best results from coated matte papers.

For this example, we'll assume you're printing to an 8.5"×11" sheet of paper that produces good results on your photo inkjet printer. Therefore, similar to the greeting card example, the first step is to create a new document with these dimensions. Select File > New from the menu, and in the New dialog box, enter dimensions of 8.5" for Width, 11" for Height, 300 dpi for Resolution, and make sure the document is set to RGB and a bit depth of 8-bit. Click OK to create the new document.

Add new vertical guides at 0.5" and 4.5" to mark the left edge of each business card by selecting View > New Guide from the menu. Then add new horizontal guides at 0.5", 3", 5.5", and 8", marking the top of each business card (see Figure 10.23). This provides a framework for you to place each business card into this document.

Figure 10.23
Add guides to the page layout for your business cards to provide a reference for where each individual card should be placed.

If you don't still have the business card layout document open, open it now. Then create a working copy by selecting Image > Duplicate from the menu. Select the Duplicate Merged Layers Only check box to flatten the image in the process and click OK. Then use the Move tool to drag this flattened duplicate into the new document you created for your print layout.

Drag this business card layer to the top-left position defined by the guides you added to the document (as shown in Figure 10.24). By default, the layer snaps into the corner identified by the guides you added as you get close; if it doesn't, choose View > Snap to turn on this feature.

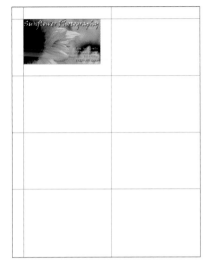

Figure 10.24

Move the first business card into the print layout in the first position at the top-left of the document.

At this point, it's a good idea to add a Stroke layer style to this image layer, which makes it easier to cut out the individual business cards after printing. To do so, click the Add Layer Style button at the bottom of the Layers palette and select Stroke from the pop-up menu. Set the size to about 2 pixels, with the Position set to Outside (see Figure 10.25). Click the Color box to bring up the Color Picker and set a color for this stroke. (We recommend using black and cutting this area out of the final business cards, but you could also set a color you like and keep it as a frame for the cards.)

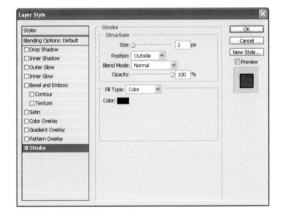

Figure 10.25

Add a stroke to the individual business card layer so you have a reference for cutting each card out later.

Once you have positioned the first business card layer, copy it: click the thumbnail for this layer on the Layers palette and drag it to the New Layer button at the bottom of the Layers palette. The new layer appears in the exact same position as the first one, so it doesn't look as though anything has changed. Select the Move tool and drag the mouse on the image to move the duplicate layer into position at the next intersection of guides below the first business card. Repeat this process to place a business card layer at every position you defined with the guides you added to the document, as shown in Figure 10.26.

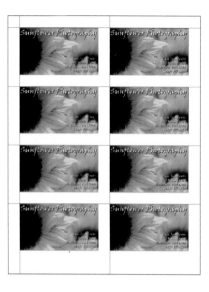

Figure 10.26
When you have placed a
business card at each
position within your
page layout, save the file
and use it as the source
for printing your cards.

When you have finished creating a complete page layout, save it as a Photoshop
PSD file so you can always refine the layout later if desired. You're then ready to print
this document as you would any other and then cut out the individual business cards.

Slideshows

There are many programs available for creating intricate digital slideshows. However,
since this is a book about Photoshop, we're going to show you how you can create a
basic slideshow incredibly quickly directly within Photoshop. It seems most photographers aren't familiar with the fact that you can create basic slideshows within Photoshop, utilizing a somewhat obscure capability offered by PDF documents.

Here's how to create a slideshow in Photoshop:

1. Select File > Automate > PDF Presentation from the menu. The PDF Presentation
dialog box appears (see Figure 10.27), which includes the basic settings for the
creating of your slideshow.

2. Click the Browse button, selecting the image files you want to include (you have
to select all individual image files rather than being able to select a single folder),
and click Open. The images you selected are added to the list of source files for
the presentation.

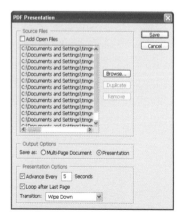

Figure 10.27
The PDF Presentation dialog box
allows you to establish the settings
for a basic slideshow that can be
played using the Adobe Reader software used to read PDF documents.

3. In the Output Options section, select Presentation so the final result is an automatic presentation rather than a simple PDF document.

4. If you want the slideshow to advance automatically rather than requiring the viewer to click the mouse for each image, select the Advance Every check box and enter the number of seconds you want the presentation to delay between images in the Seconds text box.

5. Select the Loop After Last Page check box if you want the slideshow to automatically loop indefinitely.

6. Select an effect from the Transition drop-down list if desired. The None option causes the images to switch without any effect. Some of the effects are relatively amateur in appearance. We consider the Wipe effects to be the most appropriate, but experiment with the various options to decide what you like best.

7. Click the Save button to continue. The Save dialog box appears, allowing you to select a location and filename for your PDF presentation file.

When you click Save, the Save Adobe PDF dialog box is displayed. This is a rather complicated dialog box, but you can avoid the complexity by simply selecting the Smallest File Size option from the Adobe PDF Preset drop-down list at the top of the dialog box. This ensures that the final PDF file remains at a reasonable file size, while still ensuring excellent image quality for display on a monitor or digital projector.

When you click the Save PDF button in the Save Adobe PDF dialog box, Photoshop processes your images to resize them for the slideshow, and then creates the final PDF file. The result is saved in the location you specified. You can then open that PDF file with Adobe Reader (in most cases you can simply double-click the file to do so) and the slideshow starts automatically. To return to a normal screen, use the Esc key.

Sharing Creativity

In this chapter we've presented some methods for you to both improve the efficiency of your workflow and share your images in a variety of ways. As with all of the chapters in this book, the underlying theme has been producing the very best results possible with your images and then sharing those images. Now that you have learned many techniques to help you achieve these goals, we hope you'll find an increased passion for your photography, an increased desire to share your images with the world, and a heightened level of skill in achieving exactly the results you envision for your photographers.

Index

Note to the reader: Throughout this index **boldfaced** page numbers indicate primary discussions of a topic. *Italicized* page numbers indicate illustrations.

C

Extensis, PhotoFrame, 283

Extract dialog box, 205

Eyedropper tool, Options bar, 71

eyedroppers for setting values, in Levels adjustment layer, 162–164

EyeOne Display 2, 29

eyes of birds, enhancing, 177–179

F

f/stop, and light levels, 17

Feather control, for Lasso tool, 64

Feather Selection dialog box, 75

feathering selection, **74–75**, 174

File Browser, 48

file extension, 36

file formats

    digital negative (DNG) file, 103

    JPEG vs. RAW, 5–8

File menu

    > Automate

        > Batch, 280, 282

        > Fit Image, 277

        > Merge to HDR, 197

        > PDF Presentation, 296

        > Photomerge, 189

        > Web Photo Gallery, 271

    > File Info, 34, 59

    > New, 78, 286

    > Print with Preview, 266

file size, in Camera Raw, 89–90

file types, Bridge support for, 50

Fill dialog box, *131*

film, grain of, 15

film scans, resolution for, 252

Filmstrip mode

    in Camera Raw, 105, *106*

Filter menu

    > Blur

        > Gaussian Blur, 132, 174, 220, 236

        > Lens Blur, 222–223

        > Smart Blur, 224

    > Distort > Glass, 82

    > Extract, 205

    > Filter Gallery, 228

        for borders, *284, 284*

    > Liquify, 226

    > Noise > Reduce Noise, 253, 254

    > Sharpen

        > Smart Sharpen, 260

        > Unsharp Mask, 177, 258

    > Stylize > Find Edges, 244, *245*

filtering image list, by labels, 57

filters, **218–228**

    Blurs, **219–225**

        Gaussian Blur filter, **219–220**, *220*

        Lens Blur filter, **220–224**, *221*

        Smart Blur filter, *224*, **224–225**, *225*

    distortion, 229, *229*

    Filter Gallery, *228*, **228–229**, *229*

    Liquify, **225–227**, *226*

        tools, *226, 227*

    plug-ins, *229, 229*

    Poster Edges, 229

    reducing effect, 225

    Rough Pastels, 229

    Water Paper, 229

Fit Image dialog box, 277, *277*

Flaming Pear, Goodies & Freebies, 229

flattening

    master file, 87

    panoramas, 186

    for sharpening, 257, 265

Flow setting, for Brush tool, 80

Hue/Saturation dialog box, 169–171, *170*

Hue/Saturation, to reveal color casts, **154–155**, *155*

I

image interpolation, setting for, 32

Image menu
> Adjustments, 111
>> Invert, 176
>> Levels, 188, 204
>> Shadow/Highlight, 147
> Canvas Size, 118, 238
> Duplicate, 228, 251
> Image Size, 251
> Mode
>> 8 Bit, 219
>> 16 Bits/Channel, 198
>> Grayscale, 214

Image Size dialog box, *251*, 251–253

images, names for, **47–48**

Info palette, to reveal color casts, **155–157**

International Press Telecommunications Council (IPTC), 60

interpolation, 89, 252

Intersect with Selection option, 67, 68

IPTC Core section of metadata, 60

ISO, and noise, 14

J

JPEG file format
vs. RAW, **5–8**, 242
visible artifact removal, 256, *256*

K

Kemper, Lewis, on file preparation for output, 264–265

keyboard shortcuts
for Camera Raw, **92–93**
navigating with, **45–46**
for rating assignment, 56

keywords, assigning to images, 58

L

labeling images in Bridge, **56–58**, *57*

Lasso tool, **64–66**
Options bar, 64, *64*

layer masks, 129
applying gradient to, 133–134, *134*
blurring, 132–133
and color adjustments, **173–177**
copying between layers, 176
filling with black, 175
inverting, 176
painting on, 130–131, **174–177**

Layer menu
> Flatten Image, 228
> New Adjustment Layer, 154

Layer Style dialog box, 292–293, *293*, *295*

layers, **110–112**
for dust removal, 115
for Magic Wand tool, 74
in master file, 87
soft-edged brush to blend layers, 186
in TIFF files, saving, 36

Layers palette, New Adjustment Layer icon, 111, *111*

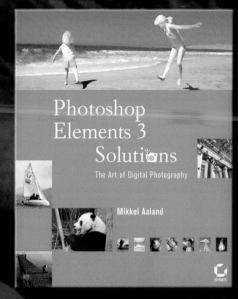

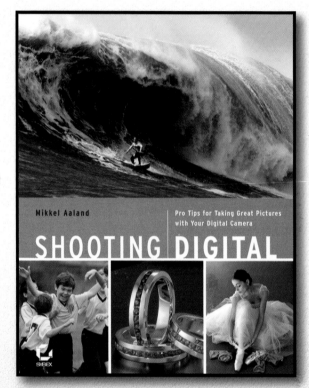